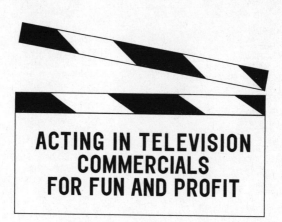

ACTING IN TELEVISION COMMERCIALS FOR FUN AND PROFIT

ACTING IN TELEVISION COMMERCIALS

FOR FUN AND PROFIT

Fully Updated 4th Edition

Squire Fridell

THREE RIVERS PRESS • NEW YORK

For Pen Dennis, my Friend and Agent-For-Life

Three Rivers Press and the Tugboat design are registered trademarks of
Random House, Inc.

Previous editions of this work were published in hardcover by Harmony Books,
a division of Crown Publishers, Inc., New York, in 1980 and 1986, and in paperback
by Three Rivers Press, an imprint of the Crown Publishing Group, a division of
Random House, Inc., New York, in 1995.

Library of Congress Cataloging-in-Publication Data

Fridell, Squire.
    Acting in television commercials for fun and profit / Squire Fridell.—4th ed.
    1. Television acting—Vocational guidance.   2. Television advertising—
Vocational guidance.   I. Title.
    PN1992.8.A3F7 2009
    792'.028'023—dc22   2008034073

ISBN 978-0-307-45024-1

Printed in the United States of America

10 9 8 7 6 5 4 3

Fourth Edition

CONTENTS

AUTHOR'S NOTE

I began writing the first Acting in Television Commercials for Fun and Profit way back in 1977, thinking I was doing pretty well in the commercial world, having shot over two hundred national TV commercials. I also thought I was undertaking a three-month writing project. When the first edition was finally published three years (and two hundred more commercials) later, I vowed I would never, in this lifetime, perch my fingers over a keyboard for that long ever again.

I was wrong. And I was wrong more than once.

In 1986, I spent a couple of months rewriting the book for the "expanded and updated" version and eight years (and another 1,400 commercials) later, I did another update. And then, in 2008 (now with over 3,250 commercials under my belt), I find myself once again with fingers poised over a keyboard. Only this time those digits are perched over a Macintosh instead of a Smith-Corona.

Those of you familiar with the earlier editions and revisions will be pleased with the new and updated data in this one. With the help of Cris Dennis of Film Artists Associates, all the information in this edition has been updated, rewritten, and revised, still focusing on the actor who wants to audition well and work often. Another big advantage is that my daughter, a graduate of the incredible Carnegie Mellon School of Drama, is now a working actor living in New York City. Her stage résumé, even at her young age, makes mine pale in comparison. Her up-to-date input has been very valuable to this rewrite.

Since this book first appeared in bookstores three decades ago, I've grown as an actor and as a teacher of acting. I've written this updated version to share what I've learned from being principal on-camera talent in literally thousands of television commercials and from teaching what seems like countless numbers of commercial acting classes.

I hope that the information, the tips, and the guidelines in this book help you get that agent, audition consistently well, land those jobs, and make some money! (Remember to send me 10 percent...)

Squire Fridell
Glen Ellen, California

INTRODUCTION

It is always foolish to give advice. To give good advice is absolutely fatal.

—Oscar Wilde

In 1941, the very first television commercial interrupted a live baseball game in New York on WNBT-TV with an endorsement for Bulova watches.* Even though WNBT probably received a few letters of complaint from baseball fans, local sales for Bulova immediately skyrocketed. Television advertising was born as a result of that ad and its success, and the television advertising industry has since grown to a multibillion-dollar business. Now, in this day of consumer awareness and the shrinking dollar, most of us buy one product over another not because of *Consumer Reports* rankings or even the cost of the product. Instead, we tend to spend our money because of the power of TV and the persuasion of television advertising.

For those who may doubt the influence of television, the following statistics may help change your mind.

- Ninety-eight percent of homes in America have at least one television; 74 percent have more than one.

- There are more TV sets in American homes than there are toilets . . . or people.

---

* The cost of that ten-second Bulova watch commercial in 1941? A whopping $9!

- After work and sleep, watching TV takes up the largest segment of our day.

- The average household in America has a television set turned on for 7 hours and 45 minutes each and every day. ("Not in MY house!")

- This year, the average American youth will spend 1,500 hours watching television, while he will spend only 900 hours in school. ("Not MY kid!")

- During those 1,500 hours spent in front of the TV this year, that average kid will have watched over 30,000 commercials. ("That's my NEIGHBOR'S kid!")

- What's over 2 million? That's the number of commercials you'll have seen on TV by the time you reach 65. ("Yep! YOU!")

- By 65 you'll have spent 9 years of your life glued to the tube. ("Nine YEARS! That's my NEIGHBOR!")

- The country's biggest advertiser, Procter & Gamble, spent over $2.5 billion on television advertising in 2008. During that same period, the nation's fast-food industry spent another billion dollars.

- Advertisers were willing to fork over more than $2.5 million to air one 30-second television commercial during the 2008 Super Bowl. (And you were in the bathroom and missed it!) Over $5.5 million were also spent for TV advertising during the 2008 NCAA basketball playoffs.

Advertisers are well aware that American households have their TV sets turned on for close to eight hours every single day. And those advertisers (who are pretty smart folks) know that they have a captive audience in which they can effectively pitch their products. How many of us watching afternoon or late-night TV haven't fallen for the familiar pitch "BUT WAIT! THERE'S MORE!," followed by "BUT ONLY IF YOU ACT NOW!"? And tell me you haven't been the one to call that "NUMBER ON THE SCREEN!," "TO GET NOT ONE, BUT TWO!," and then get something that you didn't really need? I've ended up with everything from Ginzu knives to Bullet Blenders and *I* ought to know better! Advertising works. And television advertising works best of all.

Although there are a lot of ways advertisers can pitch their products on television, one of the most effective ways has always been to use actors and actresses, either as spokespeople for the product or acting like "real people" in mock scenarios touting those products.

When most folks are asked to think of actors and actresses, the faces and names of superstars and celebrities usually come to mind. Their faces are all over the supermarket tabloids with headlines that scream out for our attention, and we can't seem to escape their latest scandals or whom they happen to endorse for president or the fact that they are working very hard to save some whales somewhere. And, strangely enough, we can't seem to get enough of them. These famous faces and big-screen idols may be who most folks think of when asked to name successful actors, but, amazingly, if you look at the income for all the actors and actresses who are union members, those folks appearing in television commercials represent about *half* of the total revenue!

It's hard to believe, so let me repeat that.

Actors and actresses make almost as much money acting in television commercials as actors and actresses make acting in movies and television *combined!* Here's the earnings breakdown.

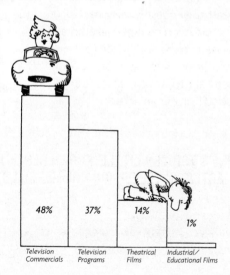

48%	37%	14%	1%
Television Commercials	Television Programs	Theatrical Films	Industrial/ Educational Films

Talking with other actors and students in classes over the years, I often hear folks particularly new to the business say that they "only want to work on the stage" or they "are only interested in doing a television series" or even they "only want to be a movie star." My response is always the same: Why on earth would you want to eliminate half of your potential income?

SIX REASONS WHY YOU NEED TO READ THIS BOOK

1. It will give you and the millions of viewers who have ever watched a television commercial and thought, "Gee, I could do that" a candid look at just what it takes to "do that."
2. This book will help you evaluate whether you've got what it takes to succeed in the business.
3. It will answer all the questions and clear up all the misconceptions you may have about what it's like to be an actor in television commercials.
4. It will tell you how to get (and keep) an agent and join the acting unions.
5. It will give beginners a solid plan of attack as they start their quest to become successful television commercial actors.
6. It will be a comprehensive guide for established actors who might be working a little but want to work a lot more and make a good living as an actor.

SQUIRE'S TOP TEN LITTLE-KNOWN BENEFITS OF ACTING IN TELEVISION COMMERCIALS

1. It's good for your humility.
   (Constant rejection may get you one step closer to enlightenment.)

2. It keeps you alert and on your toes.
   (Because you never know if and when you might be called for an audition.)

3. You'll make a lot of new friends.
   (You'll be on a first-name basis with all those other folks in the unemployment line.)

4. You'll get to see the world.
   (From some remote location or the inside of a soundstage.)

5. It's fun to live without a regular paycheck and learn to budget.
   (And still live above the garage at your parents' place.)

6. Your credit card worries will be gone.
   (Because you probably won't GET a credit card as soon as you fill out the "Where are you employed?" line on the credit application.)

7. You'll dress well.
   (Because after a job you can occasionally buy your wardrobe for half price.)

8. You'll eat well.
   (After the shoot, they might give you some of the leftover cold chicken wings or pizza they used for product shots in the commercial.)

9. A lot of forgotten high school friends will call to "stay in touch."
   (If you've got a commercial or two on the air, they'll call to ask for a loan; otherwise it's to ask if you've gotten any acting jobs lately.)

10. With a makeup professional, you'll look better on television than you do in person.
    (You'll also look ten pounds heavier.)

Admittedly, I'm at least half joking with Squire's Top Ten Benefits, but there is some truth behind it. Ask any actor. We've all got some pretty funny stories that didn't seem to be very funny while they were happening.

The first time I saw a commercial of mine on television (it was for Olympia Beer), I was thrilled! I was also *positive* that anyone who saw me on the street would immediately recognize me as the fellow wrenching under a VW bus being comforted by his wife with a cold beer. A few days later, while ordering lunch at a local fast-food place, a fellow behind me tapped me on the shoulder and said, "Excuse me. Did you . . . ?" Naturally, I cut him off and said that, yes, I was the fellow he'd seen under the VW bus in the beer commercial. After a long pause, he said he didn't know anything about a beer commercial, but that I'd left my car lights on.

A year or so later, when I started to book more than my share of TV spots, my actor roommate got his first commercial for NyQuil and was convinced that he was going to have a fistful of dollars as soon as the spot began to air nationally. After all, the agency producer whom he met on the set had told him they planned to do a series of spots using him as talent. I tried to convince him that maybe he ought to hold off on any major purchases for a while, but he was convinced that the spot was going to run on all three networks twenty times, every night for seven years.

Naturally, my pal promptly used all his session fee money for a down payment on a used Porsche. You guessed it. The commercial never aired, and someone else was driving his Porsche four months later.

HOW COMPETITIVE IS COMMERCIAL ACTING?

Very. Just like acting in television, film, or onstage. I don't believe there is another profession that is *more* competitive. For every actor in L.A. or New York who's working, there are literally thousands who aren't. So, statistically you need to be aware of your chances before deciding to travel this road.

Despite all my well-intentioned attempts to gather new statistics for this edition, the powers that be at both acting unions who handle commercial work were more than reluctant to give out (un)employment statistics. I finally had Cris Dennis, my Los Angeles talent agent, try to squeeze out a few pearls of wisdom from a buddy of his at one of the unions. I gleaned the following.

- There are a lot of people to compete with. Screen Actors Guild (SAG) membership is over 120,000, and the American Federation of Television and Radio Artists (AFTRA) members total over 70,000. (See The Unions, chapter 5.) That's an awful lot of folks who *already* have their union cards and are out there looking for work.

- Well over 70 percent of AFTRA and SAG members have to hold down other jobs to support themselves. It seems that half the folks waiting tables or tending bar in Los Angeles or New York are actors "in between jobs." (The other half are writing screen-plays.)

  I tended bar and whipped up margaritas myself for a summer at a Mexican restaurant just south of L.A. and never regretted a night's work. After all, I learned how to bartend and got to meet a lot of great people, including a terrific gal who ended up being my wife.

- The majority of SAG actors earn less than $7,500 per year from SAG jobs. If you're trying to live on that, you're living at a super-poverty level.

- About half of all the money earned by SAG actors is made by just 1 percent of the membership.

Discouraging, huh? It was even *more* discouraging not to get exact statistics from the folks at SAG and AFTRA, but you can imagine why the unions don't want folks to know their dismal employment and earnings data. All this points rather dramatically to the fact that act-ing—whether it's in commercials, TV, or film—is a very risky business for a wage earner.

But no matter how disconcerting the statistics seem to be, keep in mind that you want to be in that 1 percent of folks who *do* make a darn good living as actors.

SO WHAT DO I NEED TO MAKE IT AS A COMMERCIAL ACTOR?

You'll need a lot of things we'll cover later in this book: a terrific head-shot, a great-looking résumé, an agent who believes in you, member-ship in the unions, some improvisation classes, acting classes, and commercial acting classes, and more than your share of luck. But aside from those very important things, there are other factors that can either work in your favor or work against you. An actor once told me that to be successful as a commercial actor in L.A., you needed to be young and exceptionally beautiful, or weird-looking and excep-tionally funny. There's a lot of truth in that.

Being young is terrific, but there's not too much you can do about your age. You might be a forty-five-year-old who everyone says *looks* twenty, but let's face it—you're still forty-five. And despite what everyone tells you, no one who is forty-five looks twenty. No one. But looking twenty isn't always all it's cracked up to be. Sure, many of the commercials these days use actors who look twenty, but remember that there are all kinds of TV commercials, and they are written and produced to demographically appeal to *every* age group. So while iTunes commercials may use actors who look twenty, there are more TV spots for Procter & Gamble that use actors who are a lot older than twenty. And never forget that Proc-ter & Gamble is the biggest advertiser on television. Your age is a given—and it's also irrelevant. You can't change your age. But take heart: There are roles in television commercials for actors at every age.

It always helps to be born exceptionally beautiful, but not too many of us are. When I was first doing commercials years ago, almost everyone doing TV commercials fit into a generic mold: pleasant-looking, well-groomed, Anglo-Saxon, with nothing particularly unusual about them. Facial hair was out, actors were coiffed and combed, teeth were straight, clothes were nice and tidy, men had haircuts, and only women wore earrings. If you look at TV spots these days, that's certainly not the case. You'll see actors who look very much like the folks you'd see strolling along the streets of Santa Monica, Manhat-tan, or Atlanta . . . very much a cross-section of population. It means you no longer have to fit into a tiny pocket of model-like humanity.

You can be fat, skinny, tall, short, wear horn-rimmed glasses, be bald, or even have a Mohawk.

As far as exceptionally funny is concerned, it is more important than ever in casting for commercials. Since Robin Williams first burst onto the scene years ago, playing a quick-witted alien in a television series, there has been an explosion of commercials written specifically for actors who have comedic timing. So if you have a sense of humor and can draw upon it in an audition, more power to you. We'll explore that in more detail a little later.

So we've covered youth, beauty (or the lack of), and quick wit. But I would add a couple of very important qualities to the above actor's list of what it takes to be successful in TV commercials. The first would be determination. If you don't want to be a working actor more than the next guy, it won't happen. The fact that you're reading this book shows that you have at least some determination to succeed!

Another quality would be talent, which is difficult to describe: sometimes raw, sometimes fully developed, it is always best recognized by others. That's right, we are not the best judges of our own talent. If we were, everyone who appeared on *American Idol* would have won. Instead, it took three judges (and the viewing audience) to let these people know that they weren't as talented as they perceived themselves to be. Personally, I think the talent part has a lot to do with the Muses.

Now, assuming that you're determined and that your talent has been recognized by others, it's time to focus on the addition of knowledge, training, and skills.

This book will increase your knowledge about commercial acting, give you tips on where to go for training, and give you the groundwork to develop your skills so that you'll be able to audition better than other actors. Then, hopefully, employing those skills on the job will get you hired over and over again. And that's what this book is all about—helping you with your knowledge of the industry and helping you develop the skills necessary to succeed. These are the undeniable links between your determination, your talent, and your eventual success. And all of this will help you with your confidence, because you'll be aware that you know more than the next guy. As your skill level and your confidence increase, so will other people's perceptions of your abilities.

But remember that commercial acting is not a business that guarantees any success. An acting teacher whom I've known for a long time said there were four cardinal rules of being an actor.

1. Having talent doesn't necessarily mean that you will work. *Ever.*

2. Hard work may pay off. Or maybe not.

3. Sometimes there is loyalty in the business. Most of the time there isn't.

4. Fair happens only in Pomona in the summertime. And they charge admission for it.

(Yuk, yuk, yuk.)

SHOULD I CONSIDER TRYING TO WORK AT OTHER FORMS OF ACTING WHILE I'M TRYING TO GET WORK IN COMMERCIALS?

Definitely! Wherever and whenever there is an opportunity to do a student film, a local stage production, a reading, or a modeling job, just do it! Even if the job doesn't pay anything, you'll be gaining a lot of experience, and you'll get to meet all sorts of folks in the business. That's how your networking starts. The contacts you make now in those local amateur theatrical productions or in acting classes will, more often than not, surface and reestablish themselves at a later date. It's incredible how those six degrees of separation grow smaller and smaller as time goes by. After a while, it's hard not to work on a job where there isn't *someone* you've worked with before! *Just do it!*

DO I HAVE TO MOVE TO NEW YORK OR LOS ANGELES TO WORK IN COMMERCIALS?

When I first started working as an actor shooting commercials, 70 percent of all television commercials were shot in New York (where the ad agency headquarters were), and almost all the TV shows were cast and shot in the Los Angeles area (where the TV studios were). That meant that each summer an entire cadre of young actors (including yours truly) would exit L.A. and head for the Big Apple to live for three or four months while trying to land their share of TV commercials.

Those days have changed and for the better. Even though the majority of TV commercials are still cast and shot in and around L.A. and New York, the advent of high-quality videotape and high-tech digital has led to advertising agencies and production houses popping up all over the country. Each year, thousands of commercials are cast and shot in Chicago, San Francisco, Dallas, Baltimore, Phoenix, Seattle, Denver, Atlanta, San Diego, and Honolulu—almost every major city in the United States. In fact, there are twenty-five different regional Screen Actors Guild offices scattered all across this land: Arizona, Boston, Chicago, Colorado, Dallas, Detroit, central Florida, Miami, Georgia, Hawaii, Hollywood, Houston, Nashville, Nevada, New Mexico, New York City, North Carolina, Philadelphia, Portland, San Diego, San Francisco, Seattle, Utah, Washington, D.C., and Baltimore. And if there's a SAG office in Portland, there must be enough work there to keep the local SAG actors working!

There are definitely advantages to starting your career near your hometown: You may be able to join SAG more easily, you won't have to pack up and move to a new city, you'll be able to keep your present job, and you can dabble in acting in commercials. The more you work, the faster your learning curve sweeps upward *and* you may be able to supplement your income by thousands of dollars every year. You also won't have to compete for an acting job in a big city where thousands and thousands of other actors are pounding the pavement looking for work. Think, "Big fish, small pond"!

CAN I BELONG TO AFTRA, SAG, AND EQUITY AT THE SAME TIME? AND WHY ARE THERE DIFFERENT ACTING UNIONS?

"Yes!" to the first question and "It's a long story!" to the second. (See The Unions, chapter 5.)

WHAT ABOUT THE BREAKDOWN BY AGE, SEX, AND ETHNICITY IN COMMERCIALS?

If you've been watching as much television as the rest of America has over the last few years, you probably know the answer to this question. It used to be that young to middle-aged, Anglo-Saxon men and women were almost exclusively used as the actors in television commercials, and that "look" even became known as the Procter & Gamble look. In fact, way back in 1980, when the first edition of this book

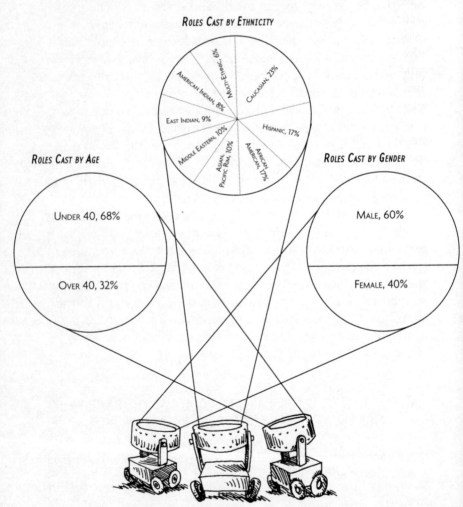

ROLES CAST BY ETHNICITY

MULTI-ETHNIC, 6%
AMERICAN INDIAN, 8%
CAUCASIAN, 23%
EAST INDIAN, 9%
HISPANIC, 17%
MIDDLE EASTERN, 10%
ASIAN, PACIFIC RIM, 10%
AFRICAN AMERICAN, 17%

ROLES CAST BY AGE

UNDER 40, 68%

OVER 40, 32%

ROLES CAST BY GENDER

MALE, 60%

FEMALE, 40%

was printed, those young to middle-aged Anglo-Saxon men and women accounted for a full 88 percent of the actors cast in television commercials. But more recently, commercial advertising has adapted to better reflect the actual demographics of our population. The enormous buying power of the increasing Hispanic population is a great example, and now there are commercial advertising agencies that cater *only* to the Spanish-speaking market. During my stint as Ronald McDonald, I shot commercials for two different ad agencies— and did one set of spots completely *en español!*

Nowadays, TV commercial casting generally reflects a cross-section of the population, meaning there is room in television advertising for actors of every color and age group. Obviously, local advertising reflects this demographic casting more specifically than national advertising. You might find lots of Spanish-speaking commercials focused on the Hispanic market in San Diego and Los Angeles, but not too many in Mason City, Iowa.

On page 12 is an actual breakdown of casting in the Los Angeles area for a given period. (The casting breakdowns even list the roles specifically by gender, age, and ethnicities. Boy, talk about profiling!)

ALL THIS DATA IS SWELL, BUT CAN'T I JUST GO ABOUT IT THE SAME WAY YOU DID?

Robert Frost may have written, "Two roads diverged in a yellow wood," but there are a lot more than two roads through those woods. And there are more ways to get to your destination than you think. My road was determined by choices I made and by choices that seem to have been made for me, and you're likely to experience that too. Plus, commercials have changed since I was cast so many times for Procter & Gamble as the "young man," then the "young husband," and then the "dad." How I started is just one way that one person traveled a road years ago.

SO, HOW *DID* YOU GET STARTED?

Okay, you asked:

Right out of The University of the Pacific and after a stint in the Marine Corps, I was hired as the drama (don't you hate that word?)

teacher at El Rancho High School in Pico Rivera, California. It was a terrific job in a very supportive school with a lot of talented kids. I directed three shows a year, and when I didn't have a production mounted, I acted at night with an incredible theater group in Costa Mesa, South Coast Repertory.

Volney Howard, my college roommate (who is still one of my best friends), came down from L.A. to see a show I was doing (Sam Shepard's *La Turista*) and brought a buddy with him. Vol's friend, Ramsay King, turned out to be a young casting director for Universal Studios. That contact led to a theatrical agent, which led to some guest-starring roles on TV shows. (Every once in a while, a residual check for a dollar will show up in the mail for a rerun of an episode of *Mama's Family* or *M*A*S*H* that I guest-starred in three hundred years ago!) This led to a commercial agent, which finally led to being hired to act in a lot of television commercials. Eventually, I quit teaching and became a full-time actor. That's probably why I've taught so many workshops over the years and why I wrote this book. I still feel a little guilty that I'm no longer in the classroom.

AND HOW SUCCESSFUL *HAVE* YOU BEEN?

Pretty successful *and* pretty lucky! To date, I've been the principal on-camera talent in over 3,250 different TV commercials and have recorded as many voice-overs for both television and for radio. I was also one of the last Contract Players at Universal Studios, a training program for young actors that the studio has since abandoned. (It was lots of fun being a Contract Player because Universal would cast me in different episodic TV shows and I would get a paycheck every week, whether I worked or not!) Over the years I starred or guest-starred in any number of television pilots, series, and shows. I even once made the cover of *TV Guide*, and was photo-featured in *Newsweek* magazine, in an edition called "A New Breed of Actors." I will admit that the week I appeared on the cover of *TV Guide*, my NBC series for Universal was canceled. I also have to admit that even though my name was number 1 across in *Daily Variety*'s crossword puzzle, only four people actually completed the crossword on that particular day: me, my agent, my wife, and my mom.

OKAY. I'M DETERMINED, I UNDERSTAND MY CHANCES, AND I'M READY TO GO! WHAT DO I DO NOW?

Good for you! Assuming you've got some talent, you understand your chances, and you have a lot of determination, we'll hope that a little luck also flows your way. Now keep reading! With the knowledge and skills you gain through the information in this book, you'll soon be on your own road in a successful pursuit of acting in television commercials. It will be a different road than others have taken, but hopefully your path will encounter the fewest potholes.

The remainder of this book will be devoted to getting you started on your journey through the often confusing, sometimes perplexing, but ofttimes rewarding world of the commercial actor.

Good luck!

part one

Before
Your Talent Agent

CHAPTER 1

YOUR FIRST HEADSHOT

It's much better to look good than to feel good.

—A makeup artist to an actor

Everyone's heard the urban myth about somebody's second cousin who happened to be walking his dog in Des Moines and was "discovered" by a traveling casting agent who just happened to be driving by. Mr. Dog Walker was then put on an airplane, flown to Los Angeles, featured in a TV commercial, and retired wealthy beyond measure. The catch: It didn't happen. That's why they call it an urban *myth*. Lana Turner wasn't *really* discovered at Schwab's Drug Store. ("Who's Lana Turner?" you ask.)

Don't get me wrong, there have been lots of ordinary folks who've actually been picked off the street to be in TV commercials, but we're talking about apples and oranges. You're reading this book because you want to make a *living* as a commercial actor, and that means doing a lot more than one job. Throughout the country there are many smaller markets where you can submit yourself for a commercial job and land an occasional spot, but you won't make a living in commercials. To do that, you need a commercial talent agent to submit you to casting directors for auditions and then represent you once you do get the job. (We'll talk more about agents in the last chapter of Part One.) Your agent is the vital link if you want to work often and make substantial money doing so. (We'll assume that you do.)

In order to get that all-important talent agent, you need to submit a headshot of yourself. And to be successful in landing that agent, you need a *really good* headshot.

OKAY—TO GET AN AGENT I GUESS I NEED A REALLY GOOD HEADSHOT

Yep. It was worth repeating!

The name of the game is *advertising*. And that means that you need to advertise yourself better than your competition. The average commercial agent is mailed, e-mailed, or hand-delivered hundreds of photos, snapshots, and JPEGs each week, either from aspiring actors hoping for a career in commercials, or from actors who already have an agent but are looking for new representation. The truth is that it takes that agent (or usually an assistant) about twenty seconds to sort through the hundreds of choices and select the four or five actors he or she feels might be worth taking a look at.

Your aim is to make sure your headshot is one of the chosen few, not one of the many that end up getting deleted, tossed in the circular file, or fed to the shredder. Before I go any further, I will say that it is *most imperative* that your headshot be an exact portrait of you and how you look right now. One of the key gripes from talent agents and casting agents is that the actor standing in front of them doesn't even look related to the actor whose headshot they're holding in their hand.

BUT I DON'T LIKE TO HAVE MY PICTURE TAKEN!

Then you're looking at the wrong career. Get over it. This is a business of getting your picture taken—and sometimes at twenty-four frames a second. When I hear someone say she doesn't like to have her picture taken, it usually means one thing—she thinks she's not going to like what she thinks she's going to see.

So before you hire a photographer to take your headshot, it's a good idea to do the following. Put on some clothes that you like and that you think might be acceptable to wear if you were cast in a commercial. Then take a good, critical, objective look at yourself in a full-length mirror. Now make a list of those things you're not particularly fond of about the way you look, and then divide those things into two categories.

1. The things you *can't* change.

2. The things you *can* change.

First, immediately forget about those things in category one. You can't change them. If you're six-foot-ten in your stocking feet or four-foot-eight with high heels on, that's the way it is. So if you *are* the former, your goal is to work more than any other six-foot-ten person! On the other hand, if you're proud of the fact that you're four-foot-eight, and you carry yourself proudly, you'll be fine. Remember that these things are the things that make *you* the unique you that you are.

The second category consists of the things that you're not comfortable with, that you *can* change, and that you would like to change. Take a look in the mirror again.

WHAT SHOULD I BE LOOKING FOR?

LOOK AT YOUR FIGURE. Most folks these days are packing a few more pounds than they should. That's not to say that you're not going to work if you're more rotund than svelte, but you are limiting your casting options. Keep in mind that the camera adds ten pounds to everyone, and if you're not completely comfortable with your weight, it will show in the way you carry yourself. So if you don't like what you see, and you think you'd feel better about yourself if you lost some weight, then do it. Walk more, skip the french fries, work out, and tighten up. You certainly don't need to be a bodybuilder to be in television commercials, but some muscle tone looks good on everyone, and you'll probably feel better about yourself if you're a little buff.

On the other hand, if you *like* the way you look, then you're fine the way you are. The days of every actor looking like a runway model are long gone. Folks are bigger these days and advertisers know it. The commercials they write, produce, and air reflect the cross-sections of our population.

TAKE A LOOK AT YOUR HAIR. If you're a fellow who is follicularly challenged, my advice is to put that in the "can't change it" category and be happy with it. Bald is fine and much better than a comb-over or a bad hairpiece. If it's a question of style, take a look at the actors and actresses in your age bracket who are doing most of the commercials you see on television. If you're sporting a spiked, multicolored Mohawk, you've definitely limited yourself to a very small category, and you're probably not going to be featured in too many Procter & Gamble spots. If an ad agency wants a twenty-year-old who sports green hair, they'll usually just hire an actor who fits the role and color his hair. Just keep in mind that styles are constantly changing and your hair should look contemporary.

TATTOOS AND BODY PIERCINGS? Your choice, but a sparkler in your nose, a ring in your lip, three rings in your eyebrow, and a Raider Nation tattoo on your neck will probably not get you a job. Usually, if the advertiser is looking for an actor sporting a tattoo or an earring, they'll have makeup do the artwork or have wardrobe come up with a temporary prosthetic for the actor. Remember that a tattoo is a long-term choice that is very difficult, painful, and expensive to remove. For the purposes of TV commercial acting, I'd stay away.

And if you do have a tattoo, it would be a good idea to mask it as best you can before you have any meetings with agents or have an audition. You should also remove problematic earring(s) and cosmetically wax over any hole(s). For women, one earring in each ear is fine, as long as they are not distracting.

The closest I ever came to a tattoo was almost getting USMC emblazoned on my arm when I was in the Marine Corps, just out of boot camp and on my first liberty in San Diego. After too many cervezas, four of us new Marines went into a tattoo shop (cleverly positioned next to the bar), and I watched as the other three got their arms jabbed with needles and painted with ink. One fellow even ended up with CYNDI engraved on his arm...and of course a week later got a Dear John. I don't know why I declined that night, much to the heckling of my buddies, but at least for my acting career, I'm glad I did. Still, I often wonder if my buddy ever found another Cyndi.

YOUR HANDS HAVE TO BE CLEAN AND PRESENTABLE. You may be handling product in some commercials, so clean hands and well-trimmed fingernails are important. If you bite your nails, stop. If you have ugly warts, get rid of them, and if you're thinking about getting LOVE and HATE on your fingers, reread my thoughts in the section above that refers to tattoos.

LOOK AT YOUR TEETH. They don't have to be perfect, but make sure they're pretty straight. Discolored or missing teeth are a no-no. If your teeth are dark and dingy, use whitening strips or get them whitened. If your teeth need some cosmetic repair, get thee to a dentist. If they *are* perfect, you may get a toothpaste commercial!

IF YOU CAN'T SEE WITHOUT GLASSES, THINK ABOUT GETTING CORRECTIVE LENSES OR HAVING LASER SURGERY. Again, if the advertiser wants someone who wears glasses in the commercial for an effect, the wardrobe person will bring a selection of lens-less glasses to wear. Real glasses with corrective lenses are very hard to light and photograph because they bounce light into the camera lens.

LOOK AT THE CLOTHES THAT YOU'VE CHOSEN FOR YOUR SELF-ANALYSIS. Are there really many actors in your age category whom you see on commercials dressed like you are? Do you always dress the same way and have one "look"? A good rule of thumb? When you're in doubt about what to wear, always dress upscale, not down.

When choosing your clothing, colors are very important. The key is to find colors that accent and complement your hair, eyes, and skin tone in order to make your color headshot pop off the page and be noticed.

Are your clothing choices flattering to your body? That area of skin betwixt pants and top may really look great on a hard body, but a bare midriff bulge on most women is unattractive. Take a critical look at yourself, and then ask for a second opinion from someone you know who dresses well. (Everyone knows someone who dresses well.) Get his or her thoughts about both your colors and your choice of clothes. Some folks are naturally gifted in this area, and some are not. (My wife picks out all my clothes...)

Now, if your list of things you can change includes losing weight, doing your hair differently, no longer biting your nails, whitening your teeth, getting your eyes fixed so you can see without glasses, or spending some time rethinking your wardrobe, the time to address all those things is *now*, before you hire a photographer for that first photo session. Then you can start telling yourself that you're going to like your photo session and you're going to like the resulting headshot! Getting your picture taken is what this business is all about!

OKAY. I'VE MADE AN ANALYSIS OF MYSELF AND I'M WORKING ON THOSE THINGS THAT NEED ATTENTION. WHAT'S NEXT?

As already mentioned, at this point in your search for an agent, you need a *terrific* headshot. These days, eight-by-ten color photos are the norm. Your friends may say that three-quarters body shots and off-center framing are in vogue and the way to go, but, for right now, the most important thing is to make sure your face is in focus and is the focus of the picture. After you have an agent, you and he might change what your headshot will look like. Different areas of the country may prefer differently framed and different-looking, off-center headshots. New York headshots tend to be more avant-garde while Los Angeles tends to be more traditional. But no matter where you live, your focus for now should be on getting a great color eight-by-ten glossy with your face dominating the photo.

It helps to keep in mind that having your picture taken isn't easy. It takes the best of us not to feel a little self-conscious and tense. Photos don't lie, so if you're feeling stress or tension, it will show. But the more you practice something, the easier it will be next time. In fact, if you have a friend who dabbles in photography and is willing to shoot some practice headshots of you, go for it. In this age of digital cameras, you can have a whole lot of shots taken without incurring any cost. If you do decide to use a buddy for your practice shoot, however, make sure you explain the framing and the other perimeters. Remember that every time you have a photo session, you'll get more used to having your picture taken. And who knows? You might just end up with a pretty good-looking headshot that a professional photographer can use as a guide.

SO, I SHOULD USE A PROFESSIONAL FOR MY *REAL* HEADSHOT SESSION?

No matter how skilled your amateur friend is at photography, you'll most likely have to use a pro. There's a big difference between an amateur photographer and someone who knows focus, framing, and lighting, and shoots headshots for a living. Above all, be *very* prepared for your photo session. Actors seem to squander more hard-earned dollars on never-to-be-used headshots than on anything else. It's your money, so spend it wisely.

WHAT DO YOU MEAN BY "BE *VERY* PREPARED FOR THE SESSION"?

This is where your practice session(s) will come in handy. You'll know more about your most flattering angles and expressions because you were able to practice, and the more you know and practice going into the *real* photo session, the more relaxed and confident you'll be. You'll know what to expect and won't be intimidated.

Make sure you meet the photographer before you pay anyone anything. You should feel comfortable and relaxed with him before you hire him to work for you. Make triple sure you're satisfied that this is the right person for you. Don't be intimidated, and feel free to shop around if you don't feel exactly right about your relationship with the photographer or the photos you see. Otherwise, you'll be wasting your money. Remember that *you* are hiring the photographer and not the other way around!

Discuss beforehand exactly what you want him to do and what the headshot is for. If you're "seeking representation" (a fancy phrase for "looking for an agent"), then let the photographer know. Find out what his ideas are, where he plans to shoot, what clothes you should bring (colors, styles, number of changes), and what he suggests about makeup and hair. And most important, look at his book, which is a portfolio of headshots he's already taken of other actors. You'll not only see the quality of his work, but you'll get some ideas about what you want your headshot to look like.

Another great advantage in getting to know your photographer a bit before the shoot is that you'll be more inclined to talk during the session. You can ask him about his family, his career, his camera, if he ever uses 35 mm anymore, or how long he's been in the business. You'll find that he'll probably slow down a little, take an interest in you, and you'll end up with better pictures. Heck, you might even make a friend.

HOW CAN I FIND A PROFESSIONAL PHOTOGRAPHER?

That depends a lot on where you happen to live, but most photographers now have websites where an actor can go to look at their portfolios and prices. If you live in New York or Los Angeles, go online to Reproductions.com and look under "Photographer's Portfolios." In the L.A. section of this site alone, there are around 250 photographers listed. In New York there are just about as many. The best part about browsing? It's free. Spend a few hours online looking at different photographers' headshots, see whom you connect with, and narrow down the field.

If you live in a smaller market, you can call any local SAG or AFTRA office and ask if they publish a list of commercial photographers. If you know any other commercial actors in your area, see if you can take a look at their headshots and ask them who their photographer was.

HOW MUCH MONEY IS THE
PHOTOGRAPHER GOING TO COST ME?

That depends a lot on where you live, too. A good professional photographer in New York or L.A. will cost you more money than if you live in Salt Lake City or San Francisco. In a larger metropolitan area such as New York, where there are a lot of actors getting headshots, a photographer will cost anywhere from $500 to $1300. In San Francisco, a medium-size market for talent, the cost will be anywhere from $250 to $500 for headshots.

SHOULD MY HEADSHOT BE TAKEN OUTDOORS OR INDOORS? SHOULD IT BE IN COLOR? WHAT SIZE IS THE FINISHED PHOTO? ANYTHING ELSE?

Lots of questions—good! The more you ask, the better your pictures will turn out. Remember, no matter how many photos you have taken, at this point you're really looking for *one* terrific headshot. Just one. And here's what it should look like.

- The finished headshot should be an eight-by-ten glossy, and in color.

- Your face should be the dominant factor in the photo. In New York and some other locations, it seems to be a fashionable trend to go with the three-quarters body shot, but in your search for an agent, I'd suggest staying with a traditional *head*shot, no matter where you live.

- Since almost all commercials are positive in nature, solve problems in thirty seconds, and have a happy ending, you should be smiling enough to show some teeth. If you don't feel comfortable smiling so that your teeth show, you don't smile enough and need to practice in front of a mirror. And practice until you feel comfortable. Keep in mind that a *real* smile is a result of a happy thought. A real smile doesn't happen when the photographer says, "Smile!" So take your time. A real smile starts in the heart with a good thought, then that thought travels to the eyes, and finally it ends up at the mouth. You can't reverse the process and look genuine; it doesn't start at the mouth with a smile and then travel to the heart. Honest. Try it both ways.

- Your eyes should be visible and in focus. You can have your face slightly turned, but make sure you are looking directly into the camera lens.

- Your pose should be relaxed, almost as if someone called to you and you turned toward the voice, and at that moment, someone snapped a picture. It sounds easy enough, but it definitely takes getting used to.

- Don't show yourself in the middle of an activity. If you play a mean game of tennis, holding a racket is fine, but snapping a photo in the middle of your killer serve isn't.

- Stay away from wearing a hat or other headgear. The advertisers want to see your head and how much (or little) hair you have. Maybe they're looking for a balding father type for the commercial. Don't make them guess whether you have hair or not.

- Don't wear an outfit that may prove to be too revealing. It might get you a date but not a job. Keep in mind that Procter & Gamble is still the largest advertiser in the world.

- Stay away from wearing lots of jewelry. If your favorite earrings tend to make the person looking at your photo focus on the jewelry rather than your face, it's detracting and the wrong thing to be wearing.

- Light, everyday makeup is fine for females. And anyone, male or female, can apply a little cover-up to dark circles under the eyes or to hide a blemish or two. Many photographers have their own makeup person who will work with you during the shoot. It will cost you more, but it will usually be worth it.

- The photo can be shot outdoors or indoors. Either way, the background should tend to be nonspecific and out of focus. A park with out-of-focus foliage in the background is a common location. Sometimes the photographer will soft—spray paint a backdrop to look like out-of-focus foliage if he is shooting indoors.

- If the location is outdoors, make sure you're not in the bright sun. Bright sun on your face produces strange shadows, makes you squint, highlights wrinkles, and makes you look uncomfortable and strained.

- Usually stay away from anything in the background that might be construed as "product." Standing in front of a recognizable Lexus would prove disastrous if you ever used that photo while auditioning for a GM commercial.

  One exception to this (and there are always exceptions to any rule) was an old headshot of mine that my L.A. agent used to submit to casting folks. My wife and I own vineyards and a winery in Sonoma Valley, and in the shot, I'm standing in front of this terrific winery truck that has our GLENLYON VINEYARDS & WINERY logo on the door. You could barely make out the logo on the truck (and on my shirt), but the photo always seemed to work as a conversation starter on auditions, and growing grapes and making wine are two of my favorite topics. There's no problem because the old '54 Chevy truck was more of a classic item of interest than a product conflict. I would not use the photo while auditioning in Utah for a Mormon ad agency, however.

- Make sure the picture you select is representative of you and how you look *now*. And question the photo that everyone says is "soooooo flattering!" That may mean it doesn't look like you at all.

- The nice thing about shooting digital is that you can see your photos as your photographer is shooting them, and you can make sure you're both on the same track.

DOESN'T ANYONE USE 35 MM ANYMORE?

Hardly ever. Digital shots look just as good, you can get your proofs online, it's cheaper to reproduce, and you don't have to fool around with sending in negatives to get prints.

HOW DO I GET TO SEE MY PHOTOS?

The photographer will usually take a couple of hundred photos with his digital camera, and then either post those photos on his website or e-mail your photos to you so you can pick and choose. The photographer may also send you a disc though the mail so you have a hard copy as a backup. I would also ask the photographer to snail-mail you a contact sheet, which has a lot of small photos on individual sheets, so you can easily compare your photos side by side with a magnifying glass. It's harder to compare and confusing if you have to download individual pictures on your computer. Just make sure to ask him beforehand if the contact sheet is included in his price.

HOW LONG DO I HAVE TO WAIT TO SEE MY PHOTOS?

Until your payment clears.

HOW DO I SELECT THE ONE PHOTO FOR MY HEADSHOT?

Pick out the three or four photos you like the best that fit the above criteria, live with them for a day or two, and show them to people and get their reactions. Then you can make up your mind on which one or two are perfect.

CAN I HAVE MY PHOTOGRAPH TOUCHED UP?

Your photo can certainly be digitally corrected to enhance colors and clarity (and get rid of that pesky pimple), but resist the temptation to digitally erase wrinkles, crow's-feet, or smile lines. Your photo should look like you. My agent told me that he once had an actor who had digitally added some hair to his headshot where there wasn't any in reality. Casting directors will have trouble with that because the photo won't look like the actor will in person. Remember, today's commercial casting is much more about "real people" anyway. Not perfect model types.

NOW THAT I'VE SELECTED MY PERFECT HEADSHOT, WHAT DO I DO WITH IT?

Once you've made up your mind and picked out that perfect headshot, you need to get reproductions made so you can submit them to agents. There are a lot of places to have that done, but a dependable and not-too-expensive favorite can be found online at Reproductions.com. (This isn't a plug for that particular company, but it's who I've used; they do a good job, they're very dependable, they're up-front, and you can do it all online.) You can either e-mail them your photo or snail-mail it on a disc after you've selected it. One of the great advantages of digital photography is that it's much easier and sharper than getting reproductions made from a 35 mm negative, and there's no loss in resolution.

WHAT DOES *THAT* COST ME?

Look online. For instance, at Reproductions.com, a hundred photos cost less than a buck per copy. If you get two hundred, the cost per photo goes down considerably. And the next time you have reprints done, they will be considerably cheaper because your photo and format are already on file.

SHOULD I HAVE MY NAME PUT ON THE FRONT OF THE PHOTO?

Yep. Have only your name professionally printed on the bottom of the photo. Right, center, or left. It's your choice. You can pick out the paper weight (I like normal instead of heavy), your font style (my daughter likes "avant-garde" and I like "impress"), whether you want to use all uppercase letters (I do), whether you want a white border all the way around (I do), and where you want your name to be on the headshot (I like lower, center in the white area, but sometimes I do it differently). Reproductions.com explains all that. You'll be attaching a résumé to the rear of the headshot, but I'd also neatly print your name and contact information on the back of the headshot.

HOW MANY COPIES SHOULD I GET?

It's up to you, but I'd start with a hundred. It's not that much more money than getting fifty, and if you don't use them all, you can give them away to your mom, dad, and uncle Tom at Christmastime.

HOW WILL I KNOW IF I'VE CHOSEN
THE RIGHT PHOTOGRAPHER?

If the photographer makes a living doing what he does, then he's undoubtedly got some talent. He may, however, not be the right photographer for *you*. That's why it's so important to look at his portfolio and meet with him before your shoot date. It makes no difference whether he's shot on location for *National Geographic*, or he's photographed movie stars for *People* magazine, if you feel intimidated or uneasy, it will show in the photo. No matter if he's the most famous photographer in the world—if he's not right for you, he's not the right choice, and it's a waste of your money.

The best example I've ever seen of choosing the *wrong* photographer is on the next page. They are my wife's old headshots that I used in the first edition of this book. Even though the two photos are black-and-white (the way we used to do it) and a bit dated, I've never seen a better example of contrasting photos that were taken just one week apart by two different photographers. The first photo (on the left) was my wife's first headshot, taken by a professional photographer whom I'd used a few times before. He always did a good job with my headshots, so I assumed hers would also be good. Unfortunately, he was in a hurry that day, and the fact that Suzy felt rushed and uncomfortable showed in the photo.

Suzy immediately found a woman photographer with whom she felt very much at ease, and she had another headshot session (the photo on the right). And what a difference! Even though these two headshots were taken just one week apart, the actress on the right got her agent. The actress on the left wouldn't have had much of a chance of getting an interview. I've taken the liberty of reprinting them in this edition to show you the differences between the two.

WHAT ARE THE MAIN DIFFERENCES
BETWEEN THE HEADSHOTS?

LEFT PHOTO	**RIGHT PHOTO**
*A tense, forced smile	*A relaxed, natural smile
*Background too sharp and patterned	*Background out of focus and soft
*Contrast is too high	*Contrast is soft and shows shading
*No highlight on hair for depth	*Hair has shadings and texture
*Shot in bright sun—eyes are squinting	*Shot in shade with reflected light
*Turtleneck makes subject look closed up	*Open plaid shirt looks casual with a layered effect
*Dull and lifeless	*High energy and alert
*No agent with this headshot!	*Got her agent with this headshot!

GOT A GOOD EXAMPLE OF A CURRENT HEADSHOT?

Yep. Below is Lexy Fridell's headshot (note the coincidence of the last name) that she used while searching for her agent in New York. Keep in mind that it was for the New York market so it is more of a three-quarters look. As far as attitude and energy, I guess she *did* learn something from her old man. (Keep in mind that it was originally in color and it has been reduced from an eight-by-ten for this book.)

Lexy Fridell

WHY IS IT A GOOD HEADSHOT?

The photo has that if-someone-called-your-name-and-you-turned-around look to it. Her face is the focus of the photo, and she shows teeth; she has a nice, relaxed, natural, nonforced smile that appears to be the result of a positive, happy thought. The background is colorful but soft and out of focus, with contrast that shows shading. Her hair has texture and the earrings are subtle enough not to draw attention away from her face. The choice of clothing shows layers, and the top is casual and flattering. It's a high-energy photo and it got her an agent and some work! Ultimately, that's why it's a good headshot!

OKAY—I'VE GOT A GREAT HEADSHOT! WHAT'S NEXT?

Turn the page. You need to work on your résumé.

CHAPTER 2

YOUR FIRST RÉSUMÉ

In the beginning of their careers, Marilyn Monroe did an ad for Union Oil, Clint Eastwood was a spokesman for the Milk Advisory Board, Jodie Foster frolicked for Coppertone, and Joe Mantegna pitched Ragú spaghetti sauce.

In the same way that a good, clear, easy-to-look-at, up-to-date headshot is vital to attracting a commercial talent agent, a good, clear, easy-to-look-at, up-to-date résumé is also extremely important. Most agents and casting directors will not even consider an actor who doesn't have a professional-looking résumé either posted online or printed.

GOT AN EXAMPLE OF A GOOD RÉSUMÉ?

Yep. On the next page is Lexy's actual résumé that she used in New York when she was looking for commercial representation. It is reduced for the book, but normally would be eight-by-ten, the same size as her headshot.

SHOULD MY RÉSUMÉ BE ATTACHED TO MY HEADSHOT?

Yes. Remember that your résumé and headshot should always be exactly the same size. If you print your résumé at home, your paper will be 8½-by-11, so keep that in mind when you're formatting your mar-

LEXY FRIDELL

AEA / AFTRA / SAG

(555) 555-5555 LexyFridell@nyc.net

Height: 5'3"   Weight: 105   Hair: brown   Eyes: hazel

MUSICAL THEATRE:

DR. DOOLITTLE	Polynesia	NYC/PCLO readings/*Richard Sabellico*
GREASE!	Frenchy	Kansas City Starlight/*Barry Ivan*
HELLO DOLLY	Ermengarde	Pittsburgh CLO/*Glen Casale*
LITTLE SHOP OF HORRORS	Audrey	Summer Repertory Theatre, CA
PETER PAN	Wendy	Summer Repertory Theatre, CA
THE WILD PARTY	Dolores	Carnegie Mellon University
A MY NAME IS ALICE	Alice #1	Carnegie Mellon University
COLE	Soloist	Idyllwild Arts Academy
THE SECRET GARDEN	Martha	San Domenico Theatre, CA
ONCE ON THIS ISLAND	Ti Moune	San Domenico Theatre, CA
PETER PAN	Peter	Broadway Bound Productions, CA
CINDERELLA	Fairy Godmother	San Francisco Conservatory of Music

THEATRE:

SYLVIA	Sylvia	Summer Repertory Theatre, CA
BILOXI BLUES	Daisy	Summer Repertory Theatre, CA
THE LOYALIST	Flora	TRUE readings/*Richard Sabellico*
STREET SCENE	Mae	Summer Repertory Theatre, CA
PENSION GRILLPARZER	Man / Walks / Hands	Summer Repertory Theatre, CA
SLY FOX	Ms. Fancy	Carnegie Mellon University
SPOUSE SWAPPING	Chelsey	Carnegie Mellon University
RICHARD II	Queen	Carnegie Mellon University
BOY GETS GIRL	Harriet	Carnegie Mellon University
WINNIE THE POOH	Roo	Sonoma County Repertory, CA
OUR TOWN	Stage Manager	Idyllwild Arts Academy
CHEKHOV'S THE CELEBRATION	Mrs. Merchutkin	Idyllwild Arts Academy
KING LEAR	Fool	San Domenico Theatre, CA
THE WINTER'S TALE	Emilia	San Domenico Theatre, CA
LITTLE WOMEN	Jo	San Domenico Theatre, CA

TRAINING

—**BFA Musical Theatre/Acting, Carnegie Mellon School of Drama**
Recipient of "Adelene Roth Memorial Award" for Acting
—**Idyllwild Arts Academy**, Graduate in Acting
—**Acting:** *(your acting teachers / coaches should go here)*
—**Singing:** *(your acting teachers / coaches should go here)*
San Francisco Conservatory of Music: Merit Scholarship for Voice
American Conservatory Theatre's Young Actor's Musical Theatre Program
Point Park Summer Dance Program

SPECIAL SKILLS

Puppeteering, basic piano, American and European Dialects/Accents, Kid/cartoon voices, ballet, tap, stage combat/fencing, clowning, mask, commedia, and a nose trick!

gins. Visualize it reduced to eight-by-ten. There are two ways to attach your résumé to your headshot: My favorite is to staple your résumé to the back of your headshot with two staples at the top, always with your résumé print-side out. The second way is to have your résumé *printed* on the back of your headshot. The reason I don't like the résumé printed on the back as much is that each time you add a credit and have to redo your résumé, you have to toss the headshot. Having it printed on the back also gives the viewer a sense that you don't do enough work to change your résumé very often.

WHAT SHOULD I INCLUDE ON MY RÉSUMÉ?

Let's go back to Lexy's résumé and take a look at it, top to bottom.

Her Name
Lexy's given name is Alexandra, but she prefers and uses her nickname. It's fine to use either one, but don't include both. Whatever name you use on your résumé and your headshot should be the name you want to be called. If Lexy had put Alexandra "Lexy" Fridell at the top of the page it would leave doubt as to what people should call her. Don't confuse anyone.

Her Union Affiliation
Lexy then listed her three unions. AEA stands for Actors' Equity Association; AFTRA stands for American Federation of Television and Radio Artists; SAG stands for Screen Actors Guild. (See chapter 5, The Unions.) If you belong to any of these unions, be sure to list them. If you don't . . . then don't. And *never* fib. SAG *eligible* is not the same as actually belonging to and being a dues-paying member of SAG. If you do belong to all three unions, I'd list AEA first. Why? It's the hardest acting union to get into and it means that you have worked onstage professionally. It carries some weight because it implies that you are a well-trained actor and automatically commands a degree of respect.

Her Telephone Number and E-mail Address
Lexy's telephone number is listed near her name and should be the number where she can *always* be found at a moment's notice. For that

reason, your cell phone number is probably the best to list. Your e-mail address should also be included.

Her Vital Statistics

After your name, possible unions, your telephone number, and your e-mail address should come your vital statistics. Your height and weight should be accurate—not how tall you'd *like* to be nor what you'd *like* to weigh in two months. Along with your height and weight, include your hair and eye color. If you're a trained singer (that means you're willing and eager to sing something a cappella upon request), you should include your vocal range.

Her Credits

Usually your résumé will break down your experience into the following categories:

Your **THEATER** work

Your **TELEVISION** work

Your **FILM** work

Your **TRAINING**

Your **SPECIAL ABILITIES**

You'll notice that Lexy's résumé had no TELEVISION or FILM entries at this stage in her career, so it wouldn't have been a good idea to list either one as categories and then have no credits underneath! Since she's light in that area, she took advantage of the fact that she's done a lot of THEATER work, and she chose to divide her THEATER work into two subcategories: MUSICAL THEATER and THEATER. Good idea? In this case, I'd say it was a *very* good idea. It draws attention to the fact that she is a serious actor with a lot of stage experience. Remember that no two résumés are the same.

Under THEATER work it's customary to list the name of the play or musical, followed by the character played, and then at which theater the production took place. Sometimes a director's name is included if it might be a name an agent (and later, a casting director, a director, or a producer) might recognize. The world of acting is very small, so including a director's name might just be the spark that ignites a great conversation between you and your prospective agent! An interview that started out with "Oh, you worked with Peter Brosius on *Nemo*! We went to college together!" would probably be a very good interview.

Your TRAINING is then listed. And if your training is the biggest part of your résumé, then that's where your focus should be. If you don't have many (or any) credits, then your training shows how serious you are and how much desire you have to learn and be successful.

SPECIAL ABILITIES is usually the last category on your résumé. Just make sure that whatever abilities you list in this section you can perform at the drop of a hat!

If your résumé lists that you can juggle, you'd better be prepared to grab three balls and keep them airborne for a while. If you include that you have a nose trick, you're undoubtedly going to be asked to show your special ability to anyone and everyone who looks at your résumé. It better be a pretty good nose trick, because you're going to be doing it a lot! (Ask Lexy to show you hers!)

WHAT IF I DON'T HAVE *ANY* STAGE OR TELEVISION OR FILM CREDITS?

Even without any credits on your résumé, listing your training and workshop classes can still help a talent agent decide whether he wants to meet with you. No matter how much or how little experience you have, you can create a résumé that looks professional, is interesting, truthful, to the point, has your contact information, and is easy to read. If you don't have any film experience, then focus on television credits. If you don't have either of those, then focus on your theater roles. If you have absolutely no professional experience, then focus on your training. Be comforted that although many actors may have *more* to put on their résumés than you do, a lot will have *less*. Remember that every movie star, every television series regular, and every commercial actor with hundreds (or thousands!) of commercial credits all started somewhere, and, in the beginning, each one was sporting pretty much a blank résumé. No one is born with experience.

WHAT IF I DON'T HAVE ANY TRAINING?

Then get some. In fact, get a lot. You've already read the introduction to this book so you know how difficult it is to succeed in this business. That means you need to become very competitive. If you haven't taken any acting classes, improvisation classes, or commercial acting classes, then what are you waiting for? Almost every community college in these United States has a bevy of acting classes that are pretty much free, so get a course description and enroll in every one you have time for! Not only will you learn a lot, but you'll get to meet people who have the same interests, you'll be making contacts, you'll make friends, and you'll have something to put on your résumé!

CAN I FUDGE THE TRUTH A LITTLE BIT ON MY RÉSUMÉ?

Don't do it. One of two things will happen: You'll either get caught in your lie, or you'll be so worried that someone will discover you've lied on your résumé that you won't do well during an interview. Honest. Trust me.

Three Quick Stories
When I was just starting out my acting career in L.A., a friend of mine (who was also beginning his career) decided that his credits were lacking that little something extra to make his résumé more impressive and exciting. Since he didn't have any classic stage credits and felt it was important, he listed one. He included on his résumé that in college he had played Aeschines, one of the minor roles in Shakespeare's *Pericles*. Since the play was rarely performed and is certainly one of the more obscure of the Bard's plays (it's not even listed in the First Folio), he felt pretty safe. He sent out his headshots and résumés, made his telephone calls, made the rounds, and finally got an appointment with a commercial agent. An exciting day!

And you can guess what happened . . . He went to an office to meet with an agent, proudly presented his new headshot and slick-looking (but embellished) résumé, and was invited to sit down. As the agent began reading my pal's résumé from top to bottom, he stopped, broke out in a big smile, looked up and said, "You did *Pericles*? I did the show in college too!" It was the *only* credit the talent agent wanted to talk about. So, how'd my friend do? First came the stammering, then the flop-sweat, then the sheepish admission that he had fudged a bit on the résumé. Needless to say, he left the interview with egg on his face. The moral of the story? Don't fib on your résumé. Or you'd better be a pretty good Shakespearean scholar.

It's also interesting to note that my buddy eventually stopped trying to be an actor and changed careers. Guess what his profession is now? He's a very successful casting director in Los Angeles!

Another actor friend in those L.A. days of yesteryear also felt that *his* résumé didn't have enough television credits, even though he had an agent, had done some episodic television, and had even guest-starred on a few TV shows. So he decided to embellish *his* résumé. One of the credits he added was a guest-starring role in one episode of a long-canceled, one-season television series that had been shot on location in New York. Since he was an L.A.-based actor, he felt he was pretty safe.

When he appeared at an audition for a new episodic TV pilot, the producer looked at his résumé, got a curious look on his face, and started asking the actor a few questions about his role in the long-canceled show. You guessed it. The producer for the pilot also produced the series in New York. Again, the moral of the story? Don't fib on your résumé. Or do a lot of research on the show credits of the producer and director you're going to read for.

Because he knew I was writing a book on commercial acting, my L.A. agent collected and sent me some reject photos and résumés he received that otherwise would have gone in his circular file. One résumé caught my eye. The young man was twenty-two years old and he had listed a total of fifty-seven adult roles he had played onstage, including the title roles in both *Othello* and *King Lear.* We figured that if he'd started performing right out of high school, he'd have had to have done major roles in about fifteen productions each year! The lad never was called in for an interview. Once again: Don't fib on your résumé. Or even stretch the truth. If you've acted in fifty-seven acting scenes in an acting class, they don't count, and don't list them on your résumé. If you *have* acted in fifty-seven plays, then list your favorites that you'd like to talk about. The bottom line, and for the last time: *Don't fib on your résumé!*

IF I DON'T HAVE MUCH TO PUT ON MY RÉSUMÉ AND DON'T WANT TO FIB, WHY EVEN HAVE A RÉSUMÉ?

Even if you've only taken some acting classes and have only a few stage credits, a résumé can help agents, casting people, directors, producers, and clients remember you. It can also give you something to talk about during an interview. Even if you have only a little experience listed on your résumé, it can help be an icebreaker during an interview.

When I was first starting out and didn't have a heck of a lot to put on my résumé, I always included that I was a high school drama teacher and it was enough to start conversations. And, as I've said, if you don't have a lot of experience, don't worry. Every actor has to begin somewhere. Unless your surname is Barrymore, none of us are born with a résumé attached to our diaper.

BUT I DON'T HAVE *ANYTHING* TO PUT ON MY RÉSUMÉ EXCEPT FOR MY NAME!

Then I'd suggest you set down this book, put things on hold for a while, and get busy. How can you possibly know that you want to be an actor if you haven't ever tried acting? You need some training and you need some acting classes!

IF I'VE DONE A FEW COMMERCIALS, SHOULD I LIST THEM ON MY RÉSUMÉ?

Nope. You should be proud of each and every commercial you've done, but listing them on your résumé isn't a good idea. If you want to show that you've been in some commercials, make that entry on your résumé something like this.

Commercial list on request.

Or you might want to be a little more specific, particularly if you'd like to talk about your commercials with the prospective talent agent, and write something like this.

One or more commercials for each of the following advertising agencies:

> Saatchi & Saatchi
> Leo Burnett
> Ogilvy & Mather

If the topic of commercials that you've done *does* come up during the interview, have at your beck and call the name of the director, and at least one key advertising agency person's name who was present on the shoot. Above all, always speak with enthusiasm and excitement about how much fun it was on the shoot, what great people you met, and how much you learned. People will pick up on your enthusiasm! If you say how hard the job was, how much you hated the rude director, and the fact that the day was a bust because the spots never aired, people will pick up on your negative energy.

WHY ISN'T IT A GOOD IDEA TO LIST THE COMMERCIALS I'VE DONE ON MY RÉSUMÉ?

Two Reasons

A PERCEIVED CONFLICT: If I listed a commercial that I had done for Miller Beer, and then went in to audition for a Bud Light spot, I probably wouldn't be considered for the job. This would be true even if the Miller spot had been released two or three years before. Advertisers are funny that way.

A PERCEPTION OF OVEREXPOSURE: If I were to list the thousands of commercials I've done over the years (see the appendix of this book if you're interested), the advertiser would definitely feel that I was "overexposed." The perception would be that I had done so many commercials, the viewing audience might associate me with a product other than their product.

SHOULD I LIST MY AGE?

Adults shouldn't list their birth dates on their résumés. The picture should speak for itself. That's why it's enormously important to have your photograph look exactly like you do right now. Almost every actor thinks he looks younger than the age on his driver's license. One of my agent's key gripes is to have a forty-year-old actress in his office who has listed an age range on her résumé of 18–25, but he knows he wouldn't be able to sell the actress anywhere under thirty-five. He says that even though he's been in the business of marketing and selling people for a long time, sometimes an actor will even choose to argue the point with him. He's had even one résumé cross his desk where an actor listed an age range of 20–65!

CAN YOU REVIEW THOSE *GREAT* RÉSUMÉ TIPS?

Sure.

- Always have an electronic file of your résumé saved on a word-processing program on your computer so you can easily update it and tweak it when need be.

- Adjust the margins on your electronic file to eight-by-ten, the same size as your headshot. If your program won't reduce the size to eight-by-ten, after printing, use a paper-cutter to cut your résumé exactly and squarely to eight-by-ten. Don't use scissors.

- Use an easy-to-read font style and size. You can adjust the size of the font depending on how much information you have to put on your résumé. Just make sure it's easy to read. Size 6 font isn't a good choice.

- Always have someone else proofread for spelling and punctuation to pick out something you may have missed. Take a good look at Lexy's résumé. No mistakes!

- Your résumé will, most likely, be stapled to the back of your headshot. That way, all someone has to do is turn over the headshot and see the résumé on the back.

- Your résumé should *never* be more than one page. If it looks too busy or the font size is too small to read, you need to either eliminate some credits or rearrange and categorize the data so it's easy to look at and absorb.

- Decide what your name is going to be, then use only that as your name. If your christened name is Michael and you want to be known as Mike, then that's what should be on your headshot and your résumé. Try not to confuse the agent or anyone else. If your name happened to be Tom Cruise and you went down to join SAG, the union would tell you there was another Tom Cruise who was already a union member. So, from that point on, you might have to join the union as Thomas Cruise and be known by that name.

- Make sure your contact information, both day and night, is correct and current. If someone wants to get ahold of you, he should be able to do that with no effort. These days, a cell phone number is the best choice.

- Leave out any unnecessary information. Marital status, astrological signs, and whether you like puppies and work to save whales are all no-noes.

- It is best not to include your measurements or your sizes. They are important for modeling but not for television commercials. You got your agent because he thinks you look like someone who is going to be employed in commercials, and that means a 10 percent commission for him. Your look is more important than your exact size. Later on, when you *do* get a commercial and they need to fit you into clothing for the shoot, a wardrobe person will collect all your current size information.

- List all the information on your résumé in very separate categories.

- Tell the truth when you're listing anything on your résumé, including your real height and weight.

- Make sure your résumé is absolutely perfect in both the content and the way it looks on the paper. It should be easy to look at and read. If it's less than that, you've wasted your time, effort, and money.

WHAT ABOUT USING A BIO INSTEAD OF A RÉSUMÉ?

After years of credits and establishing an extensive résumé of work, sometimes it might be more appropriate to use a bio instead of a résumé. At this stage in your career, however, stick with the résumé. In case you're interested, my bio looks like the sample on the next page.

SQUIRE FRIDELL

Squire Fridell has been a professional working actor since 1969 and may hold the distinction of being the only actor to have never drawn unemployment benefits. He holds a Master's Degree in Acting/Directing and for forty years has taught and directed both professional actors and young actors at every level: elementary school to the professional stage.

Mr. Fridell is also one of the most successful actors ever in television commercials. For almost four decades he has performed as principal on-camera talent in over 3,250 TV commercials and appeared in some living room, somewhere in America, on the average of once a night selling something to someone . . . doing everything from squeezing toilet paper, smiling over a cup of coffee, asking for a light beer, jumping in the air for Toyota, or even chasing the Hamburglar around McDonaldland as television's Ronald McDonald. He is the author of four published plays, has written a couple of screenplays that have yet to find their way to the big screen, and wrote the definitive commercial acting text, *Acting in Television Commercials for Fun and Profit*.

He has starred in twelve television pilots (mostly short lived) and five big-screen features (mostly unmemorable films). He was also one of the last "Contract Players" at Universal Studios and has starred or guest-starred in any number of television series and shows over the years. He has been on the cover of *TV Guide*, photo-featured in *Newsweek* magazine, and says his true claim to fame was once being "# one-across" in the *Daily Variety* crossword puzzle.

Squire and his wife, Suzy, now live in Glen Ellen, California, where they grow grapes and reputedly make "The Best Syrah On The Planet."

You can visit them at GlenLyonWinery.com anytime.

CHAPTER 3

THE PUBLICATIONS AND POOPSHEETS

Anthony Hopkins couldn't remember his lines during his first outing as an actor and was fired.

Now that you have a terrific headshot and well-done résumé, it's time to find out as much as you can about this industry. Before the advent of the Internet, actors relied a lot on the U.S. Postal Service to deliver daily, weekly, or monthly publications to tell them what shows were being cast, which schools were available, who was teaching the classes being offered, where the jobs were shooting, and what actors who were working a lot had to say. We pored over the latest copies of *Daily Variety,* the *Hollywood Reporter, Commercials Monthly* magazine, *Back Stage West, Drama-Logue, LA Casting* magazine and a host of others. Even though some of those publications are still snail-mailed out to actors, producers, talent agents, directors, and casting agencies, today most of the folks who choose to subscribe do so online. It's cheaper, it's much faster, and it saves a tree or two.

Because most actors who want to work in commercials also want to work on TV, in film, and/or live theatre, there aren't any publications, online or otherwise, that devote *all* their energy solely to TV commercials. Even though your interest may be focused only on television commercials at the moment, I think it would be a good idea to take a look at what other work might be available to you as an actor. You never know . . .

Many of the subscription services below are better utilized if you already have your agent, but you should be aware of them and what they offer right off the bat.

First, both SAG and AFTRA have national and regional magazines and fliers that they periodically send out to their members. You can usually get copies of these by calling your regional union chapter and nicely asking for a copy. It might cost you a few dollars, but it's worth it.

Next, use the Internet and check out the sites I've listed below to pick and choose which other publications and services you might want to subscribe to. Sometimes there is no charge for posting your headshot and résumé, but be aware that each of the sites is in the periodical business to make a profit, and I've yet to see one that didn't eventually have some sort of a subscription fee involved. I have not listed each and every service, but the ones below are pretty tried and proven. (I'm registered with the first two.)

I've also taken the liberty to ask Cris Dennis (my Los Angeles agent) his opinion of a few of these that he uses, and I've included his response. (What better source than from the agent's mouth?)

Casting Networks
CastingNetworks.com

- Membership required.

- Four geographical regions to choose from: Los Angeles, New York, San Francisco, Miami.

- You can submit yourself electronically.

- A very good way to get your headshot and résumé seen by agents because you can post your headshot(s), résumé, and reel online as part of the service.

- You can access lists of the agents and casting directors who subscribe to Casting Network's services.

- Good source for each of the above regions and a good service for both nonunion and union talent.

- Casting notices are sent via e-mail directly to you.

Cris Dennis says:

> LA Casting is part of Casting Networks, and currently LA Casting gets the lion's share of commercial projects. I like this resource and guesstimate that 98 percent of all commercial casting directors in the Los Angeles market post their projects on LA Casting.
>
> A great resource that they offer to talent (both union and nonunion) looking for representation is their "Talent Scout" feature. Actors can post themselves in this section and agents in their geographic area (and even other areas) are able to peruse at their leisure. I try to personally log on to this feature every day. I can enter in the parameters that I am looking for, such as age ranges, ethnicity, gender, et cetera, and get a list of available actors in those categories who are looking for an agent to represent them. I can view their résumés and pictures, union affiliations, and in some cases, demo reels.
>
> And no personal information is given out to the agents. If I see some talent that my agency might be interested in contacting, I put those names in a folder and then send each of them an e-mail from me directly through Casting Networks. Casting Networks then contacts the actors so I never even see their e-mail address.
>
> My note to them will be something like "My name is Cris Dennis with Film Artists Associates and if you are interested in commercial representation I would like to set up a meeting. Please call me at 818-883-5008. I look forward to hearing from you."
>
> I've found and signed a few working actors for my stable this way. As I said, I like this service.

Actors Access
ActorsAccess.com

- Part of a parent company, Breakdown Services, used by casting agents and agents.

- Membership required.

- Geographical: LA, NY, FL, HI, CO, UT, TX, the Southeast, Chicago, Vancouver, Toronto.

- You can submit yourself electronically.

- Another good way to get your headshot and résumé seen by agents, because you can post your headshot(s), résumé, and reel online as part of the service.

- Good source for each of the above regions and a good service for both nonunion and union talent.

- Casting notices are sent via e-mail directly to you.

Cris Dennis says:
I also like this site and it is the other main website that posts commercial projects for agents to work on. The site posts some print work and commercial projects that are both union and nonunion and still holds the monopoly on theatrical break-downs.

Many casting agents will post their projects on this site and there are one or two casting directors who will use only the parent company, Breakdown Services, exclusively. They offer a similar service (like LA Casting) to their members looking for representation and will e-mail a "talent link" to agents.

Clicking on the link brings up a page of actors looking for representation. Agents can view pictures, résumés, demo reels, and be able to contact actors to set up a meeting.

Ross Reports
RossReports.com

- Established in 1949.

- The best and most current guide to all the names, addresses, and telephone numbers of casting agents and agencies.

- The big plus to Ross Reports is the amount of detail given on each individual agent within the agency, the actor types whom they handle, and how they accept submissions for representation.

The listing in Ross Reports for Cris' agency (and my agency), Film Artists Associates, looks like this.

ROSS REPORTS TELEVISION AND FILM LISTING
PUBLISHED BY VNU BUSINESS MEDIA (THE FILM GROUP)

770 Broadway, 4th Floor
New York, NY 10003
(646) 654-5729
FAX (646) 654-5471

FILM ARTISTS ASSOCIATES (SAG-EQUITY)

21044 Ventura Boulevard, #215
Woodland Hills, CA 91364
Phone: (818) 883-5008
Fax:
E-mail:
Website:

Designated Agents: Cris Dennis (Adult—Commercial); Pen Dennis (Over Scale/Celebrities); Martha Dennis (Business Affairs). Actors/ actresses, comedians, ethnic/foreign types, seniors (mature), spokespersons. Interviews by appointment only. Accepts photos/resumes by mail only. Do not send demo tapes unless requested. Attends showcases.

CRIS DENNIS

Film Artists Associates
Serving the commercial casting industry for almost 40 years
818-883-5008

Cris Dennis says:
> *I highly recommend Ross Reports. They update their information on agencies very regularly and the information they publish is accurate. Ross Reports is a great site for actors looking for representation!*

Backstage
Backstage.com

- Three subscription levels (the middle level includes Ross Reports).

- Membership required.

- A weekly *Back Stage Magazine* (sort of a *People* magazine for the industry) is offered at the most expensive subscription level.

- You can post your headshot, résumé, and reel.

- Geographically lists a lot of nonunion and union commercial submissions and audition opportunities; lots of commercial acting classes are posted.

- Like the other services, you can easily customize your job search so that specific casting notices will be sent to you via e-mail.

Screen Actors Guild
Sag.org

- Even as a nonmember of SAG, you can go to their site and pick up a lot of information.

- They list all their regional SAG offices (over twenty) and contact information.

- You can access their current lists of agents, both franchised and ATA/NATR (see chapter 6, The Talent Agent) and get a lot of information.

- Unlike Ross Reports, where a full explanation is given, SAG uses only abbreviations to indicate an agency's specialty. (FS: full service, C: commercials, and so on.)

Players Directory
PlayersDirectory.com

- Since 1937!

- This is both an online service and a physical publication for actors primarily in L.A.

- Virtually every established actor who wants to work in TV and film has his headshot in here.

- There are a myriad of acting classes listed, but otherwise not very useful for the commercial actor.

The Casting Frontier

CastingFrontier.com

- This new service is worth taking a look at, even though at this point in your search for your agent, it's not a service that will do you much good.

- It goes one step further than Actors Access or Casting Networks, because casting agencies actually handle their auditions online. (Whether online auditions will eventually replace actual in-person auditions remains to be seen . . . only time will tell.)

- You get all the benefits of being able to post your headshot, résumé, and a reel, plus have access to your auditions.

Other Sites You Can Search

Aftra.com

CastingCall.com

Variety.com

HollywoodReporter.com

There are several websites besides the ones I've listed that promise to get your headshot, résumé, and reel in front of agents, casting directors, and producers. Most have a subscription fee and most are not used by industry professionals for casting. At this stage in your search for an agent, you might think about using Ross Reports for a good up-to-date list of agents and their specialties and Casting Networks to get your headshot seen by an agent if you're in the right geographical areas. But before you spend your money to sign up, I'd finish reading the rest of the book. That way you'll have much more knowledge about what you want to do and how you want to do it.

It's important that you understand what talent agents do, how the submission process works, and how to submit your headshot for representation, so spend some time online and get familiar with the different industry websites.

IF I'M NOT YET REPRESENTED BY A TALENT AGENT, SHOULD I HAVE MY HEADSHOT(S) AND RÉSUMÉ POSTED?

Definitely. It's a good way to get your face in front of a talent agent and there are a lot of nonunion postings that would be useful to know about. If you're not yet represented by a talent agency, however, there's not much chance you'll be called in by a casting director for a union audition.

WHY DON'T THE UNIONS HAVE THIS SERVICE FOR THEIR MEMBERS?

SAG, for one, just realized they were a few years behind the curve and they have started a digital base service as part of their website.

SPEAKING OF ONLINE, SOME OF MY FRIENDS HAVE THEIR OWN WEBSITES. WHAT DO YOU THINK?

At this stage in your journey, I'd say forget it. A personal website might be a nice addition to your overall sales package, but right now it's not necessary, and no talent agent or casting director is going to take the time to look at it. Instead of putting your energy into creating a website, focus your attention on getting that perfect headshot and résumé.

If you *do* choose to have a website (again, I wouldn't waste my time at this point), its purpose should be to enable someone to find out more information about you and/or see the level of your professional work. You could include some production shots of you from stage shows you've been in, favorable reviews, and even a section devoted to audition material or, better yet, some existing professional footage of you. Think of a website as an embellishment of your headshot and résumé. However, it might not be a good idea to include an actual commercial you've done. If you showed a scene from a Toyota commercial, a casting director, a client, or an ad agency for Ford might construe it as a possible conflict of products.

Your website must be professional-looking, easy-to-navigate, and have a sensible address. Instead of a clever moniker such as IAma VeryCoolDude.com, use your first and last name if it's available. If someone else is using that address, just add your age or the last digits of your phone number after your name. Feel free to visit Lexy's website if you'd like: LexyFridell.com. I think she did a good job with it! I don't have a personal website for Squire Fridell, but feel free to log on to our winery website at GlenLyonWinery.com. A good friend, Clarke Smith, did it for us, and we think it's informative, easy to navigate, fun, and has some humor. Again, my recommendation for you at this stage is to put your energy into your headshot and résumé and worry about a website later.

HOW ABOUT A BLOG?

Although a lot of recognizable TV and film stars use blogs as a fan club tool, for most of us, a blog is a poor man's website. It's generally much more informal than a website, and for the commercial actor, it's a waste of time. It may be interesting and fun for you and your friends, but no agent or casting director is ever going to spend time logging on to your blog.

CHAPTER 4

YOUR KNOWLEDGE, PERFORMANCE SKILLS, AND TRAINING

Talk low, talk slow, and don't say too much.

—John Wayne (advice to a young actor)

Any commercial actor, whether he is a beginning actor just starting his career or an experienced actor with hundreds and hundreds of commercials under her belt, can learn more about the craft and the industry. I learn something every single time I teach a class and whenever I work on a job—and that's after teaching a zillion workshops and after having been principal actor in a whole lot of TV commercials.

Over the years, I've learned from my agents, from other actors and extras on the set, the production staff, the makeup gal, the wardrobe gal, the lighting guy, the cameraman, the assistant cameraman, the grip, the gaffer, the director, and the assistant director. I've even learned things from the production assistant, the craft-service gal, and the honeywagon driver. You can learn from everyone in the industry and everyone on the shoot—every single time. In the process, you're gaining valuable information and increasing your knowledge. For an actor who wants to work in television commercials, that information can be broken down into two categories: very *general* knowledge and much more *specific* knowledge.

WHAT'S THE DIFFERENCE BETWEEN *GENERAL* KNOWLEDGE AND *SPECIFIC* KNOWLEDGE?

If you're learning general things about the business, you're learning about things that will help you overall as an actor, but won't necessarily help you specifically in TV commercial acting. For instance, there's the art of makeup. Stage actors usually apply their own makeup when they're doing a play or a musical, but the actors in commercials, television, or film don't. When you are hired to act in a television commercial, a professional makeup person will also be employed to properly apply and touch up your makeup. Most actors just sit in the chair and close their eyes. So it's not imperative that you know much of anything about how to apply makeup.

But does it help you to know how makeup can create highlights and shadows on your face? Does it help you to know why rouge is used or why there is that final application of powder? Does it help to know why eyeliner is applied below your eyes? The answers add up to a resounding yes. The more you know about makeup, the better you'll look on camera, even if you do have a makeup person doing the application. So instead of sitting in your chair with your eyes closed when you have a makeup person working on you, ask your makeup artist questions. Trust me. You'll learn an enormous amount about makeup and about the specific characteristics of your face and what kind of makeup works best on you. You'll also learn a lot about your upcoming day's work. Makeup folks usually know more gossip and scuttlebutt than anyone on the set, and they love to chat. You also just might make a friend and an attentive ally for the day!

So knowing about makeup may not be considered specific knowledge that is going to make you a better commercial actor—but you'll sure look better on camera and you'll know why you look better. In the same way you can gain general knowledge about the application of makeup, it behooves you to know as much about what goes on during a shoot as possible. All of those folks on the set have very specific jobs and their collective wealth of knowledge is enormous. Will it help you generally as an actor to learn all the names and purposes for those lighting instruments? Will it help you to know why the director uses different lenses during the shoot day? Will it help you to know why they slate each shot and why they roll sound before film? You bet! Everything that happens on the set may be general knowledge to a commercial actor, but it's knowledge that will increasingly serve you well every single time you work.

SO WHAT'S *SPECIFIC* KNOWLEDGE?

Specific knowledge is what you're learning by reading this book and every other book you can get your hands on regarding commercial acting. It's listening to folks who know more than you do about television commercial acting. It's doing research about commercial acting. It's listening to your photographer during your photo session. It's learning things that will specifically make you a better commercial actor. Training (which we'll discuss a little later in this chapter) is the kinetic application of specific knowledge you've gained when you take commercial acting classes.

OKAY, I UNDERSTAND KNOWLEDGE. WHAT ARE PERFORMANCE SKILLS?

There are many physical skills that you can learn that may not seem important for the commercial actor, but they are. I call these performance skills, and they are *always* physical. Some may be more difficult to learn than others, but you don't have to be a master at any of them, just be competent enough to look like you know what you're doing for a bit.

GOT ANY EXAMPLES?

Lots of them.

- Learn to tap-dance enough to do a simple routine.
- Learn to play a couple of tunes on the piano.
- Learn to play a couple of songs on the guitar.

- Learn to perform a simple pantomime routine.

- Learn to juggle three balls.

- Learn a couple of simple magic tricks.

- Learn to shuffle cards skillfully.

- Learn to roller-skate.

- Learn to ride a pogo stick.

- Learn to ride a motorcycle.

- Learn to ride a horse.

- Learn to sing a song a cappella and on pitch.

I could go on, but all of these have one thing in common: They are all physical skills that you might use at some point in your career as a commercial actor. They also are things in which almost anyone can learn the basics. And when you take a class in voice, pantomime, juggling, fencing, piano, guitar, yodeling, belly dancing, and magic, you might even discover that you have a real interest and an undiscovered talent! My advice is to learn anything and everything that might be used as a performing skill. What's amazing to me is how many of these skills have a trickle-down effect to improve your depth and castability as a commercial actor.

I've been hired for lots of TV commercials over the years when I've been able to incorporate performance skills during the audition. I auditioned for a United Airlines commercial that called for an actor who could ride a pogo stick. I spent the entire audition not only jumping around the room on their pogo stick, but jumping around using only one foot and no hands! (Figure that one out!) I've also danced in commercials, sung in commercials, juggled in commercials, played piano in commercials, done magic tricks and rope tricks, ridden motorcycles and bicycles (not at the same time), done flips on a trampoline, thrown a football spiral, paddled both a boat and a canoe (again, not at the same time), swam against the current, climbed a rope, done pantomime, and even recited poetry and Shakespeare. (I haven't yodeled or belly danced in a commercial yet, but I'm ready if need be!)

WHAT ABOUT TRAINING?

There are two specific classes that an actor who wants to work in television commercials should take.

- An improvisation (or improv) class
- A class specifically geared to learning how to successfully audition for and perform in TV commercials

WHY IS IMPROVISATION IMPORTANT?

For decades, since the advent of Chicago's Second City, *Saturday Night Live,* and the explosion of comedy clubs all over the country, comedy and improv have been big parts of our entertainment landscape. Talent agents are always looking for those actors who have an on-camera flair for improvisation, because that ability will help the actor book jobs. During an audition, the ability to be extemporaneous and provide think-on-your-feet physical action and verbal patter gives you a real advantage over the other actors with whom you are competing. We often think of improvisation skill as something that is a "natural" ability, but it's a skill that can be learned. And, like any other skill, when you practice it, you get better at it.

There are improv groups all over the country. In Los Angeles, there are a myriad of performing companies with names like Second City, the Groundlings, Acme, Upright Citizens Brigade, bang., and Improv Olympic, where the public pays admission to see the actors perform. And almost all of these groups offer classes where actors can learn from accomplished improv actors. I suggest that you check out the entertainment section of your local newspaper, find an improv group in your area, take a night off, pay a few bucks, go watch what they do, and have some fun. Then see if they have classes and workshops and sign up.

Just remember that taking four weeks of an improv class doesn't necessarily mean that commercial jobs will start rolling in. It *does* mean, however, that you can put the class on your résumé, and it will show that you're working on your improv skills. It also means that you'll get to meet and work with some terrific actors. And while you're looking around for that improv class, pick up a copy of Steve Martin's book *Born Standing Up*. Steve is an enormously talented co-median who spent years and years developing his improv skills and his own style of comedy, all the while drawing on and perfecting the skills he learned as a youngster in a magic shop at Disneyland and as a young melodrama performer at Knott's Berry Farm. It's an inspirational book and a great read!

WHAT ABOUT COMMERCIAL ACTING CLASSES?

The fastest way to learn more about the specifics of auditioning for and acting in TV commercials is to find a class that specifically teaches you those audition and acting skills. There are lots of classes, schools, personal coaches, seminars, and books (and even a correspondence course or two!) devoted to the skills required to learn to audition for and act in television commercials. Many of the schools and classes are legitimate. Unfortunately, many are not. One version I just spotted ad-vertises a commercial acting class that is conducted online, suppos-edly "simulating the actual audition process." Apparently the actor, in the privacy and comfort of his own home, is sent audition material; the actor then sets up his own video machine and simulates an audi-tion. He then records it and digitally ships it off into cyberspace, where it is reviewed and evaluated by the teacher. It's an interesting concept, but it makes me think of taking a swimming class by correspondence course and learning the Australian crawl in your living room without the benefit of a pool. My suggestion is to forgo any Internet classes, and before you pay to attend a live class, make darn sure that it is a bona fide class that is more interested in you than in your billfold.

In major cities, including the New York and Los Angeles areas, many of these classes and schools are now being accredited by the state to ensure their validity and effectiveness. If you have *any* questions about the reputation of a school or a class, call the Better Business Bureau in your area or call the state attorney general's office. Ask for the consumer fraud division to see if their office has received any complaints.

WHAT SCAMS SHOULD I LOOK FOR?

There are a bunch of them. Here are some general rules about those classes or schools from which you might keep your distance.

- Stay away from schools that advertise "all types of training for the actor." Keep in mind that acting onstage is very different from acting in front of a camera, acting in a television sitcom is very different from acting in a dramatic TV show or in a film, and acting in any of the above is very different from acting in a television commercial. To learn how to audition for and how to act in TV commercials means you need to take acting classes geared specifically for acting in the television commercial.

- Beware of any class that advertises the taking of their class will "guarantee to get you into commercials." Nobody can do that. Honest. It'd be nice if it happened that way, but it doesn't.

- Seriously question any school or class that states you'll receive a diploma or a letter of recommendation upon graduation from their program that will help you get work. It might look nice on your wall, but you and your mom are the only folks who will ever see it. Any talent agent or reputable casting agency will get a big laugh (at your expense) if you claim to be qualified to act in television commercials because you have a diploma from a commercial acting school. It sounds like a setup for an old *Saturday Night Live* routine.

- Some schools say that you'll receive a DVD of your auditions for mock TV commercials upon graduation. It's pretty useless and no one will ever see it. Again, except your mom.

- Don't be fooled by a terrific-looking letter in the mail saying that a photograph of you or your kid was "seen and selected" and you or your kid has potentially a "great future in commercials." It's a scam.

- Don't be sucked in by a newspaper advertisement stating that the Sure Catch Casting Agency is desperately searching for folks (especially children) to place them in TV commercials. It's also a scam.

- Ditto when you walk through the mall and get a friendly solicitation from a good-looking gal with a video camera in a rented kiosk space. With a look of genuine amazement, she'll say that you or your kid "are perfect for being in TV commercials." Scam, scam, double scam.

- Be very careful of any school that wants a "small up-front fee" for a photo test of some kind that will (amazingly) reinforce the fact that you or your kid have a "great future in commercials!" After you've signed on the dotted line and paid good money, there will be another "small fee" for consultation and another "small fee" for classes and another "small fee" for your photographs. And then the cycle keeps going for more consultations, more fees, and more classes until you're broke.

It always amazes me how many folks fall for this stuff, but they do—particularly when their children are involved. We parents always want to think that our little guy or gal is exceptionally attractive, enormously talented, amazingly photogenic, makes everyone laugh, and would be perfect doing television commercials and making a lot of money. Be very careful—not only with your hard-earned money, but, most important, with your child and his or her well-being.

Take a look at the last chapter in this book (chapter 15), titled The Life of an Actor, before you decide to throw your kid to the lions. To quote *Annie:* "It's a hard-knock life!"

WHERE CAN I FIND LEGITIMATE COMMERCIAL ACTING CLASSES?

There are several bona fide, legitimate (and some are relatively inexpensive) classes, schools, and seminars you can take that will specifically help you in your quest to become a successful commercial actor. And there are a lot of sources for those classes. Always make sure you ask about the fees and fully understand what those fees do and do not include.

- Many commercial acting classes are taught through community colleges, colleges, and universities all over the country. Get your local community college class brochure for the upcoming semester and look under Acting. You might get lucky and find one, and it's usually *very* inexpensive! Check out the credentials of the teacher, make sure he or she is qualified, and go for it. I've taught scores and scores of classes (ofttimes gratis) in many community colleges and colleges all over the country.

- There are lots of classes taught by your fellow commercial actors who have had some success doing commercials. Go online or call them to find out as much as you can about them and their classes. I've taught a gazillion of these "How to Audition" and "TV Commercial Acting" classes over the years. I always tried to give everyone the most for their time and money spent, and I always tried to have a casting director or commercial agent sitting in on at least one of the auditions and evaluations.

- My favorite option for commercial acting classes would be to take a class taught by an actual commercial casting director. Taking classes from a working casting agent is a terrific way to learn not only the craft of commercial auditioning but to learn from a person who actually casts commercials. It's a great way to have a person of importance see your work. And if he likes what he sees, he can bring you in for a real commercial audition. It's a win-win. You'll learn from an expert, *and* you'll learn from an expert who has the ability to bring you in on an actual audition!

An old pal of mine who is a very successful casting agent in L.A. at one time taught twenty-eight different commercial acting classes every single week. He *loved* to find new talent in his classes, coach them until they knew what they were doing, and then bring them in on actual commercial auditions. If and when they actually got jobs (and it happened often), these actors would be walking testimonials that the classes they took actually *worked!* They got a job! And that's why my buddy's classes were always filled to capacity!

WHAT SHOULD I LOOK FOR WHEN CHOOSING A GOOD CLASS?

You can find a lot of information online, but after you've done all that research, talking to a human being is invaluable. Ask questions. If the teacher sees that you're an intelligent person who is seriously trying to investigate and evaluate which class to take, he'll be interested in you. Just make sure that you don't waste his time. If the pay structure information is online, then don't ask what the fees are. And when you do ask questions, be eager, enthusiastic, complimentary, and always act humble and innocent. Act as though you *really* want to know answers to your questions and you are *so pleased* that this *very important person* is taking the time to answer them. It makes no difference whether you are talking to a sommelier in a nice restaurant about a wine choice or talking to the guy in the plumbing department at Home Depot when you're trying to figure out which widget wrench to buy to fix your leaky kitchen sink. Always be respectful and gracious. And make sure you write down the questions you'd like answered beforehand.

WHAT SHOULD I KNOW ABOUT A CLASS BEFORE I SIGN UP?

- Ask who is teaching the class and what his/her credentials are.

- Ask if you can audit a class session so you can see if it's going to be worth your time, energy, and money. I don't know many successful teachers who will not allow a prospective student to sit in on a class. If the teacher is reluctant to let you do so, I'd ask why.

- Find out what percentage of the class time will be devoted to lecture about the business, what percentage will be dedicated to mock, on-camera auditions, and what percentage will be spent evaluating the on-camera work. The majority of class time should be spent with students doing mock auditions followed by teacher evaluations.

- Ask how many classes there will be in total and how long each class is.

- Ask how much the class will cost you and if there any other costs. Once you know the total hours of instruction and the total cost, just do the math. That's what you're spending per hour.

- Ask how many students will be in each class session. The more students, the less time *you* will get to spend on camera. It's nice to watch others make mistakes in their mock auditions and learn when they are corrected, but you really won't absorb much until you jump into the pool yourself and see if you can swim.

- Ask if any insider folks from the commercial world are coming to talk to the class. And, most important, are those folks going to sit through the on-camera portion of the class and actually watch, work with, and evaluate actors when they do mock slates and auditions on camera?

HOW DO I LOCATE THOSE GOOD CLASSES?

You can look in all the logical places for TV commercial acting classes: the community college bulletins, the trade papers, the trade magazines, and the online sources. Word of mouth is a usually dependable source, so ask anyone you meet who is in the business if she has any suggestions. And, again, keep notes. Another good source is TVI Acting Studios. It's legitimate and the classes are often taught by reputable casting directors and other industry pros. It has been around since 1988, and although it's based in New York and L.A., it's been taking the classes on the road to many cities across the country for over two decades. You can check them out at TVIstudios.com/ info/about.asp.

There are lots of classes to choose from in New York and Los Angeles, but don't be discouraged if you happen to live in Tucson. Remember that Screen Actors Guild has over twenty union chapters across the country. That means that there is definitely enough work in those areas to warrant those twenty-plus offices, so those same sources—community college bulletins, online resources, and word of mouth—can help you in Tucson, too.

IF I'VE ALREADY TAKEN CLASSES AND DONE SOME WORK, WHY WOULD I WANT TO TAKE ANOTHER CLASS?

There are actors who may have booked some jobs in the past but, for some reason, may be in a slump now. The best way to get out of that slump is to get back on camera in a class, work out the problems, fix them, and get reenergized. Ofttimes, the folks teaching those classes are casting directors, and the actor in the slump will get his on-camera face in front of them. I've always found that singers, dancers, and musicians have one thing in common: In their downtime, they are continually taking classes to get better at what they do. Actors should do the same thing!

CHAPTER 5

THE UNIONS: SAG AND AFTRA

The first strike on record was in Rome in 309 B.C. A Greek conductor named Aristos pulled his orchestra out because they weren't allowed to eat in the temple where they were performing.

There are two unions that on-camera actors in commercials need to be aware of: SAG (Screen Actors Guild) and AFTRA (American Federation of Television and Radio Artists). Basically it works like this.

SAG: If you are an actor who is hired as on-camera talent for a commercial originally shot in a "filmed" medium, you must belong to Screen Actors Guild. This is the case even if that commercial might be later digitally converted for editing.

AFTRA: If you are an actor who is hired as on-camera talent for a commercial originally shot in a "videotaped" medium, then American Federation of Television and Radio Artists should be your union.

If it sounds cut and dry, it's not. There are no absolute rules regarding whether you should belong to AFTRA or SAG when shooting videotaped commercials. It's quite hazy. Sometimes you'll be signing a SAG contract, sometimes an AFTRA contract. (I always just sign the contract and smile, because it means that I'm working.)

Most actors who act in television commercials choose to belong to both unions: SAG *and* AFTRA. The specific union chapters, addresses, websites, e-mail addresses, and telephone numbers are listed in the appendix of this book. For an absolutely current listing, search SAG and AFTRA online, because, like everything else in life, the addresses, listings, and locations are constantly changing.

HOW AND WHY DID SAG BEGIN?

A history lesson: The year was 1933, television was a ways away from being invented, radio was at its heyday, "talkies" were the new rage in motion pictures, and silent films were no more. Profits by the studios were substantial and actors were pretty much thought of as hired help. Except for the few stars of the day who commanded those hefty salaries, the majority of actors were underpaid and over-worked. Actors had unrestricted work hours, no turnaround time, no required meal breaks, no insurance in case of an accident, and they were paid according to the whims of management. It was a tough time for actors in this new Southern California suburb known as Hollywood. Attempted negotiations by actors, including the act-ing elite, proved worthless, and the all-powerful studio boss Irving Thalberg openly decreed: "I will die before some union guild tells me what I can and cannot do." His words were ominous, and in 1936, he did just that. He died. One year later, the studio heads of Holly-wood collectively signed the first contract with the Screen Actors Guild, guaranteeing some rules and regulations that finally gave ac-tors a sense that they controlled their working conditions and their careers.

In the years that followed, actors soon learned the advantages of collective bargaining. The Screen Actors Guild became increasingly powerful and proved instrumental in breaking the old accepted rules that actors could not choose their own roles nor could they work for anyone whom they wanted to. A bit later, when television was gaining momentum in its popularity with the American public, SAG was re-sponsible for securing residual payments for actors for reruns. That meant every single time a show was replayed on the air, the actors in that show would receive a percentage of what they'd been paid ini-tially. In 1953, when advertising on TV was becoming commonplace,

SAG was instrumental in securing its first television commercial contract, thereby creating residual payments for actors when they appeared on camera in television spots. The term *residual payment* was soon shortened to the single word we use today for replay of TV commercials: *residuals.* Everything from pension and health plans to safety guidelines for the actor soon followed.

These days it is not uncommon for actors to own their own production companies, or to write, produce, direct, and act in their own films. Most important, for the commercial actor, our rights were fought for and protected by the early action of SAG in the fifties.

HOW DID AFTRA BEGIN?

AFTRA's story is very much a parallel of the SAG story, but it begins with radio instead of film. In the early thirties, radio was the king of the airwaves. Live music by the big bands of the era, personality-hosted variety shows, and radio dramas gathered much of America around their huge home radios each night to "watch" the evening broadcasts. To protect the artists appearing on radio, two guilds were created, one on each coast: Radio Actors Guild in Los Angeles and Radio Equity in New York. By 1937, it had become obvious to the guilds that they would have considerably more power if they combined forces. So they did, and the American Federation of Radio Artists was created. Chicago, then the epicenter for radio soap operas, quickly joined its bicoastal brothers and AFRA membership soon soared to over two thousand members, covering almost 90 percent of all radio artists in those key broadcast cities.

Then in 1938, the huge radio superstars of the day, Edgar Bergen (Candice's dad), Eddie Cantor, Jack Benny, and Bing Crosby, joined forces and successfully negotiated with the two big networks at that time, CBS and NBC, to create a wage pay schedule and union security.

In the late forties, during the post–World War II prosperity, phonographs began popping up in American homes, closely followed by television sets. To cover these new mediums, AFRA negotiated contracts for actors who performed on records and on television where the majority of the television programming was done "live." Finally, in 1952, realizing that there was something missing in the AFRA moniker, the union split the *AF* and the *RA*, stuck in a *T* for "Television," and AFTRA was born.

Sometimes leading, sometimes following, and sometimes parallel-ing the success of SAG in negotiations with the studios, networks, and advertisers, AFTRA made headway in areas of pension, health, and welfare. Early television, which AFTRA had jurisdiction over, was all live television, meaning the actors would perform in real time. Later, in the mid-fifties, videotape was successfully developed to the point where programming could be recorded on tape for later showings and could then be broadcast repeatedly. Residuals, which had already been created and negotiated by SAG, now became the norm for both unions.

In 1960, SAG and AFTRA, realizing again that there might be more power in collective bargaining, decided to loosely join forces to ne-gotiate together rather than separately. They mostly continue to do so to this day. The two unions have been talking merger for years and someday it might (and should!) happen, but the wisdom of the collec-tive SAG membership seems to vote the merger referendum down each and every time it's proposed. In 2003, the idea was proposed again to the members of both SAG and AFTRA and needed approval by 60 percent of both memberships to pass. AFTRA voted for consol-idation by 75 percent; SAG's membership vote, however, was only 58 percent. Thus, they are still two separate unions. Go figure.

HOW DO SAG AND AFTRA NEGOTIATE WITH THE ADVERTISERS TO ESTABLISH THE FEES AND RESIDUALS FOR COMMERCIALS?

Whenever contracts expire, there are negotiations between the two unions and the advertisers, who also bring a couple of other players to the bargaining table. Not to be outdone by the collective eight letters of SAG and AFTRA, the advertising industry is represented by the Joint Policy Committee (JPC) of the Association of National Advertisers (ANA) and the American Association of Advertising Agencies (AAAA). So on the one side of the bargaining table you have JPCANAAAAA and on the other side there is SAGAFTRA. Ten to eight is my score.

Under union guidelines and agreed-upon contracts with the ANA and AAAA over the years, standard fees have been established that pay for actors' services in every imaginable situation. There are different rules and different fees when actors are asked to work out of town, work with animals, do stunts, work overtime, or work on weekends. And there are rules that govern how long the workday will be, how often there are meal breaks, what the rule-infraction penalties will be, and so forth. The current SAG commercial contract isn't *War and Peace,* but it's over 235 pages using very small font size.

The biggest negotiation impasses always have to do with money: the amount of money an actor is paid for a workday (his session fee), and how much money an actor will be paid when that work is replayed (his residuals). As any commercial actor will tell you, residuals are the bread, butter, and dessert of doing TV commercials. Since 1953, when the first commercial contract was negotiated and TV rerun payments were made, the majority of money that has been paid to members of both unions has been in the form of residual payments. The first house that my wife and I built on the beach in Sunset Beach, California, had an address plaque built into the front façade. I had it made in Mexico and it read "Casa Residuales." A little humor, but it gives credit where credit is due.

SO HOW DO RESIDUAL PAYMENTS WORK?

Even though the basic day rate might be the same for actors in commercials, there is a huge difference in the residual scale each time the commercial is replayed. It all comes down to the number of projected viewers. If a commercial is scheduled to air during the Super Bowl, the potential viewing public is huge. If that same commercial airs in the late morning during a *M*A*S*H* rerun on one of the local cable channels, the purported number of folks watching is negligible. Thus, a sliding scale was established for each of the scenarios based on the potential number of folks who might be watching that particular commercial at that time.

It used to be a pretty simple formula when the television-viewing world revolved around the three networks NBC, CBS, and ABC. Formulas based on projected number of viewers during different times of the day and night could be easily calculated. A Class-A TV commercial, for instance, was a television spot that ran on one of the three networks nationwide and during prime time.

In recent years, however, there has been an explosion of smaller cable networks that have popped up, with many of them gaining ground and popularity with their share of viewers. That, coupled with the advent of video recording devices such as TiVo and DVRs that allow viewers to eliminate commercials, makes it increasingly difficult to figure the potential number of viewers at any given time. As such, calculating the reuse and residual factor has become enormously complicated for the ANA/AAAA and for SAG/AFTRA.

So every few years when it's that time for contract renegotiations, SAG and AFTRA join forces and demand more from the advertisers. (Radio commercials are still negotiated solely by AFTRA.) Profits are being made, the rules are vague, and the unions want what they consider to be their fair share. On occasion, they've gone as far as taking their membership out on strike, hoping the work stoppage would force the advertisers to cut them a larger piece of that increasingly vague profit pie. Sometimes it's worked; sometimes it hasn't. The last few strikes by SAG and AFTRA have encouraged the advertisers to look elsewhere for talent and for locations. These days it is not uncommon for TV commercials that will air in the United States to be shot in Canada, Mexico, Europe, and Asia. It all comes down to the almighty dollar.

HOW DO I JOIN SAG?

To protect the huge membership of SAG, the union has made membership pretty difficult.

These are the three ways to join.

Way Number One

To become a SAG member, you must first audition for a commercial (or a television show or a film) and get the job. Once you're hired, the production company or the casting agency has to make a formal request to the union so you can work in a union commercial as a nonunion member. This is officially called a Taft-Hartley waiver. (For you trivia geeks, the Taft-Hartley Act was passed by Congress in 1947, overriding President Truman's veto.) Whoever is hiring you must, at that time, justify in writing why you were hired over a dues-paying guild member. Once you receive notification of the waiver by letter, you must start the job within fifteen days. After you finish the job, you then have the option to pay your membership fee and join the Screen Actors Guild. If you don't want to join the union immediately, you may join at a later date but you're known as "SAG eligible." The problem is that it's difficult to get a job if you're not in SAG and almost impossible to get into the union without having a job. (This is how I joined the Screen Actors Guild way back in 1969. I was hired to do three days' work as a guest star on a hit television series with David Hartman, E. G. Marshall, and John Saxon titled *The Bold Ones.* I did my first commercial a year later.)

Way Number Two

A performer may also join SAG if the applicant is a paid-up member of an affiliated performers' union (ACTRA, AEA, AGMA, AGVA, or AFTRA) for a period of one year and has worked and been paid at least once as a principal performer in that union's jurisdiction. (This is the way my wife joined the Screen Actors Guild. She had been a company member of the Nikolais Dance Theatre in New York for ten years and had to join AGMA because the company did a yearly New York season. Our daughter, Lexy, also joined SAG this way because she was a dues-paying Equity union member.)

Way Number Three

As of 1990, there is a third way to join SAG. If you obtain a minimum of three vouchers by working as an extra on a SAG job, you then become eligible to join the guild. But there are a limited number of vouchers per job on the set and an extra must do some scrambling to get one. Although I'm sure it's happened, I don't personally know anyone who joined SAG by collecting vouchers.

WHAT'S IT COST TO JOIN SAG?

Initiation and semiannual fees will probably be higher by the time you read this book, but currently the initiation is $2,277, plus your first dues payment of $58. The total is $2,335. The fee may be lower if you're joining one of the twenty-plus smaller branches outside of New York or Hollywood. To find the current fee structure, visit Sag.org. Your subsequent semiannual dues will then be determined by how much money you earned the previous year as an actor doing jobs under SAG's jurisdiction.

HOW DO I JOIN AFTRA?

Easy. Just find your local AFTRA chapter, contact them, do the necessary paperwork, pay the initiation fee, and join.

WHAT'S THAT COST?

The membership fee to join AFTRA is currently $1,300, and the semiannual dues are $63.50. Before writing a check, take a look at AFTRA's website at Aftra.org and contact your local chapter to make sure you have the correct fee. Just like the semiannual dues for Screen Actors Guild, your AFTRA dues structure will be determined by the amount of money you earned the previous year as an actor under AFTRA's jurisdiction.

IS THERE ANY ADVANTAGE IN JOINING AFTRA FIRST?

You eventually will want to belong to both unions anyway, so by joining AFTRA first, your later SAG initiation fee will be reduced, depending on the location of the chapter where you joined and their initiation fee structure. Also remember that working an AFTRA job then makes you eligible to join SAG.

DO I HAVE TO JOIN A UNION TO WORK AS A PRINCIPAL ACTOR IN A TELEVISION COMMERCIAL?

Good question and the definitive answer is yes. And no. The answer is yes if you are going to be working for a production company, an advertising agency, or a client that has signed a union contract. The answer is no if you are hired by a production company, an advertising agency, or a client that has not signed a contract with SAG and/or AFTRA.

Twenty-two of our states are also considered right-to-work states where SAG and AFTRA membership may not be necessary. As of this writing, those states include Alabama, Arizona, Arkansas, Florida, Georgia, Idaho, Iowa, Kansas, Louisiana, Mississippi, Nebraska, Nevada, North and South Carolina, North and South Dakota, Oklahoma, Tennessee, Texas, Utah, Virginia, and Wyoming. It's best to take a look at your state's laws and how you might be affected. A good source is nrtw.org/rtws.htm.

Many smaller clients and advertising agencies in lots of cities across the country choose to shoot nonunion commercials, and for those jobs you need not be a union member. In fact, if you do belong to SAG or AFTRA, they will probably choose not to hire you. If they did hire you as a union member, they'd potentially create all sorts of problems for both the actor and for themselves. I've worked with and talked with many actors all over the country who have chosen not to belong to either SAG or AFTRA, particularly in those right-to-work states. I've worked (as a union actor) with nonunion principal actors and extras in Alabama, Arizona, Florida, Georgia, Nevada, Oklahoma, Tennessee, Texas, Utah, and Virginia, and it's no coincidence that those locations were chosen by the advertisers. When I've spoken with the actors in those states, they say that if they *did* join the unions, they wouldn't get any work because no one would hire them.

ONCE I AM A UNION MEMBER, CAN I BE HIRED TO DO NONUNION WORK AS AN ACTOR?

This one is dicey. According to SAG, members should not agree to work on any project that is not under the union contract. SAG refers to this as Global Rule One, which specifically states that "no member shall work as a performer or make an agreement to work as a performer for any producer who has not executed a basic minimum agreement with the Guild which is in full force and effect. This provision is worldwide." Sounds pretty ominous, huh?

Cris Dennis, my Los Angeles talent agent extraordinaire, told me that the issue has come up more than a few times during his career. He said that he has booked union actors in the past on projects that were shot in right-to-work states. He said that it had always been his understanding that if you are working in a state that has a law on the books that says you have a legal right to work, then you do, in fact, have a legal right to work, no matter what a union's rules are. He also said that he recently had an offer for an actor in the above situation and when the actor checked with his Los Angeles SAG office for their opinion, they informed the actor that his union status would be in jeopardy if he took the job. The logic of the union was that their bylaws would take precedence over the laws of the right-to-work state, and that by joining the union, the actor is bound by those bylaws. Obviously, this is a very gray area that only a lawsuit will eventually provide the definitive answer for. (Me? I wouldn't have called the union in the first place.)

If you are a union member, there is another option you have to become eligible to work both nonunion and union jobs without fear of union repercussion. It's a topic that SAG and AFTRA don't like to discuss very much. It's called "Financial Core."

WHAT'S FINANCIAL CORE?

A little history: Financial Core is in reference to the U.S. Supreme Court decision allowing a performer who is a dues-paying union member to work on nonunion projects with a guarantee of absolutely no repercussions from the unions. (The actual case in 1983 was called *Communications Workers of America v. Beck.*) The case set precedent for the idea that an actor's individual liberty is fully protected by the Supreme Court. It's a decision every actor can make, and if you opt to be Financial Core, you will pay a bit less in union dues (the union may not take out money donated by the union for political causes or candidates), and you will still receive all your retirement, health, and welfare benefits. What you may *not* do is run for a SAG office, vote in a SAG election, or participate in SAG-related functions. You also may not carry your SAG card or include the fact that you are a SAG member on your résumé. You may, however, include on your résumé that you are a "Dues-Paying, Fully Vested, Nonmember Financial Core Member of the Screen Actors Guild."

There is an interesting piece written by Mark Pirro, a very successful independent filmmaker who has been making nonunion theatrical films for twenty years. He addressed the issue of Financial Core from his perspective as follows.

There have always been nonunion films and they have always used union actors. It was never that important before when we were in the minority.

Welcome to the new millennium where the little guys are taking over. The day of the nonunion films grossing upwards of $100 million is upon us and will not be going away soon.

DV (direct-to-video) is making it possible for people to produce movies and as of this writing, there are over 400 DV movies in some phase of production, many using SAG and non-SAG talent. Many films are being shot in Canada and Mexico to avoid the restrictions of unions and these numbers will get bigger as the number of filmmakers increase. SAG is trying to stop this, but what they don't seem to realize is that scare tactics won't work anymore.

You want to act and if the opportunities are slim, you can either wait tables, wait for Martin Scorsese to call, or work in a nonunion film.

Now, if you are an actor who has appeared in any of our films and are being hassled by your union, I'd like to inform you of your rights as an actor and a worker. There is something out there called "Financial Core" which SAG would rather you not know about. But this is a legal way for you to work in both SAG and non-SAG films without any hassles from the unions. This is how you can continue to work in your chosen craft regularly and not have to turn down jobs that you may desperately want.

Sure, nonunion films don't pay anywhere near the SAG day rates, and the payoff may not be as big, but the payoff will be steady and the bonus is that you can STILL take those higher paying SAG gigs when they come along. You're not giving up much, you're just enhancing what you have.

Many SAG actors have done it (it's a well-kept secret), Charlton Heston endorsed it, and it's your legal right to enact it.

On a personal note, during the early eighties, I first recognized that my trusted SAG was taking political stands on important issues that I felt they had no business being involved with. Also, it seemed that during negotiations with the advertisers, SAG and AFTRA were growing more and more militant and dogmatic, and I felt my unions were headed in the wrong direction. I became increasingly alarmed under Ed Asner's tenure as SAG's outspoken and extremely left-leaning president. In 1982, President Ronald Reagan (also a past president of SAG), openly criticized Mr. Asner and the SAG board for taking it upon themselves to donate substantial SAG membership funds to the Sandinistas, a leftist guerrilla group attempting to take over El Salvador. Where in the world was my trusted union headed?

Long-term union members such as the late Charlton Heston (another past SAG president) were outraged and took the union to task. Many of my fellow union members (including Mr. Heston) declared Financial Core in protest, thus turning in their coveted SAG cards to become "Dues-Paying, Fully Vested, Nonmember Financial Core Members of the Screen Actors Guild." When the publicity proved too much for the SAG board, and when union members actually began picketing their own guild offices, most of the in-your-face political leanings stopped. Following that debacle, Ed Asner was amazingly reelected for a second term. Of course, so was Ronald Reagan.

Then, three scant years later and still under President Asner's tenure, negotiations began anew with the advertisers over payment for actors in TV commercials. I again began to feel that my union was fighting a misdirected battle. I thought that some of the demands they were making to the advertisers would further increase our union unemployment, an issue I considered to be SAG's biggest challenge. We were also informed in a newsletter that SAG would be "lending its support to all union organizations" whether the strikes were by teamsters, airline pilots, nurses, air-traffic controllers, or sanitation workers. Individual cases and issues were no longer going to be argued. If any union demanded more from any employer, then SAG members were to unite and support their cause. For a while, I thought I was living in France.

The issue at hand preceding the inevitable 1985 strike was, again, a substantial increase in pay for commercial actors, which I felt would increase our unemployment base even further. I finally took exception and wrote the following letter, which was published in the June 1985 issue of our *Screen Actor News:*

Each time our commercial contract comes up for renegotiation, the same nagging question comes to mind . . . Do we continue to demand that our daily rate as principal performers be increased, or do we, at last, begin to confront ourselves with the real problem at hand? Our failure as a union is that we seem to focus our efforts on those few who do work, when we should be focusing on the many who do not. The unemployment rate is an ugly ever-dominant fact we live with and unfortunately encourage.

I believe I speak for those of us who make a successful income from the world of the television commercial. We need not demand more money per actor per spot, but we need to give advertisers the financial incentive to use more principal performers instead of fewer. If we utilized a scale (as we do for "group performers") of decreased session rates in proportion to the number of principals used, advertisers would be encouraged to use more actors per commercial and more members of our union would be working. I know of no actor who would not be willing to reduce his scale session fee of $333.25 to $317.40 if three or more of his fellow union members were used, even a lesser amount if six were used, even less if nine were used. Both commercially and theatrically, only when we actors act to make the unemployment situation more equitable for our fellow artists will the ever-present unemployment situation begin to improve.

Let's encourage management to hire more of us, not demand that the few of us who do work receive a higher daily rate.

Squire Fridell
Sunset Beach, CA

Believe it or not, most of the feedback I received from my fellow (mostly nonworking) union members was negative. Everyone wanted more money per day for those few who did work, regardless of the repercussions, and who was I to deny them that? My fellow union members, I believed, were cutting down all the trees and burning them, not taking into account that the forest was disappearing. I didn't think that those of us who worked steadily as actors needed to make more money. When you worked, you made a terrific wage, and I felt that SAG's focus should have been to do whatever it could to decrease our huge unemployment base and get more actors working. The more we demanded in pay for the few who *did* work, the fewer of us *got* to work. I thought it was as simple as that. When the strike was finally over, our session fees and residuals went up. And so did our unemployment.

Unfortunately, the saga continued long after the 1985 strike. In 1998, SAG and AFTRA struck again. Same issues; same results. When that strike was finally over, as expected, our pay and our residuals went up substantially. Also, as expected, even fewer actors were hired per commercial shoot.

And then came the failed negotiations in late 2000. The issue on the table this time was cable television advertising. The unions (and rightly so) wanted their share of this runaway cable-market beast. Television commercials were now being played over and over on cable channels in small markets with literally no residual reimbursement to the actors involved. This time SAG wanted part of the unregulated cable industry pie and told the advertisers. So far, so good. But then it got ugly.

The AAAA and ANA made a reasonable starting offer and things looked pretty good. Then SAG and AFTRA countered, demanding cable residual payments that were exorbitantly ridiculous. The advertisers did the math, recognized that the unions were not bargaining in good faith, and walked away from the table. Since negotiations were at a standstill, SAG and AFTRA decided to call a commercial actor strike. What resulted was a lengthy, worthless strike and some very disgruntled union members. (I probably became the most disgruntled.) At this point, I got out my calculator, did some homework, and came to a startling conclusion: If the advertisers agreed to the unions' outrageous cable replay demands, they would go out of business. I went from disgruntled to downright angry. I went to guild meetings to voice my complaints and wrote letters to both my unions, citing the ridiculous residual numbers the unions had come up with. Below is a letter I sent to both unions' headquarters in New York, L.A., and San Francisco.

August 2, 2000

I am a 30+ year member of SAG and AFTRA, have been principal talent in over 2,500 television commercials and have never, in those 30+ years, drawn unemployment benefits. And I am angry.

I attended the joint SAG/AFTRA meeting in San Francisco Monday night, spoke and posed some questions during the question/answer period. I did not get satisfactory answers. It's nice to hear that a new Second Interim Agreement has been offered by SAG/AFTRA. The pressing question is WHO CAME UP WITH THE RIDICULOUS FIRST PROPOSAL? Obviously our negotiators did not do the required math . . .

CCAA, one AD Agency in Cincinnati that I've worked with for years, however, DID do the math. Cathy Deka of Highland Talent was asked by CCAA to calculate the increases they would have to pay to have me continue to be their spokesman for Toyota. Cathy calculated that for me to do the same number of spots per month, my salary would have to be increased $100,000. That's not $100,000 a YEAR . . . that's a MONTH! That amounts to an increase in pay of $1.2 MILLION A YEAR! It would be sudden death for CCAA to sign such an agreement, and it's no wonder the Ad Agencies walked out of the negotiating room after hearing your first proposal.

So, my question is this: was SAG/AFTRA simply making an impossible, antagonistic proposal so that there WOULD be a strike . . . or was SAG/AFTRA just stupid and decided not to do the math? It'll be interesting to hear what Cathy Deka has to say about the new Interim Agreement . . .

I'd like an answer to the above. Does SAG want a strike or is my union math-impaired?

I, like many other actors who make a very good living doing commercials, did NOT vote for this strike. I am having a great deal of trouble rationalizing WHY I'm staying at home and not working.

Squire Fridell
Glen Ellen, CA

Because of my meeting appearances and letters challenging the unions' untenable position (and a lot of other members being as vocal as I), SAG and AFTRA finally said they would be coming back to the table with a counterproposal: Interim Agreement #2. After a period of time, I was assured that the first residual calculations were the result of a "technical and mathematical glitch" and that SAG/AFTRA would shortly be coming up with a very realistic counterproposal that would be "well thought out and workable." I waited and waited and, finally, the "well thought out and workable" Interim Agreement #2 appeared.

Again, I did my homework, attended another union meeting in San Francisco, and doggedly tried to have both SAG and AFTRA negotiators take an intelligent look at their newest demands. This time, CCAA calculated that my yearly fee, were I to do the same amount of work, would only give me a *half-million-dollar raise!* I was infuriated that my unions were knowingly not dealing in good faith. At that point I called my union representative (a terrific and helpful gal) and told her that if there was no hope of resolution by September 1, I was declaring Financial Core in protest to my unions' incompetence. September came and went and I declared, and remain, Financial Core to this day. It's interesting to note that my union rep in San Francisco ended up resigning from SAG in protest right after the strike was over. It's also interesting to note that what the unions finally settled for, months and months after I declared Financial Core, was *less* than what the advertisers had initially offered. The unions also publicly declared victory over their new contract. Go figure.

All this is not to say that I think all union members should declare Financial Core. The above is merely an honest and true reporting of an unfortunate sequence of events leading to my decision to become a "Dues-Paying, Fully Vested, Nonmember Financial Core Member of the Screen Actors Guild." Am I sad that I no longer am a full-fledged member of two unions that I proudly joined over forty years ago? Of course. But, for me, it was a personal and ethical decision that had to be made.

Enough whining! Time to move on to The Talent Agent!

CHAPTER 6

THE TALENT AGENT

Show business is only two percent show.
It's ninety-eight percent business.

—An anonymous talent agent

Ask commercial actors what they think of their talent agents and you get two responses: He's either a saint or he's worthless. The agent is a saint if the actor goes out on auditions; the agent is worthless if he doesn't.

WHAT IS A TALENT AGENT?

Commercial talent agents are businessmen and businesswomen trying to eke out their living much the same as we are. They are usually creative, honest, hardworking people who are the middlemen between casting directors and their stable of actors. For the commercial actor, an agent's job is to find out about auditions, submit the actors whom they represent for those auditions, and then, when their actors *do* get jobs, negotiate any unusual or overscale terms not spelled out in contracts.

WHY DO THEY DO THAT?

It's not for philanthropic reasons. They collect 10 percent of what you earn.

ARE THERE DIFFERENT KINDS OF
COMMERCIAL TALENT AGENTS?

Not for AFTRA. However, as of 2002, SAG recognizes two kinds of commercial agents: franchised and nonfranchised.

Since 1937 and prior to 2002, the Association of Talent Agents in Los Angeles (ATA) and its counterpart in New York, the National Association of Talent Reps (NATR), were the two designated negotiating bodies for all talent agents. They were known as ATA/NATR and their only difference was their respective locations. On April 19, 2002, the collective members of ATA/NATR could not come to an agreement concerning SAG's contract verbiage (Rule 16(g)) regarding the commissions, contracts, and terms for talent agents. At the end of that meeting, the majority of the talent agent members walked away from the bargaining table, taking their moniker, ATA/NATR, with them. (I always felt they sort of declared themselves Financial Core.) Knowing that these members comprised the majority of talent agents, SAG *temporarily* suspended their own contract wording and declared that there were now two kinds of agents out there who were recognized by SAG.

- Franchised agents who agreed to SAG's contract wording regarding talent agents

- Nonfranchised agents (ATA/NATR) who did not agree

Confusing? You bet.

WHAT'S THE DIFFERENCE BETWEEN A FRANCHISED
TALENT AGENT AND A NONFRANCHISED TALENT AGENT?

In practical terms, there are few differences for the commercial actor.

- Franchised agents use a standard SAG contract, and nonfranchised agents (ATA/NATR) use a general service agreement (GSA). Both contracts pretty much say the same things, but the wording can vary. As a service for their members, SAG offers to review any questions about an actor's nonfranchised agent's (ATA/NATR) GSA.

- Franchised agents can charge only a 10-percent commission to their actors; nonfranchised agents may charge their clients more than 10 percent (even though there are no talent agents on record who have done that).

IS THERE ANY ADVANTAGE TO BEING SIGNED WITH A FRANCHISED TALENT AGENT OVER A NONFRANCHISED TALENT AGENT?

So far, it's an even playing field in terms of the 10-percent commission. As far as the other terms of the GSA contract, SAG encourages actors to negotiate any terms they don't agree to. As of today's date, there appears to be little difference between signing with a franchised or a nonfranchised talent agency, and SAG is currently working to bring the ATA/NATR nonfranchised agents back to the bargaining table so that all talent agencies working the commercial contract will be franchised once again. It's in their best interest to do so.

DO I REALLY NEED A TALENT AGENT?

Yes. For the commercial actor, a talent agent is not only desirable but an absolute necessity. The talent agent is the middleman, and a vital one. It would be impossible for every actor to call every casting agency every day to find out if there are any jobs coming up for which they might audition. There are 120,000 people in SAG, and virtually no casting agent will take the time to meet an actor for a specific job unless he or she has agency representation.

WHAT'S THE DIFFERENCE BETWEEN A TALENT AGENT AND A CASTING AGENT?

Think of it this way: A *talent* agent represents you as an actor and submits you to a *casting* agent who has been hired by the advertiser to cast a commercial.

IS THERE ANY DIFFERENCE BETWEEN A CASTING AGENT AND A CASTING DIRECTOR?

Same thing. Different nouns and you can use them interchangeably.

WHAT ARE THE UNION RULES GOVERNING CASTING AGENTS?

There aren't any because they are not associated with SAG or AFTRA in any way. Unlike talent agents, casting agents can do whatever they like as long as they adopt and comply with local laws, covenants, codes, and restrictions. In most cases, after you get a business license, if you want to hang up a shingle that says you're a casting agency, you may do so.

CAN CASTING AGENTS AND TALENT AGENTS TEACH COMMERCIAL ACTING WORKSHOPS AND CLASSES?

Yes. And no.

Since casting agents are not under any rules that the unions set, they often have classes and workshops for commercial actors, and it's a terrific way to have a casting director get to know you and see your work.

Franchised SAG talent agencies, however, are governed by rules set down by SAG and they may not conduct their own commercial acting workshops or lend their names to any commercial acting classes. Nonfranchised SAG agents work independently but generally adhere to SAG's rules about teaching workshops and classes. Talent agents may recommend classes but cannot receive any sort of kickback from the workshops. The stance of the unions is that if talent agents were to conduct workshops, it would be perceived as a conflict of interest, and a talent agent could use her position to take an actor's money with an assumed promise of representation.

It is rumored that SAG is considering relaxing this rule for talent agents as long as the commercial acting school is accredited. Talent agents, however, often are invited to come to workshops and classes as guests to talk to actors and even direct actors during on-camera training. For this, SAG allows them to accept an honorarium for their time. The amount is nominal and varies depending on the school or workshop.

HOW DOES THE ACTOR-TALENT AGENT-CASTING AGENT PROCESS WORK?

Glad you asked. It's a ten-step plan.

Step One
The *client* hires an *advertising agency* who writes and develops a commercial for that client.

Step Two
The ad agency awards a *production company* the job to produce the commercial.

Step Three
The production company hires a *casting director* to conduct auditions for talent who might be right for that particular commercial.

Step Four
The casting director posts the commercial breakdown through one or more of the online services so that *talent agents* will see that breakdown. Los Angeles is currently the leader in online casting. In some other markets, particularly smaller markets, casting directors may still simply telephone talent agents, but the move to online casting is growing very quickly.

Step Five
The talent agents look at the posted commercial breakdown online (or look at the perimeters set down during the casting agent's contact) and then submit their suggestions of *talent* back to the casting director online (or via a hand delivery).

Step Six

The casting director will look at the suggested photos, reject some, select others, and come up with a master list of the *actors* from a number of different talent agencies.

Step Seven

The casting director then calls and/or e-mails the talent agents, giving each of them the list of actors from that agent's stable whom he'd like to have audition. He will also give the product name, the location, the date and times each actor should show up for the audition, as well as a character description and any pertinent wardrobe information. He will also include the shoot dates and state whether the actor may have access to the script beforehand.

Step Eight

The talent agent then contacts the selected actors via e-mail with all the above information. He will follow up the e-mail with a phone call to make sure the actor knows she has an audition and to tell her to check her e-mail for the details.

Step Nine

The actor goes on the audition and competes with all the other actors.

Step Ten

One actor is chosen for each scripted character in the commercial.

Complicated? Yes. That's why agents go crazy when actors call back and want a different time slot to audition.

WHAT DOES A COMMERCIAL TALENT AGENT DO ALL DAY?

In the old days, commercial agents would get telephone calls from casting directors with commercial breakdowns. These days, in most parts of the country, commercial agents receive those commercial breakdowns through online services throughout the day. Sometimes, they might also receive calls or e-mails from casting directors about auditions. The talent agent then tries to figure out which actors from their client base might be right for those roles in that particular commercial breakdown and submit them, again, mostly online. Once the casting directors give their thumbs-up or thumbs-down to each of the actors, it's the job of the talent agents to make sure the selected actors get to the audition.

That means that commercial talent agents also have to be scheduling experts (sometimes trying to figure out how to get an actor from a Studio City audition for Taco Bell at noon to a Santa Monica callback for McDonald's by 1:30). They must also be sure that this commercial doesn't product-conflict with a commercial the actor may have already done and is currently being held for. That means that if an actor is still receiving a holding fee for a car commercial he did (whether that commercial is on the air or not), he may not take another job for a competing car spot until he is officially released.

Commercial talent agents also spend time working with and nurturing their stable of actors, becoming part business partner, part advisor and counselor, and sometimes part psychologist. They constantly meet with and identify new talent, sign new clients, eliminate clients who don't seem to be working out, negotiate contracts for jobs booked, and chase down payments that are either late or incorrect. Agents are very busy people. If you're going to call your agent, it better not be to chitchat.

HOW DO I FIND A COMMERCIAL TALENT AGENT TO REPRESENT ME?

There are essentially three ways an actor looking for representation will submit to an agency.

Way Number One

The first way is a good method and is called "industry referral." That means that someone who knows the talent agent personally suggested you. This can come from a variety of sources, and many times it comes from a telephone call and personal recommendation from one of the agent's working actors. The call can also come from a casting director or any industry professional. (Another good reason to take a commercial acting class from a casting director!)

Way Number Two

The second way is to have a talent agent see your work in a commercial acting class during "agent's night." (Another good reason to ask if your commercial acting class has bona fide talent agents come into class!)

Way Number Three

The third and most common way to find a talent agent is through a normal submission process: submitting your headshot and résumé with a short cover letter. While it is true that the majority of talent agencies are located in Los Angeles and New York, you'll be surprised how many are scattered throughout the country.

Listing all the talent agents in America would take up *way* too much appendix space in this book, so I suggest subscribing to Ross Reports (see The Publications and Poopsheets, chapter 3). It will give you the most current and easy-to-use talent agency listings available. With Ross Reports, you can go to the website, log in, select your state, choose the talent type ("Actors") and representation ("Commercials"), and it will give you a very complete and empirical commercial agency breakdown in your area. You can also call SAG/AFTRA in your area (see appendix A) and ask them if they have an up-to-date list of the agents in your area. If they do send one or tell you how to download it, be aware that it will not be as complete and current as Ross Reports.

Once you have a master list of all talent agents who service your geographical area, start eliminating those agencies that do not represent actors for commercial work.

Some agencies have separate divisions that handle actors who have different specialties. For instance, some talent agents only handle actors for television commercials; others only for actors in TV shows and film; others only for the legitimate stage. Other agencies specialize in actors who do stunt work, dance, print work, or sports, and some only handle celebrities. Agency specialties are generally listed along with the agency names in your reference material. It's also a very good idea to talk to any fellow actor or teachers you may have gotten to know to get their suggestions.

At this point, compile your now-abbreviated list and investigate each agency's submission policy, which can easily be found if you're subscribing to Ross Reports. Other publications, including SAG's, will usually just give the initial C if the agency handles actors for commercial work. Most agencies also have websites. If you can't find the answers you're looking for, call the agency to ask what their submission policy is. But do your homework to try and avoid those calls, if possible. Talent agents are busy folks and don't like general "fishing" calls.

HOW DID YOU GET YOUR COMMERCIAL TALENT AGENT?

I signed with my first commercial agent because of a referral: my theatrical agent's telephone call and recommendation. I then followed it up with my own phone call, set up a time to meet, went in for the interview with my headshot and résumé in hand, read some copy for the agency staff, and was signed. That was in 1970.

Cris Dennis told me a great story about one actor he knew who was seeking representation. Seems that this actor kept sending Cris his headshot and résumé in the mail. He even dropped them off at the agency in person, but to no avail. He refused to give up and decided to do some creative marketing, so he called the agency and asked the gal manning the phones what kind of pizza Cris liked. He then hand-delivered a large pizza with all Cris' favorite toppings, wearing the clothes a pizza delivery guy would wear. When Cris opened the box, there was the actor's headshot and résumé taped to the inside cover staring back at him. Cris said he was so impressed by the actor's creativity and effort that he immediately called him to tell him so, set up a meeting with him, and eventually took him on as a client! Sometimes persistence does pay off! But we're getting a little ahead of ourselves...

OKAY, SO I'VE NARROWED DOWN MY LIST OF TALENT AGENTS I WANT TO SUBMIT MYSELF TO. WHAT'S NEXT?

First, pat yourself on the back! You've already done a lot of work and now you're ready to start your search!

Now type out all the names of the talent agents you'd like to contact for possible representation on a list, with ample room after each entry for your notes. Make sure everything you do is documented and organized neatly. Depending on whether you're right-brained or left-brained, some folks will find this organization part easier than others. When your list is finished, pick a name to begin your submissions. I'd stay away from attacking your list alphabetically, however. Those agencies starting with the letter *A* get a lot more submissions than those beginning with the letter *Z*. Select up to six talent agents from your list every few days and make your mail-in submissions. Snail mail is still the norm, though it will cost you postage. With all the online viruses going around, an unsolicited e-mail with a photo and résumé attachment will most likely not get opened.

WHAT DO I INCLUDE IN MY MAILINGS?

Snail-mail each talent agency the following three things, with cardboard for support so nothing arrives folded, spindled, or mutilated.

- Your *incredible* eight-by-ten glossy headshot with your name professionally printed at the bottom of the photo

- Your *terrific-looking* résumé sporting your name at the top

- A *very* brief cover note introducing yourself

WHAT DO I SAY IN MY COVER NOTE?

You aren't looking for a pen pal, so a few short paragraphs will be sufficient. Remember that talents agents are very busy folks and don't have time to wade through your short story just to find out what type of representation you're seeking. Make sure your contact information is included in the note, and if you have any industry referrals, include that info.

Here's a good hypothetical example.

<Date>

To:
Cris Dennis
Film Artists Associates
21044 Ventura Blvd, Suite 215
Woodland Hills, CA 91364

From:
Lexy Fridell
1234 Lucky Lane
Los Angeles, CA 90000
(555) 555-5555 cell

Dear Cris:
    I'm a recent transplant from New York City now living in Los Angeles and I'm seeking representation for television commercials. Your agency was suggested to me by Dennis Gallegos during a workshop at Tepper-Gallegos Casting.
    Enclosed is my current résumé and photograph for your consideration. I'd love to call your office in a few days to hopefully meet with you personally.

    Thank you for your time.
    <Signature>
    Lexy Fridell

After snail-mailing the packets with your note, your eight-by-ten glossy, and your résumé to each of the selected agents, be sure to check their name on your list so you will remember which agents you have sent your packet to. Also enter the date their packet was mailed. I cannot overemphasize the need to keep a very accurate journal of your submissions.

THEN WHAT DO I DO?

After you've figured the appropriate amount of time for the package to arrive, you'll want to follow up your mailed submission with a well-rehearsed telephone call to the talent agency. Don't wait for them to contact you; they probably won't. The best times to call are between ten a.m. and two p.m., Monday through Thursday. Before ten o'clock, you'll get the answering service, and after two, you'll be told to call back. Late afternoons and Fridays are generally pretty busy times for agents.

Your telephone call will usually be handled by a secretary, some-times by a subagent, sometimes by the talent agent. Be polite and to the point. Ask the person you're talking to if they got your submission packet, then ask if the agent is available to speak with you. One of three things will happen.

The First Thing That May Happen
You'll be told that the talent agency is not looking for any new clients. Cross them off your list and enter the information. Don't let yourself focus more than one minute of negative energy in their direction.

The Second Thing That May Happen
You'll be told that the talent agency isn't looking for any new clients right now but to call back sometime in the future. Try to verbally secure a month's perimeter for that next telephone call. Log that information on your list and enter the date you will need to make that future call.

The Third Thing That May Happen
You'll be told that the talent agent received your submission and would like to set up an appointment to meet with you. Yippee! You did it and your foot's in the door! Make the appointment and enter that informa-tion in your journal and your appointment book. Then keep up the ad-ditional calls to the other talent agents until you've had your interviews and decided which talent agency is a perfect match for you.

HOW MUCH DO TALENT AGENTS GET PAID?

Nothing. Until you work. A talent agent who represents you and sends you on commercial auditions will receive no money unless you get a job. Then, when you do get paid, the agent takes 10 percent of the gross amount of your earnings. No more, no less. For more specific details, see chapter 14, The Money. Remember that the agent makes money only if and when you make money. If someone tries to tell you otherwise, he's a crook.

CAN I HAVE MORE THAN ONE COMMERCIAL TALENT AGENCY REPRESENT ME?

Yes. And no. The rules change depending on the geographic area. In New York you may have more than one commercial agent represent you at the same time. On the other hand, in the Los Angeles area, you can have only one talent agent represent you for television commercials. You may have more than one talent agent, but only if those agents are not competing in the same area of representation. That means you might have agent A rep you for commercials, agent B rep you for theatrical work, and agent C rep you for print work. Those three agents could all be from the same agency or three different ones.

WILL A COMMERCIAL TALENT AGENCY REPRESENT ME EVEN IF THEY DO NOT OFFICIALLY SIGN ME?

That depends on the talent agency, and it's quite a common practice in New York but less common in L.A. "Signing you" means that you are exclusive to that talent agency. In New York, many actors will freelance and take audition calls from more than one talent agency. Different agencies have different policies. Some will agree to represent you only after you've signed a general service agreement (GSA) or a SAG contract with them. Others allow you to freelance.

WHAT IF I ALREADY HAVE A COMMERCIAL TALENT AGENT BUT I'M LOOKING TO CHANGE REPRESENTATION?

It happens all the time. If you already have a talent agent and want to change agents, then it might be best *not* to include the name of your current agency on your résumé. Let that come up in your conversation during the interview. You can, if you'd like, include that information in your cover letter during submission, but my advice is not to do it. The world of talent agents is a small one and many of them see one another socially. It would be an unpleasant way for your current agency to hear that you're dissatisfied. That would be a lose-lose.

WHAT HAPPENS WHEN I DO SIGN THAT GSA OR SAG CONTRACT?

A standard SAG commercial contract, which must adhere to SAG's Rule 16(g), is initially good for one year with subsequent terms up to three years. Within any ninety-one-day period, if you have not earned at least $3,500 generated from the bookings from your agency, you may terminate the agreement. It also states that your agent may not collect more than 10 percent of commissionable income. SAG's Rule 16(g) also prohibits commissions on travel expenses and living expenses, forced call, and rest-period violations.

Under the general service agreement, the ATA/NATR agencies can offer one- to three-year initial contracts to actors, and even though they can ask for more than 10 percent commission from their actors, thus far, 10 percent is still the norm. Under the GSA, an actor may terminate his contract only if the actor has not been offered one day's employment within any four-month period. Also, under the GSA, every penny of the actor's income, including travel and living expenses and work violations, are commissionable. It all depends whether your talent agency is franchised or nonfranchised, but remember that everything is negotiable. I don't think the important thing should be nickels and dimes, but to find a good talent agent whom you believe in and who believes in you. There are other varying conditions and terms in the general service agreement, and a lot of it also has to do with how the agency writes up its contracts.

HOW OFTEN SHOULD I CALL MY TALENT AGENT TO CHECK IN?

I used to suggest that you call your agent once every few weeks to remind him in a positive way that you're around. When I posed this question to Cris Dennis, his answer was emphatically "Don't call us! We'll call you!" Looking at it from his perspective, I can see his point. If every one of his clients all called him once every few weeks, he'd have no time for anything other than "how's the weather" chitchat. Agents spend their time each day trying to get their actors auditions and they have to be able to devote their time selling you to casting directors.

Cris, however, did add that if you have not heard from your agent in a month or so, it might be a good idea to send him a quick e-mail (or one of your headshot postcards) to let him know about something that just happened to you. Maybe you just finished a commercial workshop, you're performing in a show you'd like him to see if he has time, or maybe you and your wife just had a baby girl. But whatever you write, be sure you relate it quickly, concisely, and positively. However you let your agent know your good news, make sure your agent feels good about the fact that he has you as a client. *Never, ever* ask why you're not going out on auditions!

MEETING WITH THE PROSPECTIVE COMMERCIAL TALENT AGENT

The talent agent is meeting with you for one reason: because he saw something in your photograph and/or résumé that made him think that you might make him some money. He wants to make 10 percent of your earnings. That's the only reason he's meeting with you.

WHAT SHOULD I TALK ABOUT DURING THE INTERVIEW?

Be as warm, friendly, and relaxed as possible. Remember that there is nothing the agent would like more than to find someone who potentially will make him some money. Make sure you bring an additional headshot and résumé with you. He may not even look at your résumé and just have you read some copy. He may look at your résumé and then ask you about something on it. Mostly he wants to see how you perform during the interview.

Undoubtedly, sometime during the interview he'll say the following to you: "Tell me a little about yourself." What you do *not* want to relate is a lengthy chronological regurgitation of all the things that happened to you in your life. That's boring. The idea is not to see how much personal information you can squeeze into the interview, but to try and find an area of common interest and expand on it. How much you say during your interview isn't half as important as how you say what you say and how excited you are talking about it. You might tape-record a normal telephone conversation that you have with a friend or your mom and listen to it in playback. Do you use the phrase *you know* or the words *totally* or *like* a lot when you talk? Don't! Never try to fill in dead space in speech with words that don't go anywhere. ("I was, like, totally happy to be cast in the show! It was, like, a dream come true, you know" isn't a good way to sound very intelligent or professional!)

If he asks about your schooling and you discover that he was also a graduate of Carnegie Mellon, the entire interview can stay focused on your four years living in Pittsburgh, Pennsylvania. If you can find *any* topic both of you can relate to on a personal level, and it's an area you enjoy talking about or have some knowledge of, then the interview for both of you will be interesting, and you'll be much more relaxed and at ease.

Years ago, when I was teaching at a high school near L.A. and trying to squeeze in my auditions and interviews during my lunch and free period, I would inevitably be asked during the audition or interview the same thing: "Tell me a little about yourself." My response? I would say that I just finished teaching my third-period class, was on my lunch break, and was on my way back to teach my fifth-period class. We'd then get into a conversation about what I taught (high school drama and television production), where I taught (El Rancho High School in Pico Rivera), how long I'd been teaching, what I liked about teaching, and so forth. I soon discovered that almost everyone had something to add about teaching. They had either taught a seminar class during their spare time or their sister or father taught school, whatever. All of a sudden, "Tell me a little about yourself" turned into a conversation instead of a monologue.

On one commercial audition, as soon as I mentioned to the director of the commercial (a very talented and nice fellow named Bob

Gips) that I taught school, his face lit up. It turned out that he had also been a teacher, and we spent most of the interview talking about teaching. To make a long story short, he not only ended up hiring me *seven* different times that year as an actor for his commercial shoots, he also took the time to come to my school during his free time to guest-lecture to my classes about filmmaking. He even ended up hiring one of my television production students to work in his studio at FilmFair in Los Angeles!

On another occasion I had an audition to guest-star for a role in a popular TV series. By doing a little research (this was a lot harder before the Internet), I discovered that Herm Saunders, the producer, and I were graduates of the same small college. During the audition, I mentioned that I had graduated from University of the Pacific during the "Tell me a little about yourself" part of the interview. His face lit up, we enthusiastically chatted about our shared alma mater, and (to my great joy!) we soon discovered that both of us had also been members of the same fraternity! The entire conversation stayed focused on Rhizomia/Phi Sigma Kappa, and a lot of laughs were shared. Did I get that job? Yep. And over the next two years I ended up being a guest star on *three* different episodes of that series! Rhizomia Booms!

During an interview, if you can get the interviewer to do more than listen, you're both going to have a pretty good time, and it probably will pay off. It's so easy these days to Google the name of an agent, a casting director, a director, or a producer and see if you can discover something that you have in common.

If you strike out, look around in the office while you are waiting to go in for the interview. If there are multiple photos on the wall of World War II airplanes and you have an interest in flying or World War II history, then you've got a clue that *someone* who works there does too. You've got a common interest that might pay off for you. If there are five magazines that have to do with hang-gliding, or sailing, or horses, and you know a little about any of those, use it! "I notice there are a lot of hang-gliding magazines out in the waiting room. Are you a hang-glider?" Bang! Your interview is off and running! You may not even get to say anything else during the entire interview because she's excitedly telling you about the thrills of jumping off a cliff somewhere. As soon as you leave the room, her thoughts will be "What a nice guy!" One more reminder: Make sure you don't fib. There's no need to give the impression that you're an avid hang-gliding fan if you're not. Just tell the truth, be energetic, interested, and interesting.

HOW SHOULD I LOOK FOR MY INTERVIEW?

It's extremely important to look exactly like your headshot, so don't all of a sudden decide to grow a beard or a mustache, dye your hair, get your nose pierced, or sport day-old facial hair. You also might be

asked if you have any other photos with you, so if you have any additional professional photos that show you with a different look, take them along.

WHAT SHOULD I WEAR?

Apply the same criteria you did when you had your headshot done. Keeping in mind that the biggest advertiser in the world is Procter & Gamble, you should look like you could be taken off the street and put right in a commercial. Wear clothes that you feel comfortable in. You don't need to wear the same clothes you wore for your head-shot, but definitely wear the same style that you wore for that photo session.

ANYTHING ELSE I SHOULD KNOW ABOUT THE INTERVIEW?

You'll hear this many times during your career, but try to have fun with it! The whole process happens over and over, and you must have a mind-set to enable you to enjoy the interviews, the auditions, and eventually the jobs.

WHAT ABOUT YOUR LOYALTY TO YOUR COMMERCIAL TALENT AGENT?

Good question. Many actors are approached or solicited by other talent agents after they start to book jobs, often forgetting the agent who got them their SAG card and believed in them when no one else did.

Film Artists Agency has been my commercial agent for a thousand years, first with Pen Dennis and now represented by his son, Cris. Over the years, Pen has always been trustworthy, loyal, and had my best interests at heart, and Cris is the spitting image of his old man. I'm a loyal sort of guy. Even when my theatrical agent was negotiating for a TV series I'd been cast in, I always asked that my commercial agent, Pen, be included in all meetings. When Universal put me under contract and wanted complete exclusivity, Pen was there to make sure the contract clearly stated that I would still be able to do television commercials. They balked, but Pen was adamant and it all worked out. If he had not been present, things would have turned out differently.

Cris tells a great story about a talented actress whom he met in a class who was looking for representation. During their subsequent meeting, Cris asked what other talent agencies she was interested in and she said that she had submitted herself to a very high-profile agency that expressed some interest, but the agency kept giving her the brush-off whenever she called to try to make an appointment. Cris said he felt that she was very talented and he thought that he could help her find work. She ended up signing with him and soon she had several national spots on the air. About six months later, the actress called Cris, laughing. It seemed that the high-profile agency that wouldn't pay her any attention earlier had seen her commercials and called to set up a meeting. The agent was gushing with enthusiasm and wanted to know where she had been hiding! Knowing that the agent had a reputation for trying to snag away working talent (to the point of hanging around on commercial shoots!), she kindly thanked him for his interest and told him she already had loyal representation who returned her calls.

WHAT ABOUT HIRING A PERSONAL MANAGER?

Not needed and not a good idea for a commercial actor. Managers are not bound by any rules and regulations and can take upward of 20 percent of an actor's money. If you have an agent (necessary) and a manager (not necessary), you could be shelling out *30 percent* of your gross earnings! After Uncle Sam gets finished with you, you'll be bringing home less than your agent's commission.

ANYTHING ELSE?

That about covers it and, hopefully, your search for that elusive talent agent has been fruitful!

Good job so far!

Now it's time to talk about what happens *after your talent agent!*

part two

After
Your Talent Agent

CHAPTER 7

THE AFTER-AGENT HEADSHOT

What's an actor need with a conscience, anyway?

—Jiminy Cricket

ANOTHER HEADSHOT? WHAT'S WRONG WITH THE ONE I USED TO GET MY TALENT AGENT?

You might be able to use it, depending on what your agent thinks. Sometimes the agency has a certain look that they prefer for their clients' headshots. Your talent agent will be the best judge and he has your best interests in mind, so don't argue; just do what he says.

WILL HE RECOMMEND A PHOTOGRAPHER FOR ME TO USE?

Agents can't recommend just one photographer. According to SAG Rule 16(g), talent agents must suggest more than one photographer, and they are not permitted to make a commission from their referral. So if your talent agent says he'd like you to get a new headshot and suggests a couple of photographers, you'll know it's in your best interest to have a new headshot taken. You may even choose to have the photographer you used before take your new headshots. Talk to your agent about it.

HOW MANY PHOTOS DO I NEED?

Good question. That depends. In many areas around the country, some talent agents feel that you should have more than one look with some different headshots. This is particularly true if you're in an area like Los Angeles where a lot of casting is done through online posting services, and, in that case, you probably should have a total of four or five. One will be your main headshot that you will carry and use for most submissions, online or otherwise. The other headshots will be used to show you with different looks when appropriate.

WHAT DO YOU MEAN BY "DIFFERENT LOOKS"?

I'll cover that in more detail starting on page 114, but it's a good idea to talk to your talent agent before having this set of photos done, because he'll have his own ideas and preferences. He'll take a look at the photos you've already taken, show you some examples of what other actors have done and what he'd like you to do. Then you'll know how to proceed. You can also go back online to look at some photographers' examples to see what other actors did for their different looks and get some ideas. But right now, let's focus on your main headshot.

WILL MY COMMERCIAL TALENT AGENT HELP ME PICK OUT MY NEW HEADSHOTS?

He should. That's part of his job. Once you've narrowed down the possibilities from all the digital shots your photographer did, make an appointment with your agent if he has the time to sit with you, and take in the disc. If he doesn't have the time, you can send the ones you like best to your agent electronically. Then you both will make the final choice. Unless your agent recommends otherwise, the guidelines for your main, or *hero*, headshot are pretty much the same as we talked about earlier in chapter 1, Your First Headshot.

SHOULD I HAVE MY NAME PRINTED ON THE FRONT OF MY MAIN HEADSHOT?

Yep. Just your name, usually below your photo, left, right, or center.

SHOULD I HAVE MY TALENT AGENCY'S CONTACT INFORMATION PRINTED ON THE HEADSHOT?

Nope. Your talent agent information will be on your résumé, which will either be printed on the back of your headshot or stapled to it (my preference). If you have only your name on your headshot and you staple your résumé to the back, you might be able to use the same headshot in auditions for both theatrical work and commercial work, even if you have different agents for each. I would suggest, however, that you clearly print your talent agent's name, the agency name, and your agent's phone number and e-mail address on the rear of your headshot if you go the staple route, just in case your headshot and your résumé get separated.

DO I GET MY AFTER-AGENT HEADSHOTS REPRODUCED THE SAME AS MY FIRST ONE? HOW MANY COPIES DO I NEED FOR MY AUDITIONS?

Yes. Again, I suggest going to Reproductions.com and checking out their current prices. Ask your agent what he thinks about quantity, but keep in mind that the more copies you have made, the cheaper they are per copy. I'd say a hundred of your main headshot is a good place to start.

THEY ALSO OFFER POSTCARDS AND BUSINESS CARDS WITH MY PHOTO. A GOOD IDEA?

That, again, depends on what your talent agent suggests. Don't get postcards made before you talk with your agent, because he will have his own ideas and you may just have to get them done differently. My L.A. agent, Cris Dennis, *loves* postcards and thinks color postcards are great public relations tools for the commercial actor. That's because if you have postcards with your headshot and contact information on the front side, whenever you have some positive career information to impart, you can address the back side, write (neatly) your piece of industry good news, and do a mailing. Whether you have your talent agent information printed on the postcard is, again, your agent's choice, but I'd suggest only your telephone number and perhaps your e-mail address. That way, if you have more than one agent, you can use the same postcard for a myriad of mailings.

What you write should be of interest. "I just played the dead body in next week's *CSI Miami!*" might not be worthwhile enough to send out a mailing, but "I was just cast to originate the role of Dory in *Finding Nemo—The Musical* for an extended run!" definitely would be. Even a bit of personal news: "My wife and I just had our first baby! She's a seven-pound bundle of joy and has the good fortune to look just like her mom!" would be cute and nice. Not even the biggest curmudgeon casting director in the world could help but smile a little at that.

You can most likely expect your postcard to get glanced at and then tossed into the circular file, but the goal is to be seen, remembered, and called in for an audition. Stranger things have happened. The more you're out there, the more chances there are for success!

The next page shows both Lexy's postcard and mine. Be aware that in reality, they are 6-by-4½-inch normal postcard size and in color.

As far as the business card is concerned, these days you can get a business card that is actually a disc with your reel on it. Not only does it have all your info printed on the front, it also makes your work viewable to anyone who is as technologically savvy as you are. Cris says, "It's the wave of the future and it's very cool!" (A little too high-tech for me, however.)

HOW OFTEN SHOULD I HAVE A NEW PHOTO FOR MY HEADSHOT?

Obviously, you should have new photos shot whenever you look different from your current headshot. It is absolutely essential that you

Lexy Fridell
AEA AFTRA SAG

(555) 555-5555
lexyfridell@nyc.net

SQUIRE FRIDELL
(555) 555-5555

look like your headshot, so the minute you go from brunette to blond or from 115 pounds to 130 pounds, make an appointment with your photographer. Even if you don't dramatically change your weight or your hairstyle, as a rule of thumb, you should get a new headshot at least once a year. You may not think you look much different from your high school graduation picture, but you do. Another reason to change your headshot once a year is simply because casting directors get tired of looking at the same shot of you over and over again. If you keep the same headshot for too long, it gives the impression that you're not working much and can't afford a new photo session. It's always good to show your face with a fresh look.

OKAY, I UNDERSTAND WHAT MY MAIN HEADSHOT SHOULD LOOK LIKE. NOW, WHAT'S THE CRITERIA FOR MY DIFFERENT LOOK HEADSHOTS?

If your agent suggests getting other headshots with different looks, then it's a good idea. This is particularly true for casting done through online casting services. Let's suppose that you're a guy and your talent

agent receives a breakdown from the casting director, either through an online casting service, an e-mail, or a phone call. The breakdown says they are shooting a Brawny paper towel commercial and they want a dad type who is off in the woods camping and bonding with the mom type and their kid type. (In actuality, it would be more specific than the above, but that's a broad stroke of what they're looking for.) Now let's suppose that your agent has one headshot of you and you are dressed wearing a tie and sport coat. Kind of a stretch and not your best foot forward for this commercial. Now let's suppose your talent agent has more than one headshot of you, and one of those shots has you dressed in a casual denim shirt with your sleeves rolled up.

You think you have a better chance? You bet, and that's the headshot he's going to submit. He wants his 10 percent!

WHAT ARE THE OPTIONS FOR MY DIFFERENT LOOK HEADSHOTS?

The biggest difference is in the clothing. The clothes you are wearing for your main headshot should be not too formal, not too casual, not too winter, and not too summer. No particular statement. Just a good headshot. The clothes you are wearing for your different looks headshot should be the opposite. A housewife shopping at the market dresses differently than a secretary at work, and a secretary dresses differently than her boss. Your choice of clothing makes a statement. The photos will show you looking good and feeling comfortable in different settings, whether it's at a formal dinner party, out in the garden, or getting ready to go out and jog. All the photos should also have that someone-just-called-your-name-and-you-turned-around look. It used to be common for actors to hold some sort of unidentifiable product and look like they were doing a print job, but that's no longer the case.

If you are a man, the clothes you should wear for these headshots might include any of the following.

- A jacket and tie for a "going-out-to-a-dinner-party" look

- A sport coat with loosened tie for a "just-got-home-from-work" look

- A nice casual open shirt or maybe sweater for an "it's-the-weekend-and-I'm-off-to-the-hardware-store" look

- A denim work shirt for an "it's-time-to-work-in-the-garden" look

- Jeans and a work shirt for the "blue-collar construction worker" look

- Horn-rimmed glasses for more of a specific "nerdy" look, or a white jacket and/or a stethoscope around your neck for a "professional" look

- There is a lot of casting now for the "office worker/cubicle dweller," which is a bit different from the secretary/executive.

- If you were in the military, a shot of you in uniform might pay off, but don't make it look like a recruitment poster. Make sure you're smiling.

- A generic, dark blue shirt for a "fireman/police officer" look

If you're a woman, you would choose some similarly themed outfits. For instance:

- A formal dark dress with simple jewelry for that "elegant dinner party" look

- An upscale suit for the "businesswoman-at-work" look

- A skirt, shirt, or sweater (and holding or wearing glasses) for the "overworked secretary" look

- Khakis and a plaid work shirt holding gloves for the "working-in-the-garden" look

- Jeans and a work shirt for a "blue-collar worker" look

- Something in your wardrobe that might give you a "ditzy blonde" look

There are a whole lot of variations on these themes, but, hopefully, you get the idea.

Also, think of items you might use to embellish your clothing to help tell the story of your character. Holding gloves or a hard hat as a construction worker, or holding a trowel and a plant as a gardener, might work well. Tell your agent your ideas and ask what his preferences are.

And even if you *do* choose to have more of a three-quarters shot for your main headshot, these different look headshots are usually tighter and tend to show less of the rest of *you* and more of your face, unless you're doing a three-quarters shot for a particular reason. Why should your different look shots be tight? These photos will be typically viewed online in a smaller JPEG thumbnail format, thus making your face *very* small if your photo is a three-quarters or a full-figure shot. And, again, don't feature any specific product in *any* of your headshots.

SHOULD I HAVE DUPLICATES MADE OF MY DIFFERENT LOOKS?

It's not necessary for your agent to have copies if your headshots are posted online and the casting director utilizes the online casting service. In that case you'll need to have only one of each of your different looks posted online. However, if the casting is still done using hand submissions, your agent will need to have eight-by-ten duplicates of each headshot (with your name printed at the bottom) to be submitted. You, on the other hand, *will* be taking your selected headshots into your auditions, so I'd carry at least two of your headshots with you. (I carry four.)

I'VE HEARD ABOUT "COMPOSITES." WHAT ARE THEY?

Up until 2005, in Los Angeles and some other areas of the country, composites were the norm. Composites were inexpensive, three-hole-punched, 8½-by-11 alternatives to the eight-by-ten glossies that actors always have used in New York. They were printed on a newsprint paper, had a main headshot on the front with usually four smaller different look photos on the back. We actors would carry them in during auditions and give them to casting directors. Now composites are kaput, and the eight-by-ten glossy is the norm everywhere.

HOW MANY HEADSHOTS DO YOU HAVE?

I have five different headshots that are currently posted online, and I've included them on the next two pages. (Keep in mind that all the headshots are eight-by-ten and in color.) The first headshot is my main headshot, and the other four on the following page are my other looks. A terrific photographer and good friend, Clarke Smith, took the shots. He's based in New York and you can visit him at ClarkeSmith.com.

Squire Fridell

Let's take a look at my five headshots and discuss why each is a different headshot and why Cris Dennis might submit one over the others.

- My main headshot that Cris uses for submissions—and that I always carry with me—is my most casual and my favorite: I'm holding glasses and wearing an open shirt, relaxing in front of some possible conversation-starter wine barrels. ("Are those wine barrels? Do you own a winery?")

- The top-left shot on the next page presents a more "presidential" look, with dark suit and tie. The shot also has a generic, out-of-focus background, and Cris would submit that headshot for more of an upscale "business-suit" spokesperson audition. You'll also notice that I wore an American flag/USMC lapel pin. ("Is that a Marine Corps flag?" might be a good conversation starter.)

- The top-right headshot is a more casual shot with an open shirt and loose jacket. This could be submitted for any number of auditions. You might also note that my Model A Ford is definitely recognizable in the background to use as a possible conversation starter. ("Is that your car?" or "What kind of old car is it?")

- The lower-left photo is a simple, slightly upscale generic headshot and is probably the most versatile for my age group. I'm smiling, in an open shirt and sports jacket, and could be cast in any number of commercials as a casual spokesperson. There is a plain, out-of-focus exterior background and the photo doesn't make any statement.

- The final headshot, lower right, shows me in my USMC dress blues for a "patriot" look. It's an unusual, in-actual-uniform headshot, and Cris would certainly submit it only for a specific audition. But it also works as a terrific conversation starter. ("When were you in the Marine Corps?") Note also that this is the only headshot that doesn't sport a show-your-teeth smile. (I tried a few shots that way but it looked out of place in uniform.)

Again, all five headshots are eight-by-ten, in color, and have my name printed below. Even though they are used for electronic casting in Los Angeles, and Cris has them posted online with LA Casting and Breakdown Services, I also carry individual eight-by-ten copies of four of the headshots for auditions.

DO YOU HAVE AN EXAMPLE OF A WOMAN'S HEADSHOT?

Glad you asked. Below is the headshot that Lexy currently uses in New York. Note the slightly off-kilter look that's very common in the New York market. Remember that it is also in color and eight-by-ten in size.

Lexy Fridell

CHAPTER 8

BEFORE THE AUDITION

Sir Laurence Olivier, one of the greatest actors of all time, in his first professional stage appearance, tripped over the scenery and fell into the footlights.

You're heading for your first audition! Pretty exciting...but it also sounds a little scary, doesn't it? Just remember that the more you know about what will happen during the audition before you actually have that first reading, the more relaxed you're going to be and the better you'll perform. At this point, there are three things you should take the time to purchase that will greatly help you.

- The first thing to buy is an appointment book. I may be old-fashioned, but I still carry a Week-at-a-Glance rather than put my appointments into a BlackBerry or my iPhone calendar. It's just a matter of preference, but whatever you use to keep track of your appointments, keep track of them with a vengeance. Be sure to keep an accurate record of every commercial audition, every trip to see your agent, your photo sessions, even your trips to the dentist. If you are audited by the IRS (and many actors are), you'll need proof for deductions, and your appointment book will stand up as proof during an audit. The first year I was audited, my records weren't too organized and I suffered because of it. The second year (and subsequent years) I did much better. Keep good records!

While we're talking about appointment books, it's a great idea to find out your agent's birthday and enter it in your book each year ... How many actors know the birthday of their agent? Pen Dennis's birthday is June 23 and I've sent him a card every single year! I can hear you now: "How about finding out the secretary's birthday, too?" *Great* idea!

- The second thing you should purchase is a journal. Use this to log all the information about everything concerning the acting business that might one day help you out. Make an entry for each of the casting people you meet, the date you had an audition, the product that you were auditioning for, the name of the gal in the outer office, whether that particular casting director likes you to mention your talent agent's name during your slate, whatever. As soon as your agent e-mails or calls you with your audition information, you can cut and paste that information in your journal. That way you'll have a good record of the original audition in case there *is* a callback. The more you know, the more you can use. This is a very competitive business, and anything that can give you an edge over other actors may mean the difference between working and not working.

- The third thing to purchase is a portfolio carrier. This is for carrying the above items and extra copies of your headshots and résumés. It can be a portfolio bag, a briefcase, or a computer-type carry case ... just something that looks professional and is big enough for what you need to carry for auditions. Is your birthday coming up? Ask for a nice leather one that has your name embossed on the outside. My wife's gotten me a couple over the years.

WHAT WILL HAPPEN WHEN MY COMMERCIAL TALENT AGENT CALLS?

Hooray! It's what you've been waiting for! Depending on your market and whether online casting services are used, you'll probably first get an e-mail followed up by a telephone call from your talent agent notifying you that you have an audition. The following six items will either be in that e-mail or your agent will give them to you over the phone. Write them down in your journal.

1. Where the audition will be held

2. What time you are scheduled to audition

3. The name of the casting director

4. Which commercial product you'll be auditioning for

5. A hint of the character you'll be portraying

6. A hint of appropriate clothing for that character

You may also ask your agent if the script is posted online. If it is, download it, print it, and take a good look at it. Even if you don't have words to say in the spot, carefully read everything in the script and what your role is in it. I'll cover how to break the script down a bit later in chapter 10, Acting and the Script.

Let's go over each one of the above six pieces of information in detail.

1. Where the Audition Will Be Held

Make sure you understand exactly where the audition is going to be. Look up the address online as soon as you get it. It can be unnerving trying to navigate the city streets in Los Angeles if you're not used to it, so don't assume it'll be easy to find your location if you've never been there before. You can ask your agent about easiest routes (that can change depending on the time of day), what the cross streets are, any landmarks, where available parking might be if you're driving, the closest subway or bus stop if you're not. Don't be afraid to ask beforehand. Figure out your route before you start your car or get on the bus or subway. And always leave yourself plenty of extra time. If you're driving, make sure you bring lots of quarters for street parking. Better yet, keep some stocked in your car's glove compartment.

2. What Time You Are Scheduled to Audition

Be early! There is *nothing* that unnerves a casting director more than an actor who is late to an audition. And if the casting director is unnerved, you will be unnerved and not do as well as you should. It's a good idea to schedule even more travel time than you need, and then you can relax and have extra time to work on the copy. A good tip? Arrive early but do not sign in until your scheduled call-time. It will give you ample opportunity to go over the copy until you feel secure. Often the auditions will be running ahead of time or another actor will be running late. If you've already signed in, the casting director may take you early and you won't be as prepared.

3. The Name of the Casting Director
A lot of actors show up at auditions, sign in, sit down, and never greet the casting director or the outer-office secretary in a friendly way. If you're unsure whether the person behind the desk is, in fact, the casting director—introduce yourself and ask. Sometimes the person may appear a bit gruff, but just smile and be polite. It'll pay off.

4. Which Commercial Product You'll Be Auditioning For
This is a good time to talk about conflicts. There is an enforceable rule that an actor may not appear on camera in more than one commercial at a time if the other commercial might be perceived as a conflict of product. Simply stated, if you act in a Toyota commercial and have not been released from that commercial, you may not audition for or perform in a Chevrolet spot. A holding period is thirteen weeks (see chapter 14, The Money), and if you haven't received residuals or a holding fee after those thirteen weeks, you're probably released, but it's still a good idea to have your agent double-check. Be very careful. Avoiding conflict of product is *your* responsibility and not your agent's, so it's up to you to remember to ask him to check on it. The penalties are incredibly steep and you could be forced to pay for an entire recasting session and even the shooting of another commercial if you're in violation. Never assume that you are released from a commercial just because it's no longer on the air.

5. A Hint of the Character You'll Be Playing
If your agent says that you'll be auditioning for the part of a computer nerd, conjure that up in your mind and that's who you'll want to be. You'll be a guy who looks just like you, but acts and dresses like a

nerd. (It's not hard—we've all been nerds at one time or another.) I always hear stories about actors who want to "go against type" and think they need to show the ad agency or casting director that some nerds are suave and cool, but that's not what the writer *wrote*. Otherwise he would have written that in the description: "A computer geek who is trying hard not to be a nerd." If it says *nerd*, be a nerd! If it says *dumb-blonde type*, don't take offense, just be a dumb-blonde type!

6. A Hint of Appropriate Clothing for That Character

- Try to dress for the part as much as you can. A computer geek will be dressed differently than a spokesman for a bank, and neither one will be dressed like a tennis player touting a sports drink.

- When you are given that general suggestion about what to wear, relate it specifically to clothing that you own. If you're in doubt, ask your agent if your outfit will be appropriate for the audition.

- If the audition is for the part of a tennis player and you don't feel comfortable wearing shorts and a tennis shirt on the subway in Manhattan in January, then take the clothes with you and arrive early enough to change in the casting director's bathroom. Don't be embarrassed—you'll find a few other just-as-smart actors in there with you!

- I always carry a selection of small character props with me for auditions. I can't tell you how many times over the years I was able to use those horn-rimmed glasses (without lenses) or that clip-on bow tie I had in my carry case.

- Even if the commercial is for a blue-collar guy, I always carry a sport coat with me that I can throw on *just in case*.

- Successful actresses I've auditioned with seem to always have a scarf hidden somewhere that magically appears and is used as rain gear or a neck scarf or a bandanna when they needed a different look.

- The Boy Scouts say it best: "Be prepared!"

WHAT IF I'M NOT GIVEN ANY SPECIFICS ABOUT WHAT TO WEAR TO THE AUDITION?

Your agent should give you some idea of what the part is that you'll be auditioning for. If he doesn't, then ask. If you're still in doubt and no one seems to have a clue (*very* rare), just dress like other actors you see on TV commercials who are in your age group. Procter & Gamble is the biggest advertiser in the world, so watch those laundry detergent and toothpaste spots and see what the actors are wearing. Those clothes are very carefully hand-selected by the wardrobe gal and the ad agency folks. Some good tips in general:

- A layered look is good.

- Open-neck shirts, not-too-busy sweaters, and a jacket are great for many auditions.

- Long sleeves are better than short sleeves.

- Stay away from clothes that are too busy.

- If you wear shirts that have sharp, close-spaced horizontal lines, those lines will jump up and down during video playback and be distracting.

- Solid white or black may be your personal choice, but it doesn't do too well on the video playback.

- Unless you are specifically asked to do so, don't bare your shoulders or wear suggestive clothing or clothes that would be considered too trendy.

- Unless you are asked, keep your jewelry, gold chains, big earrings, or any observable piercings at home. If something draws attention away from you, lose it.

- It's always a good idea to bring along some clothing to change your look if need be. Even if you're auditioning for the role of a plumber, carry a sport coat to the audition. You probably won't use it, but it's smart to have just in case. Very often, there will be two auditions for different products going on at the same location, and it's not out of the question to be asked if you'd like to audition for the second product as long as you're there. That sport coat over your work shirt will change your appearance completely.

- When in doubt, always overdress and bring along some embellishment items and a backup outfit.

- Always be prepared to go on an audition in a last-minute emergency. You might be at the gym, but make sure you have acceptable clothes with you so you don't have to make a trip home to change. Sometimes a casting agent will get an emergency call for a casting session (or an actor replacement on a shoot day!) and you might have an audition with little or no warning. If you're prepared, it's a good thing to have happen! Most of the other actors won't be able to do the turnaround time to go home and change, so they'll choose not to try. Less competition for you! Our daughter once made the mistake of going in for a voice-over audition in New York directly from the gym (her agent had told her it was fine). She showed up at the audition, and the casting agent informed her that it was an on-camera audition! She said she wouldn't make *that* mistake again. More than a few New York commercial actors who live way uptown, downtown, in Brooklyn, or in Jersey belong to health clubs and rent lockers to stash a few wardrobe choices just in case.

I'M OKAY ABOUT AUDITION WARDROBE. ANY OTHER TIPS ON APPEARANCE?

- Your fingernails should be of acceptable length, nicely trimmed, and neat. Women should wear clear or conservative nail polish. If your fingernails are too long or you have cute little flowers painted on them or have them painted an interesting shade of black, you're drawing too much attention to your hands and away from *you*. During the audition, you're often asked to hold up your hands so the casting director and ad agency people can see how they'd look in a close-up. Especially if the commercial is for a food product and you're going to be handling the packaging, your hands are going to be on camera and they have to be photogenic. If you have ugly or inappropriate fingernails, you just lost the job.

- Women's lipstick and makeup should be on the conservative side unless someone requests otherwise. Usually the "less is better" adage applies. If in doubt, ask your agent. Dark lines and shadows around the eyes and slight blemishes can be erased with a cover-up, but be sure that it blends well with your skin and is not noticeable. Men can use it too.

- Generally, men should be closely shaved and not sport a fashionable two-day-old growth unless your agent thinks it's a good idea for the spot. The unshaven look goes in and out of vogue, and if the client wants it, he'll ask for it. Remember: Think Procter & Gamble!

- Your hair should be an acceptable length and color. A ponytail or a buzz cut in men or green spiked hair in women might make a statement that the client may not want to make. For men and women, if your hair is dyed, make sure it looks natural and that no roots show.

ANY LAST REMINDERS BEFORE I LEAVE FOR THE AUDITION?

- Again, leave yourself plenty of travel time to get to the audition so you won't have to be concerned about being late.

- Double-check to see that you have your eight-by-ten headshots and résumé with you and always carry a few extra sets.

- If you have a chance to download the copy beforehand, do it.

- If any props seem like they might be useful during the audition, bring them.

- Finally? Just look in the mirror and be pleased with what you see!

WHAT ABOUT ON MY WAY TO THE AUDITION?

- Be satisfied with your choice of wardrobe, your hair, and your makeup. It's too late to change anything, so feel confident in your selections.

- Remember that it's natural to feel a little excited. I prefer the word *excited* instead of *nervous*. *Excited* is a positive word and acts as a catalyst; *nervous* is a negative word and acts as an inhibitor. Remember that your excited feeling is a physiological reaction to stimulus, not a psychological one. It's caused by the adrenaline your body is producing; it's a legal drug, it's totally organic, and it's a good thing. The body releases adrenaline when it knows that you need to do something special, so treasure that feeling! During all the years I was teaching acting and directing in high school, whenever my kids were about to do a show, I'd talk to them about the excitement of performing and I encouraged them to always say they were excited about going onstage. *Never* say, even to yourself, that you have stage fright or you are nervous.

- Be happy that you're going on an audition and be confident that you'll do the best job you know how to do. Just take the whole process one step at a time.

- Make sure your vocal instrument is in good working order before you get to the audition. If the first word out of your mouth for the day is your greeting to the casting director, something disastrous might happen. Vocal cords are muscles, so loosen them up. It's a great idea to do a vocal warm-up on your way to the audition, particularly if you're in your car. If you're on a subway or a bus, it might be a little more difficult, so you'll have to warm up before leaving your apartment or house.

GOT ANY EXERCISES THAT WILL LOOSEN UP MY VOCAL CORDS?

You asked for it! Loosen up your facial muscles by sticking your tongue out as far as you can, then blow your cheeks up so you look like a chipmunk with a mouth full of food, and then stretch open your mouth as wide as you can and flick your tongue in and out. Then choose a speech, a poem, a tongue-twister, or a song that you know the words to and recite it at full volume, varying the pitch, enunciating each syllable, vowel, and consonant. My favorite is the "Trouble in River City" patter-song from *The Music Man*. It takes about five minutes to get through it, gets my voice ready, loosens up my face, and gets my energy level up. I did the role in four different Equity productions and it always makes me smile when I slip into Harold Hill while driving on the freeway.

Here are a couple of other exercises for you.

This one is for developing flexibility in the tip of your tongue.

> *Theophilus Thistle, the successful thistle sifter, sifting a sieve full of unsifted thistles, thrust three thousand thistles through the thick of his thumb. Now, if Theophilus Thistle, the successful thistle sifter, in sifting a sieve full of unsifted thistles, thrust three thousand thistles through the thick of his thumb, see that thou, in sifting a sieve full of unsifted thistles, thrust not three thousand thistles through the thick of thy thumb. Success to the successful thistle sifter.*

(Fifteen seconds with no mistakes is excellent!)

This next one will help you increase flexibility of your lips.

> *I bought a batch of baking powder and baked a batch of biscuits. I brought a big basket of biscuits back to the bakery and baked a basket of big biscuits. Then I took the big basket of biscuits and the basket of big biscuits and mixed the big basket with the basket of big biscuits that was next to the big basket and put a bunch of biscuits from both baskets into a box. Then I took the box of mixed biscuits and a biscuit mixer and the biscuit basket and brought the basket of biscuits and the box of mixed biscuits and the biscuit mixer back to the bakery and opened up a can of sardines.*

(Fifteen seconds with no mistakes is again excellent!)

This next one is fun and easy to memorize. It's the end of the nightmare sequence from Gilbert and Sullivan's *Iolanthe*. See if you can make it through in one breath.

> *You're a regular wreck, with a crick in your neck, and no wonder you snore for your head's on the floor, and you've needles and pins from your soles to your shins, and your flesh is a-creep for your left leg's asleep, and you've cramps in your toes, and a fly on your nose, and some fluff in your lung, and a feverish tongue, and a thirst that's intense, and a general sense that you haven't been sleeping in clover.*

Now do it *twice* through in one breath!

Another favorite warm-up piece, on the next page, is "Jabberwocky" from Lewis Carroll's *Through the Looking Glass*. Carroll made up many of these "portmanteau" words by putting together parts of other descriptive words. For instance, *chortle* was a new word that Carroll created by combining the words *chuckle* and *snort*. Look it up! It's now in the dictionary.

I love this poem. Memorize it and if you can act it out and have a group of first graders captivated, you're doing it right. I've always been a sucker for poetry and have memorized a lot of it over the years. Trust me, you'll be amazed at how many times you'll be able to use just about anything you can commit to memory. We had to memorize all the presidents in a row in order to graduate from the sixth grade in Westfield, New Jersey, and I still know them. I can't tell you how many times it's come in handy. Growing up, my secret wish was to go on a quiz show and have the topic be "Presidents." ("For every U.S. president you can name we'll give you $10,000.") I've also done "Casey at the Bat," "Jabberwocky," the nightmare sequence from *Iolanthe*, and speeches from Shakespeare a zillion times for a zillion different reasons. I even do the Act V, Scene ii, death scene from *Othello* where the title character enters his bedchamber to smother his wife, Desdemona. I have a half-and-half wig, blond and Afro, and play both parts in profile. It's pretty funny—but it's *my* bit, so don't steal it!

Now you're off for your first audition! Good luck out there!

T'was brillig, and the slithy toves
Did gyre and gimble in the wabe.
All mimsy were the boroughgroves
And the mome raths outgrabe.

"Beware the Jabberwock, my son;
The jaws that bite, the claws that catch.
Beware the Jub-Jub Bird,
And shun the frumious Bandersnatch!"

He took his vorpal sword in hand;
Long time the manxome foe he sought.
So rested he by the Tum Tum tree,
And stood awhile in thought.

And as in uffish thought he stood,
The Jabberwock, with eyes of flame,
Came wiffling through the tulgey wood
And burbled as it came!

One two! One two! And through and through
The vorpal sword went "snicker snack."
He left it dead, and with its head
He went galumphing back.

"And hast thou slain the Jabberwock?
Come to my arms, my beamish boy!
Oh frabjous day! Calooh! Calay!"
He chortled in his joy.

T'was brillig, and the slithy toves
Did gyre and gimble in the wabe.
All mimsy were the boroughgroves
And the mome raths outgrabe.

CHAPTER 9

THE WAITING ROOM

The desire to succeed is nothing. Anybody who has ever dreamed has had a desire to succeed. The difference is when someone takes his raw talent and works his ass off.

—An anonymous agent

You've made it! You're on your way and you should be proud of yourself!

You're on time, you have your headshot and résumé in hand, you've done your facial and vocal exercises, and, if it was available, you've looked at the script beforehand.

You look good, you feel good, and, right at this very moment, the playing field is completely level. You have as much a chance of landing the commercial as anyone else. Now, take a couple of deep breaths, let out a sigh, relax your shoulders, stand up straight, put a smile on your face, and open the door.

WHAT'S IT LIKE IN THE WAITING ROOM?

Waiting rooms are usually small areas and, despite SAG's Rule 16(g), there usually aren't quite enough chairs for all the folks who wish to occupy them. If there isn't a place to sit after you've signed in and received the commercial copy, don't take it personally. Just wait until a chair is vacated. It'll move faster than you think. You may even prefer to stand. I like to stand because it seems to keep my energy level up.

HOW MANY OTHER ACTORS WILL BE THERE?

I dunno. The number of actors you'll be competing with varies at each audition, and the actors who are there at the same time you are may be just a handful of the total number auditioning. Sometimes there will be only a few other actors vying for the job; other times there will be hundreds and hundreds. There might even be auditions for that particular commercial in other cities around the country, so it can be very hard to tell just how many people you're up against. When I originally auditioned in Los Angeles for (and finally became) Ronald McDonald, there were auditions for the character at the same time in New York and Chicago. You never know ... Don't be unnerved by the number of actors in the room, who they may be (you might recognize a few from TV or TV commercials you've seen), what they look like, or what they might say to one another.

It can be unsettling if it seems that everyone (except you) in the room knows one another. You're on the same audition that they are, and you have just as much a chance of getting the job as they do, so don't be awed by anyone. The face you recognize from a TV show or from a thousand commercials may have an overexposure problem, and you may be a better choice for the job. Because competition is stiff, actors can (and will) do funny things to one another at auditions. You may pick up snippets of conversation where one actor will say she just got off of a two-week shoot for a series of national spots, and another will say he is beginning work on a huge new commercial campaign tomorrow. Let them babble away; just smile, be friendly, be positive, work on your copy, and don't let it affect you. They're actors and much of it is BS anyway.

WHAT IF I DON'T LOOK LIKE I *BELONG* ON THE AUDITION?

Don't panic if you are the only short brunette in a room of six-foot blondes. Don't try to figure out the logic or the odds. Just be yourself and do your best. If you're not right for this job, at least you had the opportunity to audition, meet some folks, and do your best. And if you're not right for this particular job, someone might remember you for a different job. You might also *get* this job because they were bored looking at six-foot blondes.

HOW DO I LET THE CASTING DIRECTOR KNOW I'VE ARRIVED?

On the following page there is a copy of a SAG commercial-audition sign-in sheet. As I mentioned before, if you get there early (and you should), you might want to wait to sign in at your scheduled call time. And always greet the person at the sign-in table; sometimes it's the casting director. More often it's the assistant, but you never know.

When you sign in, start at the "To be completed by performers" area and print all the necessary information in a clear, legible hand. The sure sign of a beginner is one who has to look up his Social Security number or his SAG membership number (you may enter either one, but it's probably best to use your SAG number), so memorize both. The sign-in sheet serves a number of purposes. It lets the casting director know you've arrived, provides your Social Security number (or SAG membership number), the name of your agent, your actual call time, the time you arrived, and whether you are on a callback. Occasionally, first-audition actors will be on the same audition as those who are being called back to be seen for the second time. It means nothing as far as your chances to land the spot, so don't let it bother you.

The SAG sign-in sheet is also important for the actor. Union rules stipulate that an actor can be at the interview for only one hour following his actual call time. After that, the actor must be paid for his time spent on a prorated scale. Casting directors try to schedule actors at intervals and keep the audition process moving along so that there will not be a problem with overtime payments. If you *are* held for more than an hour and *do* go overtime, it's almost never the casting director's fault. It's usually due to the fact that there are clients or ad agency people in the audition room and they are moving too slow. My suggestion is that if you do happen to go over an hour by a few minutes, fib a little and sign out on time so that the casting director won't get penalized by the union. If it's blatant and you've been there for two hours and all the actors are signing out accurately, then I'd go

EXHIBIT E
SAG/AFTRA
COMMERCIAL AUDITION REPORT

PAGE _____ OF _____

TO BE COMPLETED BY CASTING DIRECTOR

(X) WHERE APPLICABLE ON CAMERA ☐	PRINCIPAL PERFORMER ☐ OFF CAMERA ☐	EXTRA PERFORMER ☐ TELEVISION ☐ RADIO ☐	AUDITION DATE

INTENDED USE	UNION: SAG ☐ AFTRA ☐	Person to whom correspondence concerning this form shall be sent: (Name & Phone Number)

CASTING REPRESENTATIVE NAME	COMMERCIAL TITLE - NAME & NUMBER		ADVERTISER NAME

PRODUCT	JOB NUMBER	ADVERTISING AGENCY AND CITY	PRODUCTION COMPANY

INSTRUCTIONS: Circle the name of principal performer if known.

* SPANISH LANGUAGE TRANSLATION SERVICES

TO BE COMPLETED BY PERFORMERS

NAME (PRINT)	*	SOCIAL SECURITY OR MEMBERSHIP NUMBER	AGENT (PRINT)	ACTUAL CALL	TIME IN	TIME OUT	INITIAL	CIRCLE INTERVIEW NUMBER	SEX (X) M	F	AGE (X) +40	-40	ETHNICITY (X) AP	B	C	L	H	NA	PWD (X)
								1st 2nd 3rd 4th											
								1st 2nd 3rd 4th											
								1st 2nd 3rd 4th											
								1st 2nd 3rd 4th											
								1st 2nd 3rd 4th											
								1st 2nd 3rd 4th											
								1st 2nd 3rd 4th											
								1st 2nd 3rd 4th											
								1st 2nd 3rd 4th											
								1st 2nd 3rd 4th											
								1st 2nd 3rd 4th											
								1st 2nd 3rd 4th											
								1st 2nd 3rd 4th											
								1st 2nd 3rd 4th											
								1st 2nd 3rd 4th											

The recorded audition material will not be used as a client demo, an audience reaction commercial, for copy testing or as a scratch track without payment of the minimum compensation provided for in the Commercials Contract and shall be used solely to determine the suitability of the performer for a specific commercial.

AUTHORIZED REPRESENTATIVE SIGNATURE _____

The only reason for requesting information on ethnicity, sex, age, and disability is for the talent unions to monitor applicant flow. The furnishing of such information is on a VOLUNTARY basis. The Authorized Representative's signature on this form shall not constitute a verification of the information supplied by performers.

Asian/Pacific	—	AP	Latino/Hispanic	—	L
Black	—	B	Native American	—	NA
Caucasian	—	C	Performer with Disability	—	PWD

Mail top copy to SAG OR AFTRA on the 1st and 15th of each month.
WHITE-UNION

201

along, but you don't want to be the only one. You might make a couple of bucks in penalties today, but that casting director probably won't ever call you in again.

WILL THERE BE ANY OTHER PAPERWORK TO COMPLETE?

On some auditions you may find an information sheet and/or a size card to fill out. Again, be truthful about everything. If you wear a size 12 dress, don't say you're a size 10. If you get the job and the wardrobe gal buys some size 10 clothes, you're going to have a little egg on your face. The person at the sign-in desk will probably take the information sheet and/or size card and staple it to your headshot.

NAME _____ HOME PHONE _____

ADDRESS _____

AGENT _____ PHONE _____

SAG # OR SS # _____ AGE _____ BIRTH DATE _____

SUIT/DRESS _____ SHIRT/BLOUSE _____

SHOE _____ HAT _____ PANTS _____

BEING SEEN FOR _____

SPECIAL SKILLS _____

WORK PERMIT # _____ (CHILDREN)

EXP. DATE _____ (CHILDREN)

If the job is for a Kawasaki motorcycle commercial and you say (verbally or on paper) that you once raced motocross, you'd better be pretty good on a bike! Years ago I did a spot for Honda Motorcycles that depended on whether the actors could all ride motorcycles. After we were hired, got to location, and started filming, the production company quickly discovered that one actor couldn't ride at all.

Naturally, it created all sorts of problems and they had to stop shooting while they drove the fibbing actor back to L.A. to find another actor who *could* ride. Obviously, they were furious with the actor and I'm sure he didn't *ever* get called in to audition for that casting director, that client, or that ad agency ever again. I'm also sure that after it happened, the folks from the ad agency always had their callbacks for their motorcycle commercials out in the parking lot and put the actors on motorcycles.

WHEN I SHOW UP FOR THE AUDITION, WHY DO I NEED TO TAKE ALONG ANOTHER EIGHT-BY-TEN HEADSHOT AND RÉSUMÉ?

It's a good idea to have your eight-by-ten and résumé *every time* you're out and about—including taking it to the gym when you work out. Always be prepared. You never know. Even though your headshot has already been submitted by your talent agent and you've gotten the interview, at almost every audition (this, again, depends a lot on your geographical auditioning area), you'll be asked again for your eight-by-ten with your résumé neatly attached to (or printed on) the back. And, again, there is always the chance that you might be asked to audition for another commercial for another product while you're at an interview. Always carry spares! Some casting facilities in Los Angeles now use a bar code card that an assistant can just scan when you show up for the audition. It automatically uploads your most current photo and résumé to the casting director's database. New York (and the rest of the country) will soon follow. Go to CastingFrontier.com to see what I'm talking about. 'Tis, indeed, a digital age we live in...

In addition to you bringing in your eight-by-ten headshot and résumé, the casting director or assistant may also take a digital photo of you that they will print and staple to your headshot. Casting directors figured out a long time ago that actors sometimes don't look like their headshots. This way there will be no confusion when they are watching the audition playback and doing their final casting.

One final word about the waiting room and, later, the audition room. Be pleasant to everyone. Be pleasant to the assistant in the outer office who is giving instructions or collecting headshots. Be especially pleasant if that person seems a bit gruff, abrupt, or harried, and don't take it personally. Maybe he's having a bad day, so just smile and watch him—he's most likely that way with everyone. If you don't let it affect you, you're ahead of the other actors who are taking it personally and letting it get to them. They probably won't do as well as you will during the audition. So many times I've seen actors be rude to the casting office staff. I've seen them openly complain that they are going to be late for their next interview. I've seen them talk too loud to other actors in the waiting area. I've seen them talk loudly on their cell phones even after being asked to quiet down. Remember: That person might be a low-paid receptionist today, but he's going to be a casting agent tomorrow. And he's going to remember you. Do everything you can to make your waiting room experience a good one for both you and for the casting staff. And always remember to thank casting directors with a note after you've booked a job!

The neatest way I ever thanked a casting director? Years ago, after I finished shooting my three hundredth television commercial for Toyota, I sent Dorothy Kelly, the original Los Angeles casting director for Toyota, thirty red roses with a thank-you note.

CHAPTER 10

ACTING AND THE SCRIPT

An actor is a person who has the ability to be private in public . . . acting is the art of being real under a set of very unreal circumstances.

—Lee Strasberg

WHAT'S THE DIFFERENCE BETWEEN THE *COPY* AND THE *SCRIPT*?

One word has four letters; the other has six. In commercials, that's the only difference.

WHEN DO I GET TO SEE THE SCRIPT?

If you're lucky, you've been able to download the script beforehand, but even if you have, there will be additional photocopies available in the waiting room. Always take a fresh copy just in case the words have been changed from your downloaded version. When you pick up your script in the waiting room, there will most likely also be a storyboard taped to the wall.

WHAT'S A STORYBOARD?

A storyboard is a hand-drawn, pictorial, scene-by-scene chronological outline of the action and words in the script. Look at it very carefully, because it can tell you what the advertiser has in mind for the different camera shots, the action, the characters, the setting, the clothing, the attitude, even the time of year. (If warranted, this might be the time to run back to your car for that sports coat.) Studying the storyboard before you start to work on the script will answer some questions that may come up and will help you do a better job in the audition. If you have *any* questions about either the script or the storyboard, make sure you ask the casting director or assistant. After you've finished the audition, it's too late.

The first Toyota spot I auditioned for used a little Italian phrase at the opening. I often think that I got the job only because I was the only actor who had asked the casting director how to correctly pronounce *Non sprecare la benzina* beforehand.

ARE THERE SPECIAL WORDS OR ABBREVIATIONS IN THE SCRIPT THAT I SHOULD KNOW ABOUT?

A few. You'll usually find them on the left side of the audition copy, but there may also be some within the copy itself. They're there to help you in your audition by letting you know the size of the shot, and whether the words are said by you, your partner, or heard in voice-over (VO) by an announcer. They will let you know whether you are in an exterior or interior location, the time of day or night, and so on. If you know what the words or abbreviations mean, you'll be able to use them to your advantage, so learn their meanings.

On the opposite page, there are a bunch of the more common abbreviations.

SHOULD I TRY TO MEMORIZE THE COPY?

Generally, no. If you have an *incredible* memory for words and you were lucky enough to download the copy the day before and you have the time to memorize it, then fine; but if you only get the copy at the audition or did not have time to memorize it adequately

Video: what we see—usually camera directions

Audio: what we hear—usually the actor's words

VO: voice-over—an actor's voice, off camera

OC: on camera—what we see, the visual image

MOS: without sound—silent (stands for "mit out sound")

CU: close-up

TCU: tight close-up

ECU: extreme close-up

MCU: medium close-up

MS: medium shot

LS: long shot

WA: wide-angle shot

Two Shot: two people in the shot

Three Shot: you can figure this one out

Super: superimpose—when one image is placed on another, much like a double exposure. (At the end of a commercial, they will very often superimpose the product or logo on the screen with the final picture.)

Diss: dissolve—when one scene blends into the next

Cut: when one scene abruptly changes into the next

Int: interior

Ext: exterior

Alt: alternate—usually a reference to alternate dialogue or scene

Logo: slogan or product name

SFX: special effects

Hero: the product (not you)

at home, then never try to do it on the spot. I always hear about these amazing actors with photographic memories who can memorize their copy in a heartbeat, but I've never met one. The audition isn't a test to find out who can memorize the most words in the least amount of time. In my experience, the actor who says he has all the words of the copy memorized is trying so hard to remember the words during the actual audition that he can't do anything else. In fact, I cringe with apprehension every time I audition with an actress who says she has the copy memorized. Ninety-nine times out of a hundred the words will be wrong and, even more important for me, my *cues* won't be right and it puts a big burden on me to try and salvage the continuity of the scene. I honestly don't care if she gets a callback, but her ineptitude may make us *both* look bad.

If you're in the slightest doubt as to whether you have the ability to instantly memorize copy, practice it at home and see how you do.

It is important, however, to memorize key parts of the script, because some eye contact with your partner, or the camera in spokesperson copy, is extremely important.

HOW ABOUT SOME ACTING TIPS ON READING COMMERCIAL COPY?

A lot of well-trained actors, who've worked in television, film, and/or on the stage, find the world of television commercial acting both different and difficult. In each of these related, but decisively different mediums, the audition as well as the performance varies greatly. Stage actors, for instance, are accustomed to being very broad in their delivery. Actors who are used to playing to the last row in a large theater might just bellow themselves out of the audition room. The key is to focus that energy into that two-inch camera lens and make it much more intimate. On the other hand, an actor who is used to acting on a soap opera on a much more subdued level may have to bring more energy and broadness into the audition.

If you audition for a commercial the same way you audition for a role on the stage, in a television show, or in a film, most likely you won't get the job. Many of the acting principles apply to all forms of acting, but there are also specific rules that apply to each subcraft.

YOU MEAN ALL THOSE ACTING CLASSES I'VE BEEN TAKING ARE WORTHLESS?

Of course not. The goal of any actor, whether performing in *Coriolanus* or acting in a cornflakes commercial, is to take someone else's words and make them sound like you are saying those words for the first time. The goal is to be as real as possible in a set of unreal circumstances. Any acting class that helps you do that is invaluable.

HOW CAN YOU BE "REAL" ACTING IN A LAUNDRY DETERGENT COMMERCIAL?

Good question. It's my belief that acting has little (or nothing) to do with pretending, so let's use an example of a typical script situation and see how real we can make it look.

Let's suppose the script tells you it's an anniversary dinner with husband and wife seated in a restaurant. As the husband presents his wife with a gift, he knocks over a glass of wine, ruining his wife's brand-new dress. We then cut to the wife the following day, success-fully washing her dress in our hero laundry detergent, thus saving the dress, the relationship, and the marriage. Nice script, but there are no written words for you to say and the two of you are expected to im-provise the restaurant dinner situation. What to do?

Your task, as an actor, is not to pretend anything. If you make believe that the two of you are a married couple, seated in a restau-rant having your anniversary dinner, you'll spend a lot of time trying to create dialogue that will come out stilted and false. You'll also run out of things to say pretty quickly.

WELL, THEN, WHAT *DO* WE SAY AND DO?

Rather than trying to tell us that you are married, tell us that it's your anniversary, tell us that you have a gift for your wife, or tell us that you're at a restaurant—*show* us. Simply show us that a relationship exists between the two of you. Don't pretend anything or invent words to say, just focus on the other actor and find something about her or him that you honestly like. Look in the eye of the other actor (always the eye closest to the camera) and tell her that her hair is very pretty, and touch it with your fingertips. Look in the eye of the other actor and tell him that you like the shirt he's wearing and touch the fabric. Then put a smile on your face and continue to say other com-plimentary, *real* things. It's simple, and you'll find that the words will come easy to you, because your observations are based on reality, rather than fantasy.

You don't have to script-write or make up expository, unreal dialogue. You're not pretending anything; you're just being real. The scene will take on a dimension of reality and the folks looking at the playback later will see it.

SOUNDS EASY!

It is! All of a sudden, you're not trying to become a make-believe husband in an imaginary restaurant with a pretend wife. You're merely paying another person a sincere compliment. The pretending stops, and the scene becomes remarkably easy to play. In the same vein, when you're supposed to give your "wife" a gift, why not just take off your watch or your ring and present it to her by having her pick which of your hands it's in? It looks much more convincing than using pantomime to give her a gift that isn't there. She can't see the imaginary gift, you can't see it, and no one can see it in the playback. Using something real gives you both something to actually look at, hold, and fondle. It's easy!

We've already talked about taking classes in improvisation, and how your skill at improv will help you in auditions. Good improv actors do precisely what I just described, so follow the above tips, and with practice, it will become second nature to you.

In an acting class I once took with Lee Strasberg, we did a particularly clever exercise that has always stuck with me. Lee asked four actors to improvise a scene in which they all were in a holding cell in jail. Before they'd even had a chance to ask him any questions, he said, "Go!," and they were on their own. Everyone immediately started to make up fictitious stories and tell the others why they had been arrested. "I'm in for rape, murder, and extortion. What're you in for?" "Oh, I need a fix!" "I'm a notorious killer!" and so on. The scene was pretty funny (but not very *real*) for the first fifteen minutes, but then went downhill fast. All four actors ran out of things to say because the scene was based on fiction.

Strasberg then announced that he was going to whisper the "secret of acting" into their ears. He took the actors aside, one at a time, and quietly told each to do some real things, and not make up stories. He told one to alphabetize all the makes of cars he could think of in his head and to let out a loud laugh when he'd counted those cars in multiples of seven. Another he told to count the holes in the acoustic ceiling tile, but not let anyone know what he was doing. When he finished a tile, he would walk over to another actor and try in some way to get his attention, and when he did, go back to counting holes. He told a third one to recite chronologically to himself the names of every teacher he'd ever had and then told the actor to yell an expletive when he thought of a teacher he didn't like. The last actor he merely had do exaggerated calisthenics while he counted out loud.

What happened was truly a miracle. We saw actors onstage who could have been inmates of a jail. They all could have won acting awards, and they weren't pretending to be in a jail at all. They were doing real things and therefore *being real*. Strasberg's point was that all the actors had to do was find the right piece of real business that fit into the confines of the scene, memorize the script, say the lines when they should, and it would make for some good acting.

WHAT'S ALL THIS I HEAR ABOUT THE ACTOR *BECOMING* THE CHARACTER?

No one ever really *becomes* a character. If the actor playing Othello really believed he was the Violated Moor, they'd have to get a new leading lady every night. You are who you are, no one else. But, on the other hand, you've been in love, jealous, angry, sad, happy, afraid, gregarious, and shy. If you do an audition where your character is supposed to be a shy person, you don't have to pretend to be shy. There've been times in your life when you were shy. Figure out what physical characteristics accompanied that feeling. It's very difficult to pretend to be shy, but it's very easy to lower your voice, speak hesitantly, avert your eyes when someone speaks to you, shuffle your feet, twiddle your thumbs, slump your shoulders, and generally make yourself as small as possible and *look* shy.

You can never become someone else. Why try? Years ago, someone asked well-known actor Spencer Tracy if he ever got tired of just playing Spencer Tracy. Tracy snapped back at him: "Just who would you like me to play? Humphrey Bogart?"

Once some of the basics of acting become second nature, a whole world opens up. Auditioning for commercials and acting in them isn't difficult at all and soon you'll be able to do things you never thought possible. It's an exciting craft!

GOT ANY MORE ACTING TIPS?

Yep! Some important ones . . .

- Most acting is *reacting*. If you're doing a commercial audition with another actor, really listen to that actor and to what he is saying, and, more important, *how* he is saying it. Listen with more than just your ears. Listen with your eyes, your face, your whole body. You'll find that whatever you're supposed to be saying, your words will flow much easier because there's some logic to them. You're responding to *what* the other actor said and *how* he said it. You'll also find that if you're really listening, you won't be acting only when you're saying your lines—you'll be in the scene the entire time.

- Practice saying thoughts rather than reading words. Record yourself reading copy from magazine ads and listen to play-back. If it sounds like you're reading words, then you've got work to do. Use inflections in your voice and try not to sound flat. Doing vocal exercises before an audition can help, but the only way to become more proficient at conversation-ally saying someone else's words out loud is to practice reading aloud.

- If you're going to emphasize certain thoughts or words in the copy, don't hit the small connecting words like *but, and, so,* and *if.* Emphasize and take your time with descriptive words. If you are auditioning for a food-related commercial, slow down and emphasize words like *yummy, delicious, crunch, juicy,* and *scrumptious.*

HOW ABOUT SPECIFIC ACTING TIPS WHEN I'M WORKING ON THE SCRIPT?

There are a bunch of them, and it makes no difference whether you are dealing with spokesperson copy or a slice-of-life spot.

Transition Points

There are key moments in the script where your attitude changes. Most commercials are divided into six basic parts, as follows, and the attitude changes usually occur at the moment of transition from one part to the next. The following page shows a typical slice-of-life commercial broken down into its six parts.

Understanding the six parts of a commercial will help you break it down and make it easier to work with. In almost every piece of commercial copy (even in spokesperson copy), there are important attitude changes or transition points for each of the characters. There is at least one transition point for just about every character in almost every commercial and sometimes more, and these points usually occur when the solution is presented and/or the problem is resolved. These can be changes from negative to positive, dismayed to pleased, unconcerned to aware, whatever. Look for the exact moments in which your character changes tack.

See if you can spot the transition point in this script for the spokesperson:

SPOKESPERSON: *You'd be surprised how many people would bet that it's easier to get a telephone number by dialing 4-1-1 than it is to use the phone book. Fact is, that's not a very good bet. It's easier and faster to find and dial a number than it is to go through the operator. Next time, use your phone book. You'll save yourself time.*

Now, where is the first transition point? If you guessed just after the first use of the word *book* and just before the beginning of the next sentence starting with the word *fact*, you'd be correct. The words up to that point are the presentation of the problem; then

ATTENTION GETTER — PROBLEM — SOLUTION

RATIONALE — RESOLUTION — CLOSING

words follow that are the presentation of the solution. Try it again, only this time, put a serious look on your face before you start, and then spell out the problem. When you get to the transition point, stop, smile, establish eye contact with the camera, then start the transitional sentence on your new tack.

> SPOKESPERSON: (Very serious) *You'd be surprised how many people would bet that it's easier to get a telephone number by dialing 4-1-1 than it is to use the phone book.* (Stop and smile.) *Fact is, that's not a very good bet. It's easier and faster to find and dial a number than it is to go through the operator. Next time, use your phone book. You'll save yourself time.*

Can you spot any other transition points in the above spot? One might be stopping after the "Next time, use your phone book" line, then chuckle and look at the camera before saying, "You'll save your-self time." Remember to make those transitions complete and full *be-fore* rushing on to the next line. Try it again.

HOW ABOUT FINDING TRANSITION POINTS ON DOUBLES COPY?

You bet. They're easy to find when you know what to look for. Can you spot the logical transition points for both the husband and the wife in this next example?

Married couple on a Sunday morning at home

WIFE: Ya know, there's this guy in my aerobics class . . .

HUSBAND: Yeah?

WIFE: Well . . . he's got dandruff!

HUSBAND: Why don't you just tell him?

WIFE: Honey, I have something to tell you.

HUSBAND: You mean . . . ?

WIFE: (Nods yes)

(Scene dissolves to a shower scene with HUSBAND using the product. A few days later.)

HUSBAND: You know that "guy" in your class?

WIFE: Yes?

HUSBAND: How's he looking these days?

WIFE: Absolutely wonderful!

Obviously, the husband's first attitude change (like most husbands in television commercials, he's not too swift) is just after the wife's third line: "Honey, I have something to tell you." He must make that transition clearly and distinctly after the last word of her line. The wife, on the other hand, has her first transition point just after his second line, "Why don't you just tell him?," and she needs to make that transition before her next line starts. There are certainly other transition points for each character in this spot, but these are the obvious ones. As you practice and become more skilled, you'll be able to find transition points where others won't. Locating your transitions are the first step; making full and abrupt transitions before continuing is the hard part. Don't make the mistake of "sliding" from one moment to the next.

THAT WAS A GOOD ONE! ANY OTHER TIPS?

Physical Movement During Spokesperson Auditions

Whenever possible, use physical movement, and be sure to use it within the framing of the audition camera. (That's why it's important to look at the storyboard to see how "wide" the shot is going to be.) Think of it as talking with your hands. The next illustration shows how hand gestures might be used effectively with our spokesperson copy. Also note the transition point in the storyboard version.

Because your hand gestures must be confined within the frame line, it might feel a bit odd gesturing so close to your body, so practice doing those gestures until it feels natural. When you do use your hands, make sure you don't put them between your face and the camera.

Another way to use movement in this particular spokesperson copy would be to bring in a phone book as a prop. A clever actor might bring the phone book into frame just before the line "than it is to use the phone book." The actor could then touch the book with his free hand after the word *operator,* and before the first word of the next sentence. After that, I'd lose the phone book; otherwise it becomes a hindrance. Try it.

As with all physical actions, don't make the mistake of suggesting a touch or movement. Decide what you're going to do, when you're going to do it, and do it fully.

And always remember that any physical movement or action comes *before* the words. Think of it in terms of a sneeze. The sneeze comes first, then you say excuse me, not the other way around.

You'd be surprised how many people would . . .

. . . bet that it's easier to get a telephone number by dialing 411

. . . than it is to use the phone book . . .

Fact is, that's not a good bet.

It's easier and faster to find and dial a number than it is to go through the operator.

Next time, use your phone book.

You'll save yourself time.

HOW DO I INCORPORATE PHYSICAL MOVEMENT WHEN I'M WORKING WITH DOUBLES COPY?

Let's take the same piece of husband and wife copy and see what we can do. The opening states only that they are a married couple at home on a Sunday. That means casual and relaxed. At the top of the spot, the husband appears to be responding to his wife absentmindedly, so the actor needs to find something that would be distracting him. A folded newspaper is always a safe bet as a prop. Since the wife has the first line, as the husband in the spot, I would turn the newspaper page even before the actress started with her first line. The reason? Movement is more attention-getting than words, so the focus would be on me. I would also turn the page again before my first line responding to her opening question. Then I could drop the newspaper down just before my line "You mean...?" More movement equals more focus.

That takes care of the husband in this audition, but what can the wife do to add physical movement at the top of the spot? She might be turned slightly away from him and then turn to him just before saying her first line. She could also incorporate searching through her purse, which is always a handy prop for physical movement for women. Because one of the most effective actions an actor can take during an audition is to physically make contact with the other actor, she could be trying to get his distracted attention by running her finger along his arm. Because slice-of-life commercials usually deal with the relationships between characters (husband and wife arguing over toothpaste, two neighbors talking about fertilizers, father and son talking about the merits of thrift), the act of one actor touching the other can show an immediate relationship without words.

During the shooting of a Safeguard soap commercial, one of the advertising agency folks asked me if I knew why I had been selected as the husband. I said that I had no idea, and he told me that I had tenderly touched the actress's hair during the audition. They all felt, even before the first word had been spoken, that I had immediately established a tender relationship. All I did was touch her hair and cheek before my first line and it worked!

These are only a few of the many opportunities in this copy for physical movement. Keep in mind that most actors don't use movement to their advantage. Also keep in mind that most actors don't end up getting the job.

ANY OTHER ACTING TIPS WITH COMMERCIAL COPY?

Physical and Verbal Openings and Closings
Another device that I've found to be most effective during the audition is the use of both a physical and a verbal opening and closing.

Let's talk about the physical opening and closing first. Before you say that first word of copy, you should do something physical. For the doubles copy, it was suggested that the husband turn the page of the newspaper and the wife physically turn toward the husband. The spokesman can always make the choice to turn into the camera before starting the copy. A physical closing for the spokesperson might be a finger tap on the phone book. It could also be an insider's wink to the camera. A hug or a peck on the cheek at the end of the doubles copy would be a perfect closing.

The verbal opening and closing can be used in conjunction with or separate from the physical. Before you say your first word of script, you can make a sound of some sort. A natural grunt, a whistle, clearing your throat, or a cough can all help establish that you're engaged in doing something at the opening of the spot. In order to get her husband's attention, the wife could utter "ahem" before saying her first word to show that she's uneasy about approaching her husband about his cruddy hair. The husband might be softly whistling a tune under his breath to show us he's happy that it's Sunday morning and he doesn't have to go to work. At the end of the doubles copy, either one or both actors might let out a sigh of pleasure.

The spokesman selling the use of the phone book might let out a small sigh or a *huh* before starting the copy and chuckle or wink at the conclusion of the spot. Try eavesdropping on conversations in restaurants or at the market. You'll hear a lot of sounds coloring the conversations. People personalize their speech with grunts, gasps, giggles, and groans. Remember that every one of the actors auditioning for a commercial will be saying exactly the same words of copy in pretty much the same way. The special touches that you add before you start, during specific moments of the copy, and at the conclusion, are what makes the copy *yours*. A word of caution, however: *Never* make your verbal opening or closing actual words! Copywriters tend to get crazy when actors add copy or write real words into the script. Anything not in the dictionary is fair game, however!

Practice these physical and verbal openings and closings until they feel as though they were written into the script. Remember that very few actors are going to use them.

GREAT! ANY MORE TIPS?

A couple...

The Aside

Another technique I've used when auditioning with spokesperson copy I call "the aside." It gives the effect that the spokesperson is letting the viewers in on a little secret. To do an aside, simply lean in to the camera or step slightly toward the camera before delivering (usually) the tag line of the script. Some actors even take a quick look right and left to see if "anyone is listening" when they do it. If you were to implement an aside in the spokesperson copy about the phone book, you'd simply add an aside after the word *operator,* or you might want to do it at the end of the second-to-last line, just after the word *book.* Just make sure you start and complete the action during the moment when you're not saying words. Try it both ways and see which feels more comfortable to you. It's been working onstage for a very long time.

SPOKESPERSON: *You'd be surprised how many people would bet that it's easier to get a telephone number by dialing 4-1-1 than it is to use the phone book. Fact is, that's not a very good bet. It's easier and faster to find and dial a number than it is to go through the operator.* (Possible aside here) *Next time, use your phone book.* (Or here) *You'll save yourself time.*

Go All Out!

The biggest mistake actors make when auditioning is not being fully committed to whatever it is they choose to do or say.

Don't censor your first impulse—it's usually right on the money. Whether your character is a shy, hasn't-got-a-clue husband or an overbearing next-door neighbor, commit yourself and go for it. There is little room in commercials for subtlety. The audience has to find out who you are and what you're all about in the opening few seconds.

In all the workshops I've ever taught, rarely have I seen anyone go

too far with a character. To my way of thinking, there is no such thing as *over*acting. If acting is being as real as you can be, then how can you possibly be *over* real? (I've seen a lot of bad acting, but rarely overacting.) Usually, actors give about 25 percent of what the script requires to get the job. When you work with them in a workshop situation, you can get them about 10 percent closer each time. Unfortunately, you'll have only one shot during the audition, so go for it 100 percent right off the bat!

ARE THERE OTHER TYPES OF COMMERCIALS?

Yes, and we've touched only on two: the spokesperson and the slice-of-life commercial. There are basically five different categories, and you will approach each one differently during an audition. Digitally record an evening of network television, take a look at each of the categories below, and then fast-forward from commercial to commercial to see where each fits in. The five kinds of commercials using on-camera talent are:

1. The spokesperson commercial

2. The slice-of-life commercial

3. The one-line vignette commercial

4. The no-line vignette commercial

5. The narrative/story line commercial

There is also a sixth category called the real-people testimonial commercial. These spots do not show actors, but "real" people who tell of their experiences using the product or service. Usually, there are no traditional auditions for these spots and people are selected on the strength of their responses to a taste test, or an interviewer on the street, in a mall, or in a store. The commercial can be shot using either a hidden camera or an exposed camera.

Let's go over each of the above categories you will be auditioning for in detail.

1. The Spokesperson Commercial

A spokesperson is a representative for a product or a service. The spokesperson speaks directly into the lens of the camera and talks to the audience on a one-to-one basis, trying to convince the consumer that the product or service is the best available.

The spokesperson always speaks with authority and may play the part of a convinced consumer, a specialist, an informed party, or the president of a company. The actor must appear knowledgeable, convincing, confident, well-informed, yet be warm and sincere.

The Toyota commercial reproduced on the next page is a typical example of a spokesperson spot. In many spokesperson auditions (as was in this case), there will be no storyboard printed. The advertising agency, DFS-Dorland, Worldwide (later to become Saatchi & Saatchi), and the client, Toyota Motor Sales, Inc., were both gracious enough to allow me to reproduce this script for you.

In fact, this script is my all-time favorite. It was the first Toyota commercial that I auditioned for and led to twenty-eight years as Toyota's spokesperson. Needless to say, I *love* this piece of copy!

TELEVISION COPY

DFS—DORLAND, WORLDWIDE

CLIENT: TOYOTA MOTOR SALES, INC.   LENGTH: 30
PRODUCT: COROLLA   SHOW AND DATE:
TRAFFIC NO.   TITLE: "MAP"
                                          CODE:

VIDEO	AUDIO
Tight shot of Announcer. Pull back to reveal him walking on large map of world with price per gal stickpins. Anncr. stops by Corolla. Tag line. Music/singers up.	Non sprecare la benzina. Don't waste gas. It's a world problem . . . and here's an answer: the best-selling car in the world. The Toyota Corolla. Take the Toyota Corolla 2-Door Sedan. Its engine is designed to energize every drop of fuel efficiently. And it's also the lowest-priced Toyota. It's the answer to a whole world of problems. Hey, when you got it, you got it. MUSIC: TOYOTA

Let's review a few things you might consider doing during an audition using this Toyota spokesperson script.

- Find out if the camera operator is going to widen out his shot after the opening line and how tight the shot will be at the outset. You always want to stay within the frame line.

- Try to memorize your opening and closing. If all you can safely memorize of the opening is *"Non sprecare la benzina,"* then do only that much. If you can memorize more, then do it.

- If you're not fluent in other tongues, you may not know which language the first line is written in. It will make all the difference in the world how you deliver the words. Ask. Once you find out it is in Italian, you can say the line as you imagine an Italian would. Use your hands when you speak. Overenunciate the words.

- The attitude change would probably occur after the word *problem* in the second line, so stop, smile, and then give them the answer to the world problem.

- When you give them the answer to that world problem, you might also want to point and look off camera toward where the car would be, before starting the next thought.

- You'll notice that the script says "world problem" at the opening and "world of problems" at the end. The same gesture for both those bits of copy might work for you.

- Don't let your energy down during the bulk of the commercial. All that copy is important, so don't speed through it.

- You might want to try the aside before the last line of copy. It's a natural for that treatment.

- You also might want to try a shrug or a tongue click before the first line. Maybe a wink or a positive nod after the closing.

How's that for a few things to try? See what else you can think of.

2. The Slice-of-Life Commercial

On the next few pages is an audition script and a storyboard for a thirty-second slice-of-life commercial. In this type of commercial, it's as though the camera were eavesdropping for a few moments into some people's lives. It has a very short, single-purpose story with a very discernible plot. As in most stories, it has a beginning, a middle, and an end. There is a problem presented ("Isn't there a towel strong enough to scrub?"), a possible solution ("Try Brawny!"), and a resolution ("Brawny, you make camping easier!").

TELEVISION COPY

ADVERTISTING

WILLIAM ESTY COMPANY, INCORPORATED
EAST 42ND STREET • NEW YORK, N. Y. 10017 • 697-1600

American Can Company
BRAWNY PAPER TOWELS
:30 TV
"Campers"
ACNT 5173

AUDIO

SON: Dad!!

DAD: Wait, Bobby.

DAD: (To wife) Isn't there a towel strong enough to scrub?

  (SFX: LOUD CRUNCH)

BRAWNY: There is one.

Try Brawny.

  (SFX: MUSIC STING)

MOM: Strong enough for this griddle?

BRAWNY: Sure. Brawny's got (SFX: SMACK) scrub strength!

Even strong enough for that mess.

Because Brawny takes tough absorbent fibers and . . . bonds them
    together tightly . . . (SFX: SCRUBBING) for scrub strength.

DAD: Brawny, you make camping easier.

BRAWNY: Brawny.

In this kind of commercial, everyone apparently lives happily ever after, because the paper towel, deodorant, foot powder, aspirin, toothpaste, or sleeping aid completely solves their emotional and physical problems, and everyone's lives are altered for the better. Marriages are saved, sanity is secured, embarrassment is avoided. There's always a happy ending. (That's why we always smile and show teeth for our headshots.)

Some slice-of-life commercials have a serious tone, but most are written with a light touch. Unlike spokesperson commercials, the actors relate to each other and *never look into the camera* unless the script specifically says to.

My thanks to the William Esty Company and the American Can Company for their permission to use the script and storyboard for this Brawny paper towel commercial. This spot is a favorite of mine because my wife and I were both hired as the mom and dad.

TELEVISION COPY	:30 TELEVISION	BRAWNY

Video		Audio
1. Open on cooking area of campside. Tent and camper bus in background. Son with fishing gear beckons father. Dad is struggling to clean dirty griddle.		1. SON: Dad!! DAD: Wait, Bobby.
2. Husband turns to wife. Bobby sees Brawny. His mouth flies open. He points upward.		2. DAD: (To wife) Isn't there a towel strong enough to scrub? (SFX: *loud crunch*)

TELEVISION COPY   **:30 TELEVISION**   **BRAWNY**

Video		*Audio*
3. Brawny enters. Surprised Mom and Dad look up.		3. BRAWNY: There is one.
4. Mom and Dad still looking in amazement as Brawny bends down.		4. Try Brawny.
5. Brawny presents towel to camera.		5. (SFX: *music sting*)
6. Mom and Dad still looking up at Brawny. Dad holds up dirty griddle.		6. MOM: Strong enough for this griddle?
7. Brawny smacks fist.		7. BRAWNY: Sure. Brawny's got (SFX: *smack*) scrub strength!
8. Cut to man's hand scrubbing griddle with Brawny. Top part of 409 cleaner is visible.		8. Even strong enough for that mess.

TELEVISION COPY	:30 TELEVISION	BRAWNY

Video		Audio
9. Cut to fiber demo.	FIBERS	9. Because Brawny takes tough absorbent fibers and ...
10. Action continues.	BONDED TOGETHER	10. bonds them together tightly ... (SFX: *scrubbing*)
11. Action continues.	((SCRUB)) ((STRENGTH))	11. for scrub strength.
12. Cut back to camp. Husband presents clean griddle.		12. DAD: Brawny, you make camping easier.
13. Brawny presents roll of product.		13. BRAWNY: Brawny.
14. Brawny presents roll of designer product and holds next to first roll.		14. And designer Brawny. Both with scrub strength.

Now let's take a look at a few things that enterprising actors might be able to do with this copy during their audition.

- Because there's no indication of what the actors should be doing in the written script, it's very important to take a look at the storyboard before the audition. If not, you may not know that Dad is supposed to be cleaning the dirty griddle with a towel that's falling apart. And you wouldn't know that the loud crunch is supposed to be the Brawny Giant stepping in to solve their problem. Storyboards are very important.

- When the son "sees" the giant, he needs to make sure that he picks out a place way over the camera lens, either camera right or camera left, to look and point. This pointing makes us understand that he sees something and also gives the other actors a point of reference. And he should remember never to block his face (or anyone else's!) when he points.

- Dad needs to be busy scrubbing something *with* something. Rather than pretend to be scrubbing, it would be best to use a handkerchief (or a paper towel you swiped from the men's room before the audition) and scrub your hand at the bottom of the frame line. Scrubbing your hand isn't as good as scrubbing a griddle, but it's a lot better than scrubbing air. At least you're doing something real.

- Mom doesn't have any words until well into the copy, and it would be best if she weren't just standing around waiting for her first line. She could turn away from the other actors so that she would have some turning action to do when her husband asks her his first question. Or the actress could be packing some things into her handbag. What she does isn't very important, but it is most important that she is doing something.

- The obvious attitude change for Dad occurs after his frustrated line about strong towels, and just after he physically looks to where the son is pointing. Mom's initial transition could be shortly before or after that.

- There's a great opportunity for the son to come out with a sound like *whew!* or *wow!* just before he says his first line. Dad could let out an exasperated sigh or grunt before his first line or after his "Wait, Bobby." Being careful not to actually say any real words, Mom could begin to answer Dad's question to her before Brawny answers for her.

- All the actors must be sure that while they are astounded by the giant, they do not exhibit fear. This is very important, because the giant represents the product and the product is always a positive thing to behold.

- After Dad says his last line, he could chuckle, the son could wave at the giant, and Mom could hug Dad or she could wave at the giant. There are a lot of possibilities.

See what else you can come up with.

3. The One-Line Vignette Commercial

The vignette commercial is a commercial composed of quick scenes using different actors. Each actor says a word or phrase (usually into the camera) with energy and enthusiasm. It could be the name of the product or a word or phrase describing the product. What follows is a typical one-line vignette commercial. The product, Alpine Yogurt, is fictitious.

Looks like a pretty easy commercial to audition for, right? All you have to do is look at the camera, eat some yogurt, and say one word.

TELEVISION COPY	:30 TELEVISION	ALPINE YOGURT
Video		*Audio*
1. Open on snowy exterior scene of mountain cabin. Slow zoom to door.		1. (VO) All over the world . . .
2. Cut to woodsman eating Alpine.		2. . . . there's something that this man . . .

TELEVISION COPY	:30 TELEVISION	ALPINE YOGURT
Video		*Audio*

3. Cut to beach scene on Riviera. Attractive, thirtyish woman eating Alpine.		3. . . . this woman . . .
4. Cut to tulip field in Holland. Eight-year-old girl sitting amongst flowers eating Alpine.		4. . . . this girl . . .
5. Cut to ballet-school scene in France. Confident eight-year-old girl eating Alpine.		5. . . . and *this* girl all have in common.
6. Cut to ECU of woodsman.		6. WOODSMAN: Alpine!
7. Cut to beach woman.		7. BEACH WOMAN: Alpine!
8. Cut to girl.		8. GIRL: Alpine!

TELEVISION COPY	:30 TELEVISION	ALPINE YOGURT
Video		*Audio*
9. Cut to girl.		9. GIRL: Alpine!
10. Cut to product shot.		10. (VO) Alpine! (echo of *many* voices in unison)

Wrong! Keep in mind that if it seems like an easy audition to you, it will also probably seem like an easy audition for everyone else. You can be sure that the competition for this job is just as stiff as for any other.

The instructions from the casting director or assistant will probably be something like, "You're enjoying your yogurt at the beach [in a field of flowers, wherever], and then you say 'Alpine!'" (Even though the commercial has you in two scenes, in the audition these will most likely be done as one scene.) Use any script suggestions and follow the casting director's instructions, and then dig deep to come up with ideas that will make your audition stand out.

- They will expect you to pantomime eating the yogurt, so stop at the store on your way to the audition and pick up the actual product if it's available, and then you won't have to pretend you're eating. (You can even claim it as a tax deduction—"audition prop.") You cannot imagine how much of an impact this makes on the people who have the ability to hire you. The surprising thing is that very, very few actors think to do this. Make sure you take the food into the audition room in a paper bag. Don't let any of the other actors know what you're doing.

- Dress properly for the part. Your talent agent has already told
  you who your character is and has given you a hint of appropriate clothing. If you're in doubt about the suitability of a particular garment, ask your agent beforehand. If you're auditioning for
  the woodsman, wear your jeans and a flannel shirt. A long
  johns–type undershirt with long sleeves and suspenders might
  be welcome additions. Also see if you can find a knit hat to
  bring along (another item to hide from your competition).

    If you're auditioning for the woman at the beach, wear a
  bathing suit (a very flattering and conservative one unless specifically requested otherwise) under some casual clothes. You can remove your street clothes in the audition room. Bring sunglasses to
  wear on your head (never cover your eyes) and a ribbon for your
  hair. The girls should do the same thing as far as clothes and props
  are concerned. A leotard and tutu for the ballet student or a
  Dutch-boy hat for the girl in the field are all plus points for clothing. If you can think of something unique, use it. If you have a
  question as to suitability, always ask your talent agent beforehand.

- Anything you can do to change your body position, expression,
  and attitude is useful. Opportunities for movement and physical
  transitions in this spot are easy to find, but make sure you do
  them, do them abruptly, and do them fully. Here are some obvious changes.

    - Start by *not* looking at the camera during the first part of
      the scene. Look at the yogurt, take a spoonful, react, then
      turn to the camera for your line.

    - Change your look from a look of anticipation to a look of
      delight after taking the bite.

    - Change body positions from a slight slouch to an erect pos-
      ture after taking the bite.

- Be aware that there's very little time to build a story here. You
  can't spend time putting on suntan oil, building a fire, picking
  flowers, or dancing. The copy says that your scene starts with
  your character eating yogurt and finishes with the word *Alpine!*

Make the most of the short scenario you have. The focus here is just on the character eating Alpine Yogurt. Start by eyeing the yogurt container in your hand. Open it, look at and smell the contents, dip the spoon in, stir the contents, take the spoon out and look at the yogurt, put it in your mouth, taste it, make your transition, and *react* into camera with the line. Also make sure you have something to do after the word *Alpine*. Enthusiastically eating more yogurt would be the obvious choice.

- When you're doing food commercials, take tiny bites. Otherwise the lens of the audition camera might get a little messy when you hit the *p* of *Alpine!* Incidentally, *never* suggest in any way that you don't like the food or product. If you're a fanatical vegetarian and find yourself auditioning for a fried chicken commercial, don't let anyone know you belong to PETA.

- As in other types of commercials, utilize sounds in reacting to the product. *Mmmm* is a great one. Just don't say anything that sounds like a word. If it's in the dictionary—don't use it.

- When you say the line of copy, notice if there's an exclamation point after a word. Practice saying the word so that it comes out a positive statement and not a question. And always smile when saying the name of the product.

- Most actors tend to hurry to the punch line. Everybody's going to be saying that punch line, so it stands to reason that it's what you do *before* the line that will get you a callback.

4. The No-Line Vignette Commercial

This is the same as the one-line vignette spot, except that there are no words for the actors to say. The characters are supposedly caught "unaware" by the camera and then react positively to the product. This type of commercial is ofttimes seen with soft drink ads that show quick, high-energy shots of young people enjoying the beverage. The previous storyboard for Alpine Yogurt would be a good example of the no-line vignette, if the last line were omitted and only the actors' reactions are shown. Go back and try the yogurt script without the line. You'll notice that by not having any words at the end of the spot, you're forced to rely on the full and complete transition you must make *before* tasting to *after* tasting. Without words for you to say, the transition is even more important and you may have to dig a little deeper into your bag of tricks to do something that will make your audition memorable. Remember that the pay is the same whether you say words or not in a commercial, so make sure you apply all the other tips for the one-line vignette to these scripts. There may not be any lines for you to say, but you can still use your verbal openings and closings during the audition.

5. The Narrative/Story Commercial
While the typical vignette commercial usually requires quickness, energy, and variety, the narrative/story commercial involves a simple plot. These spots are usually the most creative with regard to direction, writing, cinematography, music, and editing. They can be used quite effectively to appeal to the emotions of viewers and can sometimes be genuine tearjerkers—like the one I made up that follows. (Maybe I'll have a new career as a copywriter!)

Auditioning for this kind of minimovie is a lot different from auditioning for any of the other kinds of commercials. This spot really is a

---

TELEVISION COPY	:30 TELEVISION	TENCO CELLULAR SERVICE
Video		*Audio*
1. Opening wide-angle shot of car on desolate highway at dusk. No other cars in sight. Headlights flick on.		1. *(haunting music up, mixed with solo car noise)*
2. Dissolve to wide-angle shot of same car. Very dark and ominous.		2. (SFX: *rain*)

TELEVISION COPY	:30 TELEVISION	TENCO CELLULAR SERVICE
Video		*Audio*
3. Dissolve to same shot. It's raining heavily.		3. (SFX: *thunder*)
4. Cut to driver of car. Woman, twenty-five to thirtyish, concerned look on face.		4. (SFX: *rain and wiper blades*)
5. Cut to gas gauge of car. Reading is empty.		5. (VO) There are times . . .
6. Cut to driver. Obviously worried. She reaches for her cellular phone and looks down.		6.
7. Cut to cellular phone: "No service."		7. (VO) . . . when cellular service is more than just a convenience.
8. Cut back to driver. Obviously worried.		8.

TELEVISION COPY	:30 TELEVISION	TENCO CELLULAR SERVICE

Video

9. Cut to car slowing down. Turn indicators on to pull over. Car comes to a stop alongside road. Rain is heavy.

10. Different angle. Car alone on side of road. Emergency flashers go on. Another car speeds by.

11. Cut to worried driver.

12.

Audio

9. (SFX: *car sputtering*)

10.

11. (VO) At least that's what we think.

12. Tenco. More service to more remote areas than anyone. Tenco.

small feature film, and the acting is on a much more subtle level. The casting director (or assistant) will give you instructions like: "You're alone in a car on a bad stretch of road. It's raining and you run out of gas. You don't know what to do." Let's see what you could do with what you're given:

- Have the appropriate wardrobe. It's storming and raining, so a scarf and coat with a big collar would make some good costume additions.

- The opening scene might be a good time to check your wristwatch. A watch is a great prop for a lot of commercial auditions, but make sure you really take note of the time and don't pretend by glancing at your watch. I always take a few seconds to say the time to myself when I look at my watch during an audition. It really shows that you care about what time it is.

- The script indicates that the character is first seen just as the rain is starting. Take a moment *before* you realize it's raining so you can make the transition from unconcerned to worried. You might even be humming a tune under your breath until the moment you react to the rain beginning.

- You might change your body position from sitting casually to more upright as the showers begin.

- There is also a moment in the script when the character realizes that she's almost out of gas. This could be an acceleration of worry and another transition spot. Perhaps interjecting an *Oh!* would work.

- Another spot for a transitional moment and some physical movement is when a car speeds by after you are stopped. Within the confines of your car, you might physically wave to catch the attention of the other vehicle as it whizzes by. When you realize that the driver isn't stopping, you have another transition.

These certainly are not the only things you could do if you were auditioning for this spot, but they're a few ideas to think about. The more ideas you have, the more you can eliminate the less attractive ones. And the more you can break down the action into specific moments and events, the easier it will be for you, the clearer it will be to the camera, and the better your chance of landing the job.

Now you're knowledgeable, armed, and dangerous, so let's go on an audition!

CHAPTER 11

THE AUDITION ROOM

AKA: THE INTERVIEW, THE CALL, THE READING

God makes the star. God gives them the talent. It's up to us producers to recognize that talent and develop it.

—Samuel Goldwyn

Acting is one of the most competitive professions in the world, and whether you get the job depends on what happens during your audition. There are a lot of actors out there looking for work. Talent is important, but frankly, I've never been able to define what that word means. I don't know if it can be taught; I tend to think it can't. Skills, however, *can* be taught. If there are seventy-five actors auditioning for the same commercial and if they all have the same amount of talent, then it is the actor with the best skills who will get the job. It boils down to what you do during the audition that the other actors don't do. You need to incorporate the tips we've talked about and practice them over and over until they become second nature. I've compiled these tips as a result of auditioning for thousands of commercials and watching other actors audition. The interesting thing I've learned in the process is that these acting tips are used only by a small and select group of actors who have one thing in common: They all audition well and they get jobs! Now it's time to apply what you just read and join the working class.

WHAT SHOULD I EXPECT WHEN I WALK INTO THE AUDITION ROOM?

Don't expect anything or have any preconceived ideas. The room may have only a video operator, a video camera, and you. Or the room may be filled to the gunnels with clients, ad agency people, production people, the director, the casting director, a video machine, a video operator, and a guy delivering sandwiches...all staring at you. Increasingly sophisticated video technology now allows some casting sessions to be conducted with the director on a video screen giving you instructions from a city three thousand miles away. No matter how many folks are in the room when you enter, smile at everyone, introduce yourself, shake hands (if hands are offered), hand over your headshot and résumé to whoever seems to be in charge, and listen to what's asked of you.

A casting director friend in Los Angeles once told me that when he first started working as a casting director, a fairly well-known actor came in for an audition. When the actor entered the audition room, there was only my friend and his video camera. When my buddy started to introduce himself, the actor cut him off and remarked how terrible it was that there wasn't anyone of importance in the room to watch his audition. My casting director friend didn't finish introducing himself. He also didn't hit the record button during the audition. Be nice to everyone! Even if it seems as though the director or casting director is giving everyone a hard time, take advantage of it. If you have a great attitude, you're smiling, and you look like you're having fun, you may be the only actor seemingly not affected by all the negativity. And you might just get the job because of that.

If there are some folks in the room, be prepared for a little small talk that sometimes happens. You can ask questions about the product ("Is this a new kind of Lego? I had a great set when I was a kid..."), or talk about their commercials that are currently running ("I've seen your Lego commercials on the air and I really like the spot with the elephant!"). Anything you can glean from the copy or storyboard might be useful. ("I noticed from the copy that you're from the Des Moines office. I lived just outside of town for three years when I went to the university.") Just remember to keep your small talk short and positive. One line is usually enough unless someone picks up the ball and engages you in a longer conversation. And if you sense that small talk may not be appropriate, then don't worry about it.

Remember that you are auditioning from the very first moment you enter the audition room, so project sincerity, confidence, warmth, interest, and success. Say only positive things and be upbeat and full of energy. First impressions happen only once—that's why they're called "first impressions."

WHAT ELSE CAN I DO TO MAKE SURE THAT THE FIRST IMPRESSION I GIVE IS A GOOD ONE?

Because of the life experiences we've had, we automatically place everyone we come in contact with in various categories. This person has an attitude, that person looks like a sloucher, this person looks friendly, and that person looks high maintenance. And *that* person looks just like your alcoholic, grizzled uncle Al.

We may not consciously choose to pigeonhole people, but we all do it and we can't help doing it. Just remember that casting directors, agency producers, directors, and talent agents *do it for a living.* They size you up instantly and they're very skilled at it. Here are some iron-clad things that you can do to project a better image of yourself.

Your Posture
If you slouch and walk with a head lead, people perceive you as weak. So stand and sit erect. If it doesn't feel right, then it only means that you're used to being a slouch. So start thinking taller and straighter. You'll look confident and in charge of yourself. When China was getting ready to host the Olympics, we all saw the camera footage of the hostesses walking around with books on their heads so that they would project an image of confidence and pride during the Olympics.

Your Walk
Are your feet pointed toward your destination when you walk? Do you shuffle your feet or do you step with confidence, looking always

as though you know where you're going? Remember to always walk like you have a destination.

Your Handshake

If a hand is offered, lean forward, extend your hand, and take the hand *firmly*. Nothing indicates more about someone's low self-esteem than a limp handshake. If you have a problem with moist hands, wipe them just before going into the room.

Sitting

Many times you won't have an opportunity to sit and you'll be meeting and talking to folks while you're standing. Personally, I like that scenario. It tends to give me more energy than I would have if I were seated. Remember to stand tall, but not stiff. If you are asked to sit, never pick a soft leather chair to disappear into. If you have a choice, sit with good posture in a rigid chair, focusing your attention toward the other person. I usually don't cross my legs, because it tends to push me back into too relaxed of a position. I'll usually angle my legs to one side, sit erect, and face forward.

When You Talk

Make sure you establish eye contact. Listen and answer questions. When it's appropriate, ask questions in a positive way. If you've done a little homework, you may know something about the casting agency or the production team or the director or the product that the other actors didn't take the time to find out. Don't be afraid to use your hands to gesture, but stay away from any nervous tics such as biting your nails or touching your hair, your face, or your clothing. And make sure you have a short and not-as-short positive reply as needed to "tell me a little about yourself." If you rehearse your response, you'll do better. And, as I mentioned earlier, stay away from filler words such as *like, totally,* and *you know*.

You may also want to read Tonya Reiman's book called *The Power of Body Language*. It shows how your body language directly relates to your success, both socially and in the workplace, and it's a good read for actors.

Your Scenario Plan

The thought of any interview or audition is bound to be fraught with a lot of scary what-if's. A good practice is to set up a plan in your own mind of how you'd *like* the interview or audition to go. It's probably not going to go just the way you imagine, but it's still a good place to start. You might say to yourself:

> *I'm going to set out my clothes the night before and repeat my affirmations after I awaken (see below). Then I'll make sure I leave early enough to have an easy trip. When I arrive, I'll collect myself and smile even before I walk in the door. When I enter the room, I'll try to make pleasant eye contact with whoever is behind the desk before I sign in. If the person in charge looks my way, I'll greet him or her with a smile, a nod, or a verbal greeting if it's appropriate before I sign in. After my sign-in, I'll get a copy of the script and look to see if there is a storyboard tacked on the wall . . .*

And so on. Even though the variables are many, the more you plan in a positive way for what might happen, the fewer surprises you'll have and the fewer mistakes you'll make.

Positive Thinking and Affirmations About the Day

I'm a very strong believer in affirmations. It's like the old adage that if you say something enough times, it eventually becomes true. Each and every morning after awakening, smile, close your eyes, visualize a terrific day, and say to yourself aloud: *This will be a new and wonderful day for me. There will never be another day like this one. Today I will prosper in everything I attempt.* It works! Try it! This positive, repetitive affirmation can and will change your life.

The bottom line is that when you make a knowing effort to incorporate the above tips in order to give a good first impression, you're not only showing the other person some respect but you're giving off an air of confidence, warmth, sincerity, interest, and success. It'll pay off in any situation. Trust me.

Once you've made your good first impression and are ready to begin the audition, it's time to get to work. The first thing you'll be asked to do on camera is to slate your name.

WHAT'S THE "SLATE"?

Your audition will almost always be recorded on video to be played back later. At the very beginning of the audition you will be asked to verbally slate your name and identify yourself on camera so that folks can identify you later on when they play back the tape. Like everything else that happens in that room, the slate is an enormously important part of the audition.

WHAT DO I DO WHEN I SLATE MY NAME?

Wait until the camera operator gives you the cue to start. He'll say something like "Slate your name, please" or "Now" or "Action," or he'll just wave in your direction (don't wave back). At that point, smile, look at the center of the camera lens, take a second, and say your name slowly and clearly, as if you're proud of it. Don't be in a hurry, and remember that people can tell a lot about you by watching you and hearing you introduce yourself.

My first name isn't very common and my family moved a lot from one city to another when I was growing up. When I would show up at a new school on my first day, the teacher would always have me stand and say my name in order to introduce me to the rest of the class. Being the new kid, it wasn't my favorite thing to do, but I quickly learned that if I hurried and slurred my name so I could sit down quickly and not be noticed, I'd invariably be asked by the teacher to stand up and do it all over again. So I learned to stand, smile, and say, "Hi. My name is Squire Fridell," as though I was proud of it. It seemed to work, and after that I didn't have to stand up and say it twice. I think because of that life lesson, I like to get a little extra time on camera by prefacing my name with a greeting.

So now when I slate, I always say, "Hi. My name is Squire Fridell," and finish with a little nod to the camera while I'm still smiling to put a button at the end of the slate. Most actors make the mistake of using the slate to merely telegraph information. Don't lose this opportunity to demonstrate what kind of a person you are and give them a taste of your unique personality. I also like to focus my attention on the script or cue cards before I'm asked to slate, and when my slate is over, focus my attention back to the copy. Otherwise you're just staring at the lens (and the camera could be running) waiting to slate or waiting for the camera to stop—doing nothing and looking a little stupid. This routine gives me movement, looks spontaneous, and my nod puts a period on my name. Practice doing it; you'll like it.

Some casting directors prefer that you also say your agent's name during the slate, but don't do it unless you're asked. If you notice *any* idiosyncrasies that a particular casting director has, make sure you write them down in your journal. After the slate, the camera operator will either continue to let the camera run and begin the actual audition or, more likely, he'll stop the camera and get set up to begin the actual audition. Either way, make sure to take the time you need to collect your thoughts before starting the copy. Don't make the mistake of going right from slating your name to the first line of copy.

WHAT IF I'M AUDITIONING WITH ANOTHER ACTOR?

Don't let your partner's shyness, gregariousness, ability, or lack of ability affect you in any way. You are being auditioned on *your* merits, not your partner's, so you don't need to look at yourself as a team member. No matter what your partner does, just be pleasant, keep that smile, and stay positive. Never correct a partner who misses a line. Even if your partner and the casting director seem to be the greatest of friends, don't let it intimidate you. I would rather audition with someone who does *not* show off her best skills in the audition. As long as she gives me my correct cues, I'm happy. The eye can only look at one place at a time, and I'd prefer that the director, casting director, or client look at *me* during the playback of the video rather than at my partner, since, oftentimes, only one person in a two-person audition makes the callback.

I always think of the slate as the time to outshine my partner, and there are a few subtle things you can do to accomplish that. Any stage director will tell you that movement draws more focus and attention than speech. When you and your partner are both asked to slate, turn your head to your partner, smile, and magnanimously gesture that he or she may go first. This works particularly well if you're a male auditioning with a female. Keep looking at your partner until he or she is finished, then, with that same award-winning smile, turn your head back to the camera and do your own slate. You'll not only look polite, generous, interested, and friendly, but you'll have those all-important people watching you most during the videotape replay later on. Be aware that the camera operator may dictate who is to slate first, or he may focus the camera in a tight shot on each of you and have you slate individually. You can still look at your partner while she is doing her slate and you'll get some head movement when the camera pans over to you. Make sure you try this before you use it in an audition, however. It can backfire if you're not sure what to do.

WHAT IF I'M AUDITIONING WITH A CHILD?

I think W. C. Fields was credited with saying, "Never appear onstage with either an animal or a child. Either one will upstage you." But if you show up for an audition and it's for a daddy and his little boy, you have no choice. Children can be particularly difficult to audition with and to work with for a lot of reasons. Here are some tips to make it easier.

- In many commercial scenarios, the child will be playing with something or eating something, and they'll want both of you to be facing the camera. Depending on the size of the child, kneel down behind him and put him in front of you, to one side of your face or the other so that you're looking over his shoulder at what he's doing. If the child gets behind you, all the camera will see is the back of your head. Hopefully, the camera operator or casting director will have your positions figured out beforehand.

- If the camera operator is vague, take command of the situation during the audition. Don't be afraid to touch the child (tell the child you're going to) and physically put him where it works best for you. Children can sometimes take over the audition completely. Just be friendly but a little on the firm side. It will make the child more secure and make you look more like the parent you're supposed to be.

- Many actors will try to get to know the child a little in the waiting room before going in for the actual audition. Casting directors sometimes even pair up "parent" and "child" beforehand. I've found that it's best not to establish a too-cozy, friendly relationship, as it may be counterproductive during the audition. I think it's much easier during the audition if I assume the role of an uncle rather than that of a buddy.

- If I know I'm going to be auditioning with a toddler, I'll bring a little windup toy or a gadget for him to play with. Don't pull it out too soon. Kids have very short attention spans. You'll also really impress those folks watching your playback!

- If the child isn't doing what she's supposed to be doing, let the casting director do the correcting. Keep your composure, your award-winning smile, and recover any way you can in order to carry out the continuity of the reading.

- Auditioning with and working with kids can be frustrating, but remember that it's just as frustrating for all your fellow actors. Just listen to the directions you are given and do your best.

WHAT ABOUT USING PROPS DURING THE AUDITION?

Great idea! Most of the time, the casting director will have props for you to use, but it often happens that there are no props in the audition room. Whenever possible, rehearse with and use *real* props. If it's a coffee commercial audition and your partner is supposed to hand you a cup of coffee, it's best to use a real cup. If there isn't a Styrofoam coffee cup in the audition room (that'd be a first!), it's okay to substitute a short, rolled-up piece of paper that *looks* like a cup, but don't ever pantomime. (Dennis Gallegos, a casting director in Los Angeles, used to call that empty hand that actors use to pantomime holding something "the claw.") Better yet, if you know you're going in for a coffee commercial, bring a cup from home. You may not use it, but you never know.

My wife took this one step further and taught me a little about props. Years ago on her way to a Lipton Lite Lunch audition, she stopped at the market and bought a package of Lipton Lite Lunch and stuck it in her purse. The casting director hadn't provided any props, and when the audition called for her character to produce the product to solve her friend's hunger problem, Suzy whipped out her newly purchased package. The casting director thought she was clever, the advertising agency and the client probably thought she "looked more real" for some strange reason, and she booked the job! Plus she was able to write it off as a prop *and* she got lunch. Moral of the story? If you're going on a Diet Coke audition, stop and buy a can of Diet Coke. Then, after the audition, you'll have a tax-deductible soft drink! And always remember to keep your props out of sight of the other actors in the waiting room. You don't want any of them stealing your clever ideas.

WHEN DO YOU USE CUE CARDS INSTEAD OF USING THE SCRIPT?

Usually there isn't a choice. In different geographic areas they tend to use one or the other. In Los Angeles, for instance, cue cards are always printed up for you, even though you first see the copy on a script in the waiting room. The advantage to using cue cards is that your head is up and your face automatically cheats toward the lens. The cards are there to help you and make your audition better. If they were scribbled by someone who got a D in penmanship, and they aren't written very clearly, just remember that all the other actors have the same disadvantage. Physically, the lines will be written out and spaced differently on the cue cards than they are on the script, so the copy will look different. Be sure you rehearse aloud once before they turn on that camera to record your audition. If you absolutely cannot use cue cards for some reason, then ask if it would be okay to use your script. You'll almost always do better, however, if you practice and use the cue cards that have been done for you.

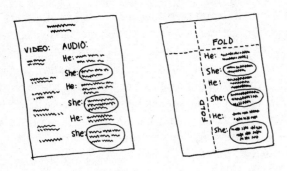

When rehearsing or reading with handheld copy, circle your lines in pencil so that your eyes can easily find the next set of words to say. It makes the usual two-character copy look only half as difficult. In spokesperson copy, circle the opening and closing lines for easy, quick reference. If there are cue cards, and the handheld copy is to be used only for rehearsing in the waiting room, circle your lines or the opening and closing anyway. It tends to break down the script and make the segue to the cue cards easier.

When you're reading handheld copy, fold the paper so that only what you need to see shows. Folding the script to the smallest possible size will not only keep your paper from shaking during your audition, but you'll be able to move the copy higher so your eyes won't have to look so low to find a line. Make sure you've read and understand any stage directions on the left side of the page before folding the copy.

Whether you are using cue cards or handheld script, it's most important that the camera and/or the people watching your audition get a clear view of your face. Always angle your face toward the camera (or them) so that *both* your eyes can be seen. If you're holding a script, try to hold it just high enough so that the camera sees your entire face, not the top of your head. Don't hold it off to one side, either. Practice at home in front of a mirror and see how you do.

HOW CAN I BEST WORK WITH THE AUDITION CAMERA?

The audition camera is a casting office fixture and something you'll always have to deal with, so learn to see the camera not as an intimidating machine, but as a friend that can help you get a callback. Even though the camera may be positioned all the way across the room, it can zoom in to a very tight shot of your face. You can sometimes see how tight the shot is on the TV monitor in the room if it is positioned right. If you can't see it, just ask how tight the shot is going to be. If you know the shot is from your chest up, you'll have to confine your gestures. Otherwise no one will see the clever things you're doing . with your hands during playback.

Make sure you stand on both feet so that you don't sway back and forth. It's sometimes a nervous reaction to go from one leg to another, but on camera, you'll look very strange rocking back and forth during the playback.

Keep your energy up from the time you enter the room until you're out the door and on your way home. Don't smile only when you think the camera is running. And if you're asked questions while the camera is running, always answer directly into the camera, as though you were talking to it. If the tape is running and you keep looking one way or another to talk to the casting director or the ad agency person, you'll look a little foolish during the playback.

This takes some practice and feels very unnatural until you get used to it. If you have a video camera and recorder at home, have a friend help you tape some mock interviews and auditions. It will get you more comfortable with the camera and will be a valuable experience for you.

ANY MORE TIPS ABOUT THE AUDITION?

Yep. Some are repeats, but they are worth repeating!

- Approach any audition enthusiastically and be happy that you've gotten this far. You aren't there by chance. Your name was suggested somewhere by someone and the casting director said yes. For every actor who finally gets to audition, there were a lot of actors who weren't even submitted; and there were a lot of actors who were submitted but the casting director said no. It's a triumph just to make it into the audition!

- Speak clearly, a little louder than you normally would in conversation, and enunciate your words.

- Note where the microphone is and don't bump into it or make shuffling noises with your script or your prop that might distract from your audition.

- If you have a regional dialect of some sort, get rid of it. If you have a good ear and can mimic someone else's speech pattern, find a novel on CD you might enjoy listening to and practice copying the recorded actor. If your dialect is severe, there are any number of speech and dialect teachers you can work with, maybe even at your local community college. It's nice to be able to do dialects when called upon for a specific audition, but an accent you can't lose will limit the number of auditions you'll get.

- Even if you feel you aren't right for the part you're auditioning for, never let anyone know that. Just do your best during the audition. Many times an actor who isn't right adds a favorable twist to the character, and the character is rewritten slightly to fit that actor. If you aren't right for this job but you audition well, the casting director may call you in for another job for which you're perfect. Never cast yourself in or out of a role. Let the casting director do that. It's his job, not yours.

- Be sure to listen very carefully to whatever the person in charge has to say. Give that person your full, undivided attention, listen to the instructions given, and implement them. You can assume that if any additional instructions are given to you, they are extremely important. Casting directors hate having to repeat what they just explained to an actor because he didn't listen.

- Even though you've memorized the opening and closing of the copy for maximum on-camera impact, make sure you don't die out on the rest of the copy in between. There's always a tendency to lose energy, particularly in spokesperson copy, about halfway through the script. Take your time and make each part count.

- You should never try to memorize the entire script, but some eye contact with your partner or the camera is extremely important. Memorize as much of the opening as you easily can and deliver those words off script to the camera or your partner. Next, you can refer to the copy for the bulk of the words and then go off script to the camera or your partner for your closing.

1. SLATE	2. OPENING LINE	3. BULK OF COPY	4. LAST LINE
LOOK AT CAMERA	DO NOT LOOK AT COPY (MEMORIZE)	REFER TO COPY	DO NOT LOOK AT COPY (MEMORIZE)

- As a general rule of thumb, it's better to have contact lenses or surgery to correct your vision problem. If you must wear glasses to read the script or the cue cards (particularly in spokesperson copy), make sure you slate with your glasses off, then put them back on, take a look at the copy, figure out your beginning, take the glasses off, and do your memorized opening. At the moment when you need to rely on the printed word, slip your glasses back on and read the bulk of the copy. Then take them off again as you look into the camera for your memorized finish or tag line. This will let them see you both ways and it will add a dimension of authority to your audition. Many actors even carry phony glasses without lenses to use for the above effect or for a character look. If you want to try this tip, make sure you practice it. It sounds simple, but it's not.

1. SLATE   2. OPENING LINES   3. BULK OF COPY   4. LAST LINE

- If you're auditioning with a partner, take a look at *your* upcoming line toward the end of *his* line. It is more important to get your cues in on time and get the copy right than it is to have full eye contact. Make sure you know what your cues are. Also take a look at the other set of lines—you may be asked to switch parts.

- Don't be afraid to take your time before starting your reading. After your slate, look at the first line or phrase you've committed to memory, look up, and start. Be absolutely sure you're ready before taking the plunge.

- If you make a mistake during the reading and have a chance to tape again, make sure you go over the mistake aloud before trying take number two. There's a reason the mistake happened, so be sure to fix it before proceeding.

- Be aware that adrenaline always makes everyone speed up, so force yourself to slow down. You'll probably have only one chance, so take your time and make sure it's right.

- If you immediately get off to the wrong start—stop; 99 percent of the time you'll be able to try again. On the other hand, if you fluff a word, just keep going and forget about it. Don't dwell on your mistakes. No one ever cares about one mistake. They will care about the second, third, fourth, and fifth mistake you make because your mind is on the first one. Don't draw attention to it. Just forget it.

- If they ask you to do the reading more than once, be happy that you get another chance. It means that they're interested. Try to find a different way to do the reading. Don't carbon-copy what you did before. Show them how versatile you are.

- If you feel that you'd like to try something a little differently and ask to be taped again, make sure that you do something very different! Most actors will ask to try something new and then repeat exactly what they just did.

WHAT DO I DO AFTER THE AUDITION IS OVER?

Congratulations on getting through your first audition! Most likely, you just had your hardest one. Hopefully, you'll find that succeeding ones will become easier and easier.

Here are a couple of additional tips.

- When you finish with the audition, no matter how you think it went, just smile, say thank you, sign out at the correct time, and leave. Don't ever comment on how you feel the audition went—not to the casting director, the other actor you auditioned with, nor to actors waiting to audition. If you want to shout for joy or cry your eyes out, wait until you get at least a mile away. Even if you feel like you bombed, *look* positive.

- If you happen to be performing in a play in town, you might mention it and drop off a flier to the casting director before you leave. Tell him if he'd like to see the show, you'd be glad to secure free tickets. It lets the casting director know that you're working as an actor and gives him something to talk about when he's reviewing the playbacks with the clients.

- As soon as you finish with the audition, enter all the pertinent information in your journal and go over each moment, from entering the waiting room to exiting the audition room. Then ask yourself the following questions.

  - What was the name of the casting director and/or assistant?

  - What do I feel I did well during the audition?

  - Was I comfortable with my clothing?

  - Was I prepared?

  - Did I allow myself enough time to absorb the storyboard?

  - Did I have enough time to work with the copy?

  - What do I feel I could have done differently?

  - What will I do differently next time I audition?

As soon as you've entered that information in your journal, work on the problem areas and fix them.

- After you've worked on the problem areas and figured out how to not make the same mistakes again, forget it. Just go about your life and put it out of your mind. You've already figured out what you can do better next time, so let it go. Then, if you *do* get a callback or a job, it will come as a pleasant surprise and you won't have lost any sleep over it. All the years I went on auditions while I was still a high school teacher, I was always so preoccupied with racing back to class, I never had a chance to dwell on my free period/lunchtime auditions. And that was a very good thing.

- Don't make the mistake of calling everyone you know to tell them that you went on an audition. If you do, they will call twice a day to see if you got the job. Keep a low profile until you're certain that you're working. Then you can shout it to the world.

- Always have somewhere to go and something to do right after the audition. Don't go home and stare at your TV or cell phone. Visit a friend, walk in the park, jog, work out—anything, as long as you don't dwell on the audition.

- Never assume anything about your audition. The job you thought you were absolutely perfect for, you're not going to get . . . and the audition you were certain you bombed may end up landing you a job.

Once, after a particularly bad audition for a Contac commercial, I wondered why I was in the business! I had a lot of trouble manipulating an eye mask up and down, I couldn't see the words on the cue card, and the audition went downhill fast. Normally, I would have forgotten about the audition after my entry in my journal, but this one was *so* bad, I thought if word leaked out I'd be washed up as an actor. After I got home, and in the middle of telling my wife about the terrible audition I'd done, my agent called to tell me I was booked for the job! I guess everybody else had trouble with the eye mask, too.

Remember, put the audition out of your mind—until you get a callback!

CHAPTER 12

THE CALLBACK

Always take your wallet on stage with you.

—George Burns (advice to a young actor)

WHAT'S A CALLBACK?

A callback is another audition, usually just like the first audition, but it's only for the finalists. Again, you will sign in using the SAG sign-in sheet and might be asked for another headshot and résumé, so make sure you bring a spare. Both the first audition and the callback are usually recorded, but the callback may have additional folks in the audition room to watch your performance, including the director, the ad agency folks, the client, and the casting director.

On the other hand, it may just be the camera operator and you. Current video technology can allow the director and/or ad agency producer to work with you from another location. It's a little unnerving when that happens, and your tendency might be to respond by looking toward the voice giving you direction. Again, don't do it. Your eye focus should be into the camera, the same as the director-in-absence does when he talks to you. If you can practice it at home, it'll be a lot easier.

Remember that if you *do* get a callback for a commercial, you're perfect for the job! And you have just as much of a chance to land that job as anyone else who is called back. Now the ad agency folks have narrowed down the field and they want to find the person they feel would be best for this particular commercial. Sometimes it will involve mixing and matching actors to see who looks best together as they create a family for the commercial, or pairing actors to create a husband and a wife. You've made it this far, so try to relax and do whatever it was that you did in the audition. You're perfect for the commercial and now it's their subjective choice as to who is the *most* perfect actor for the spot. At this point, it has a lot to do with them and little to do with you.

WHAT SHOULD I WEAR FOR THE CALLBACK?

Don't go out and treat yourself to a new set of clothes. Wear exactly what you wore to the audition. They liked the way you looked during the audition and they've watched the video playback over and over, so don't confuse them. Actors who make the mistake of getting a new hairstyle or wear a flashy new outfit for the callback are usually the ones who don't end up with the job.

WHAT SHOULD I EXPECT AT THE CALLBACK?

Don't anticipate anything. There are no givens. Again, there may be a few more people in the room and you may be asked to read the copy any number of times. Just smile and be pleasant, take the callback one step at a time, and don't try to second-guess anyone. Listen carefully and just follow directions. If the director is present (or in a monitor), he may direct you by asking you to read the copy a different way. Many times he is seeing how you respond to his direction and how flexible you are in taking direction. You may also be given an entirely new set of words, a new character to play, or a different set of tips as to how to play the character. Again, the director may want to see how you take direction. The key to a successful callback is to listen carefully to whatever you're asked to do and then to do it. If you fail to make those changes, chances are you won't be getting the job.

If your callback is for a multiple-character commercial (husbands and wives or a group of guys), there will probably be a lot of mixing and matching. Again, don't try to second-guess. Look like you're having a great time and keep a smile on your face. Remember, most commercials are booked by the actors who simply have learned to listen to what the director wants and can adjust their performances accordingly.

ARE ACTORS STILL PUT ON HOLD?

In the old days, there was the audition, followed by the callback. Then, when the selections were narrowed down to one or two actors, the talent agent would get a phone call from the casting director requesting him to put his actor on hold. At that point it was the responsibility of both the actor and her agent to notify the casting director if the actor got another job offer that conflicted with the scheduled commercial shoot date(s). She could not take the other job since she was on hold for the first one. The problem was that it was sort of one-sided. Sometimes another actor was chosen for the job and the casting agent didn't get around to releasing the less-fortunate actor(s), causing them to miss out on other opportunities to work. They abused the system, and it proved to be enough of a problem that the talent agents started insisting that actors be paid a session fee for the date(s) they were on hold. SAG finally got involved and decreed that casting directors could not place actors on hold. Doing so constituted a booking and meant the actor was to get paid. In this way, SAG essentially did away with the term *on hold.*

WHAT DOES *FIRST REFUSAL* MEAN?

In those days of yesteryear, first refusal merely meant that you were one step closer to getting the job. Now, depending on which part of the country you're in, *first refusal* is used as a synonym for the old *on hold,* which, again, means actors must not take another booking because they are committed. In New York, *first refusal* is used more often than it is in Los Angeles, where *on availability* seems to be the norm.

Semantics, semantics... These days an actor may be put on availability for a shoot date (sometimes even before the callback) so that if another offer of work comes up for the actor and the dates conflict, the talent agent has to call the casting director about the potential schedule conflict. Technically, if the casting director then insists on that right of on availability, on hold, or first refusal, the actor's agent has to honor it. Even though SAG ruled against the on hold status, there doesn't seem to be a problem with casting agents using on availability or first refusal. Go figure. SAG will most likely make another ruling someday as soon as someone gets abused and makes an issue of it.

On availability or first refusal may not seem like much of a problem for the actor, but there are huge potential payoff differences between one commercial and another. One booking might be for a regional commercial and another booking for a national class-A spot. It could be the difference between a few hundred dollars and many thousands of dollars.

HOW SOON AFTER THE CALLBACK WILL I FIND OUT IF I GOT BOOKED FOR THE JOB?

Hard to say. There have been occasions where I've found out before I left the casting office and sometimes it's taken months before I've known. There's an old axiom in this business: "No news sucks." You'll hardly ever get a call from your talent agent or a casting agent letting you know that you *didn't* get the job... so if you don't hear anything, you're probably not going to be working. Even if you think that your callback was fantastic, everyone in the room laughed at everything you did, and then they told you that you were just what they are looking for—don't assume anything. It means nothing until you actually get that call from your talent agent booking you for the job.

Once, I thought I had one of the best theatrical auditions I'd ever had for a pilot for Universal. I was told I was perfect for the role and work would start the following Monday. I was handed the script and told to go home and start memorizing my part. Guess what? I never heard from them. (The good news? The pilot bombed and never aired! Ha!)

I've also been in callbacks where I felt I was absolutely wrong for the part and that my audition was a disaster. Guess what? I ended up getting some of those jobs. Because of this, years ago I developed a defensive trick that I built in to the hard drive of my head. Whenever I would go on a callback, I would have something scheduled to do the moment I walked out: I'd go to the gym and work out, I'd go to a movie, or I'd meet someone for dinner—anything to keep me from thinking about the audition or the callback.

This forget-about-it mentality always worked well for me . . . sometimes a little *too* well. When I auditioned for the part of Ronald McDonald, I had no idea that the audition was to replace the original actor. I got a call from my talent agent saying he had an audition for a commercial campaign called "Operation Red Shoe." He said that it was a bit secretive (even he didn't know the product), but the role was for a "clownlike character." I stopped off at Hollywood Magic on my way to the audition and picked up three juggling balls and a couple of small magic tricks, just in case there would be an occasion to use them during the audition. I went into the casting office waiting room, worked on the copy, figured out where I could incorporate my magic gags and juggling, went in, and did my best. I thought I did okay, left the audition, and following my own advice, promptly forgot about it.

Some three months went by and my agent, Pen, called me again, saying that I had a callback. I could not remember the audition, but I did have the information written down (and what I'd done during the audition) in my journal, so I figured I'd repeat what I'd done before.

I took in my juggling balls and my magic tricks again, and as soon as I opened the door of the waiting room, I saw seven actors in makeup and costume, all the spitting image of Ronald McDonald. I finally got it: "Operation Red Shoe" and a "clownlike character." Someone did my makeup, I got into a red and yellow costume, auditioned again, and used the same juggling and magic tricks I'd used during the first audition. It was then an additional three months before I found out that I was about to spend a lot of time in whiteface and a red wig, chasing the Hamburglar around McDonaldland.

THE JOB

Anyone who finds acting difficult just shouldn't be doing it.
—Kurt Russell

Congratulations! Hopefully it's the first job of many for you! At some point, every commercial actor who's ever had a great career started with his very first commercial! I remember my first commercial vividly: It was for Olympia Beer and was directed by Cal Bernstein, an award-winning photojournalist during the 1960s civil rights movement. To top it off, the commercial was shot on 35 mm film by cinematographer Haskell Wexler, a two-time Oscar winner (eleven nominations!) whose credits included little B-films like *One Flew Over the Cuckoo's Nest, Bound for Glory,* and *Who's Afraid of Virginia Woolf?* Suffice to say that I was pretty much in awe of the talent behind the camera.

We spent a long, hot day in front of a house somewhere in Los Angeles shooting that Olympia Beer commercial. There I was with my commercial wife who was trying to save my day by handing me a cold Olympia Beer, while I was supposedly having trouble repairing something underneath a VW bus. It was a narrative story commercial and I had no words to say in the spot, but I think I can remember every setup and every shot. Cal Bernstein was nice enough to send me a 16 mm copy of that commercial. I had it converted to DVD a few years ago and I still have it. I hope your first job is as memorable for you!

(Trivia item: James Dean's first professional acting job was in a Coca-Cola commercial!)

But let's not get ahead of ourselves. Between the time your agent calls, notifying you that you've landed a commercial, and your first day of work, you'll usually have a wardrobe call.

WHAT'S A WARDROBE CALL?

After you've been notified by your agent that you're definitely working, usually someone in charge of wardrobe will phone you. She'll tell you what clothing she's looking for and ask what you own that might be suitable. Then you'll decide together what things you should bring to the wardrobe call. She'll also take down your sizes and probably go shopping for some alternatives to show the client, the agency people, and/or the director. Make sure you tell her your accurate sizes, not what you think you're going to weigh after fasting all weekend.

Here are some tips.

- Be as helpful as you can. Don't go out and purchase clothing, but do volunteer to bring in anything you think they might use.

- If you bring in your own clothing, make sure it fits you. It isn't too helpful to have to tell them that the shirt they like doesn't fit you anymore.

- Take notes. Then, as soon as you've finished talking with the wardrobe person, immediately get together all the clothes the two of you have decided might be appropriate. If you don't write it down and instead wait until just before the wardrobe call, you might not remember exactly what you decided to bring.

- Sometimes there is only one person at the wardrobe call, but most likely the client, agency people, director, and wardrobe person will all be present. This may be the first time you meet these people face-to-face, so write down and remember their names. Being able to greet them by name during the actual shoot can have lasting benefits. Also remember that all of them will probably be more familiar with you than you are with them. They've been looking at your audition playback over and over.

- You may feel a little like a mannequin during the wardrobe call (you basically are). Don't let it bother you.

- Don't be offended that no one likes your personal clothes. Don't be offended if you think the clothes they select are terrible. Their taste, or lack of it, may be quite different from yours.

- There may be some disagreement among the powers that be about the suitability of a particular garment or two. Stay out of the discussion. You may think your input is important, but it's not. Interfering could unknowingly make an enemy.

- You'll be paid a fee (see chapter 14, The Money) for clothes you wear in the commercial that are your own property. Clothes that they buy are theirs, so don't walk off with them after the shoot is over. If you really like an outfit or a shirt, talk to the wardrobe person about purchasing it. The going rate (if they'll sell) is usually half what they paid for it. If she doesn't want to sell it, don't pester her. (The client may also wear a 40-regular sport coat.)

ARE THERE MORE WORDS OR PHRASES I SHOULD BE FAMILIAR WITH THAT I MIGHT ENCOUNTER ON THE SET?

Yep. Here you go.

The Important People Involved and What They Do

CLIENT
The client is the company that owns the product or the service that wants to advertise to increase sales. Toyota, Procter & Gamble, and H&R Block are typical clients for products or services.

CLIENT PRODUCER
Sometimes a client representative is on the set when the commercial is being shot, but usually not. Most often, it happens when a new ad agency takes over the account. If a client producer *is* on the set, he'll be responsible for the client's best interest on the shoot.

AGENCY
Short for the advertising agency. During what's known as a "review," ad agencies will compete for the job of becoming the client's advertiser. During the review, each competing ad agency writes some commercials and develops a media package to show the client what they would do if they were awarded the job. If they *are* awarded the job, they will further develop that media package to involve television advertising, radio advertising, and/or print advertising and come up

with a very detailed marketing plan. They will do focus-group studies, develop advertising campaigns, write and produce commercials, buy airtime, and create budgets. The ad agency keeps its job when the advertising leads to increased sales. If the sales go down, the client may call for another review and one agency might lose the job to another ad agency.

AGENCY PRODUCER(S)

These are the folks on the set from the ad agency who act as liaisons between the storyboard and the director. Their group developed the concept and wrote the commercial and they are there to see that it gets done the way it was conceptualized. They're usually folks who are really good at art because they draw storyboards, and they're also good people to get to know. They work hard and they are almost always on the set. I have a lot of good friends who are agency producers. They're creative folks and fun to hang out with.

PRODUCTION COMPANY

This is the film or tape company that is hired by the advertising agency to actually shoot the commercial. Some production companies have their own full-time staff, but most often they have a skeleton crew of higher-ups and employ the freelance shoot-day crew when needed.

PRODUCTION COMPANY PRODUCER(S)

I've worked for production companies that had a full-time staff and companies that had only a production company producer who hired virtually everyone else for the shoot. The production company producer sometimes owns the production company.

PRODUCERS (IN GENERAL)

If there are ad agency producers and production company producers and client producers all on the set at the same time, there are bound to be some disagreements. Each producer has his own specific area to watch out for. One may be concerned about going overtime and over budget, another concerned with the quality (and quantity) of the shots, another producer demanding that the product has to be prominently displayed and well-lit. If there are disputes on the set, remember that it has nothing to do with you, so stay out of it. Your job is to do what the director tells you to do. He is hired to direct the spot and you're hired to do what he tells you to do. In an ideal world, everyone on the set, including the producers, would direct their comments and ideas to the director, who then passes them on to the actor. And if you see them all whispering in the corner, don't get paranoid. Sometimes that heated discussion is no more than who's going to win Sunday's football game. They could also be discussing the way a line should be read, but, again, it's the director's job to relay that information to you. Sometimes the producers will have different ideas than the director or even each other and you'll be asked to do the same scene in a slightly different way. Just smile and do as you're told. You were hired because you were the best choice in the world.

DIRECTOR

This is the person hired by the production company, usually with the approval of the ad agency, to shoot the commercial. Some directors work for or own the production company and some of them freelance. Some specialize in stunts, some are known for their ability to work with children, some are hired because they do a great job lighting and shooting automobiles. It's also interesting to note that most television commercial directors are not trained stage directors and their expertise is more technical than people-oriented. They always have a great visual sense, but many of them know next to nothing about acting and sometimes their people skills are sorely lacking. Many act as their own cameraperson, they usually have a great eye for lighting and composure of camera shots, and they usually have a lot of experience in art direction. You can bet they are all terrific still-camera photographers.

A.D.

This is not a reference to the date. The initials stand for assistant director, and he is the person in charge of keeping the shoot moving along. He's often heard yelling, "Quiet on the set!" when the camera is about to roll, and he is your off-the-set liaison with the director.

The A.D. signs you in and out, tells you when to go for lunch, notifies you when you should be getting into makeup and wardrobe, assigns your call time, and answers just about any question you might have. The A.D. can be a great help to you on the set, so learn his name and be friendly.

PRINCIPAL

An actor who is hired to act in the commercial is a principal actor, as opposed to atmosphere/background talent/extras. Usually there is an audition for the principal roles in a commercial, whether the roles are speaking roles or not.

TALENT

The term has no correlation with whether or not you have any. (That's a joke.) It's merely the name given to the principal actors hired to do a commercial. They're often referred to collectively as "the talent."

ATMOSPHERE/BACKGROUND TALENT/EXTRAS

Extras are also known as "background talent" or "atmosphere." They are background people in a commercial and they are not hired to be principal talent. Extras are directed by the A.D. rather than the director and they are usually cast by their headshots and not in an audition. They get a flat fee for the day with overtime, but they do not get residuals. (See chapter 14, The Money.) Watch car commercials. You'll see a lot of extras milling around looking at the cars. They are easy to recognize because you never see their faces on camera.

If the extra's face is seen and he is identifiable, he will be upgraded to principal talent and he will be eligible for residuals. Many times in the after-shoot editing session, the editor will have to cut a shot because one of the background extras was positioned so his face was plainly seen.

I've worked with extras who consistently tried to get upgraded to principal talent by making their faces seen by the camera, but if the A.D. is on his toes, it won't happen.

If the extra keeps it up, he'll be warned once and then asked to leave. And he certainly won't work for that production company again.

Words You'll Hear on the Set and What They Mean

UPSTAGE
On the set, it's the area behind the actor, if he's facing toward the camera.

DOWNSTAGE
On the set, this is the area between the actor and the camera.

CAMERA RIGHT
If you're the actor facing the camera, it is everything to *your* left. It is exactly the opposite in stage acting terms (where stage right means to the actor's right when he faces the audience). Confusing, huh?

CAMERA LEFT
If you're the actor facing the camera, it is everything to *your* right and, again, the opposite of what stage actors are used to.

BLOCKING
The movement and action of the principal actors planned by the director. Since there are usually many shots and setups for the camera and the lighting will have to be changed for each shot, blocking on a commercial shoot is very exact. Blocking for atmosphere talent is usually planned and executed by the A.D.

HITTING YOUR MARKS
This is the ability to physically stop on a preset mark or the ability to hold or set the product down in an exact spot. Some actors are better at this than others, but it's something that all commercial actors must be skilled enough to do. You must be able to repeat an action, stop on a mark, and set down that box of detergent exactly the same way at exactly the same angle you were instructed to do each and every time.

CONTINUITY
This is the job of the script supervisor, and it means making sure one setup and shot will be chronological with the next when the com-

mercial is finally cut together. If your hand is scratching your head in one shot, it's the script supervisor's job to make sure your hand is still scratching your head in the next shot when the commercial is finally cut together. The script supervisor, aside from being responsible for the continuity of the spot, also times each and every shot so that the finished commercial will not go longer than they want it to. Actors can help script supervisors and directors by paying careful attention to the flow of the storyboard to see where they are in the next frame.

CHEAT TO CAMERA

This is an actor's technique to turn his face toward the lens of the camera a bit so that more of his face can be seen. Watch television and find a commercial when a TV wife is talking to her TV husband. In real life, both would be in profile having a conversation, but in a commercial scene they will both cheat their faces slightly to camera. Rarely is anyone in film (or onstage) in profile. If you're ever blocked and you're supposed to look directly at another actor's face, cheat your face to camera and pick out your partner's eye that's closest to camera to look at.

KEY LIGHT

This is a small-diameter light that is set up specifically to highlight you or the product with an extra light boost. If you move slightly or don't set the product down in exactly the right spot, you'll both "be out of the key light."

HERO

Not you. That's the name given to the art-department-created perfect product, sometimes built, baked, or put together by an artist. It can be a box of toothpaste that's actually a piece of specially created balsa wood that's been painted and color-corrected to look like the product. It can be a box of detergent that's really not a box of detergent. It can be some chicken wings or pizza that's been sprayed or painted to look absolutely perfect for the camera. (Before sneaking a cookie or a french fry from a food-product commercial shoot, be very aware that the delicious-looking hero may not be edible.)

WRAP

A wrap for you is called by the A.D. as soon as your last shot has been completed and you're done for the day. Go home. Not everyone wraps at the same time, and often the A.D. will wrap the talent but the crew will still be on the set working on some additional product beauty shots. When I was finished working on location somewhere, I'd always call home tired (but happy!) after I was wrapped. My wife would always commiserate with me ("Oh, you poor guy"), but I'd always say that, even though I might be a little pooped, the guys on the crew were still on the set working. And they were working on the set that morning while I was still in the shower getting ready to go to work.

WHEN I SHOW UP ON THE SET, HOW WELL DO I NEED TO KNOW THE COPY?

You'll need to know your words perfectly. Don't make the mistake of not *completely* memorizing your part. If you kind of know the words, you're going to have a lot of trouble on the shoot day. When you show up on the set, make sure you know the script from start to finish—forward, backward, and sideways. One thing that directors will not tolerate is an actor who doesn't know his words well enough to do them a hundred different ways, a thousand times, during the shoot day. Onstage, in television, and in film you can sometimes get away with being *almost* word perfect. In a commercial, however, *each and every* word has been carefully timed and chosen and has been approved by the advertising group after multiple meetings. More often than not, those words have also been checked out and approved by a legal team.

Television commercials tend to have a lot more words in thirty seconds than thirty seconds of an onstage play, a television show, a film, and certainly more than in real life, and there are many more time constraints. Many times your mouth has to move much faster than your brain would like it to. Many times you don't have the luxury of time (as you do onstage, for instance) to completely justify what you're about to say. If your TV husband has dandruff, you can't take half an act or even ten seconds to figure out how to tell him. There is a script supervisor holding a stopwatch and she knows that you have 3.8 seconds to deliver that particular line letting your husband know he's got a problem.

The other reason that commercial copy is hard to remember is that it's not memorized kinetically. When you're hired to act on stage, before your words are memorized, you usually have a series of blocking rehearsals where the director and actors work out all the stage movement. *Then* you're expected to memorize the words. Since the movement corresponds with your words, the memorization is relatively easy. In a commercial, the blocking comes after your words are memorized, so you lose the kinetic connection. Memorizing 29.4 nonstop seconds of copy as the spokesperson for a car commercial is tough. Trust me.

But when you can show up on the set having done your homework and are feeling absolutely confident that you can repeat the commercial copy three thousand times without making a mistake, it'll be worth all the effort. You'll be better prepared to handle the detailed blocking, complicated product handling, and any changes in the script.

CHANGES IN THE SCRIPT? I THOUGHT YOU SAID THAT THESE WORDS WERE SET IN STONE!

Ad agency lawyers sometimes wait until the last second to approve the final copy wording, and the agency folks may not be given the final-final approved script until the last minute, so be aware that there are often last-minute script changes and tweaks. If you have your script absolutely memorized, it's easy to drop in or change a few new words—but if you harbor the slightest doubt that the words aren't perfectly memorized, any changes are going to throw you for a loop, particularly as the day goes long and fatigue starts to set in. Because I've had to memorize a lot of words over the years, I've learned to identify these three kinds of memory:

- Short-term Memory
- Long-term Memory
- Middle-term Memory

What's the difference, you ask? Let's take a look at each of them:

Short-Term Memory

I have pretty good short-term memory. If I'm introduced to someone at a party or at work, I can remember his name for the duration. If I'm driving and on the cell phone (only where it's still legal!) and someone gives me a telephone number I have to dial, I can usually disconnect and then punch in that number. That's short-term memory.

Long-Term Memory

I'm *very* good on long-term memory. I can still list all the presidents in a row and recite the Preamble to our Constitution (thanks to those New Jersey sixth-grade graduation requirements!). I've also memorized a lot of poetry, monologues from plays, music lyrics, and speeches and whole scenes from Shakespeare. Long-term memory is stuff that I've *committed* to memory.

Middle-Term Memory

Unfortunately, what I don't have much of is what I call middle-term memory. Middle-term memory is when you can quickly memorize the words for a thirty-second TV commercial, repeat the words correctly all day long, and promptly forget them the moment you walk off the set. It's what most actors need and I don't have it.

So how do I deal with my disadvantage? I have to take the time to commit those words to long-term memory. It's very frustrating for me, and it takes me a long time to memorize my words before I show up on the set—but in order to not flub a single word, it's what I need to do. In other words, I have to start memorizing the copy the second I can get my hands on the script. I type the script out, highlight my lines, and go over and over them. I use a small digital voice recorder and go over the copy until I can repeat my lines with no mistakes. Then I record it again at a faster tempo until I can keep up with that speed and then record the copy even faster than I would ever logically say my lines on the set. Running my words certainly helps pass the time on the freeway. I also sometimes get strange looks from other drivers as they watch me animatedly talk to myself.

You won't know what kind of memorization ability you have (or don't have) until you're on the set under all that pressure, so my suggestion would be to *over*memorize the copy until you understand how difficult or easy the process is for you.

I'VE GOT MY TERMINOLOGY DOWN AND I'VE MEMORIZED MY WORDS! NOW WHAT'S THE SHOOT DAY GOING TO BE LIKE?

Below is the schedule of events for that Brawny Paper Towel commercial that both my wife and I were principal talent in.

TUES., MARCH 27:

10:00 a.m.—Agent calls audition for both Squire and Suzy at Coast Productions (L.A.) for Brawny Paper Towels. Audition time—4:45 that day. Camping scene, husband and wife.

4:30 p.m.—Arrive at Coast. Look over script.

5:10 p.m.—Audition. Videotaped. (Thought we did poorly.)

8:00 p.m.—Agent calls. Callback for both of us the following day at 3:40.

WED., MARCH 28:

3:30 p.m.—Arrive at Coast wearing same wardrobe. Look over script.

4:00 p.m.—Callback audition with director, clients. Videotaped again. (Thought we did a little better.)

WED., APRIL 11:

10:00 a.m.—Agent calls. Both of us got the job. Notified of wardrobe call and work date. (Unusual notification in two ways: First, it's very unusual for a real husband and wife to be cast as a commercial

---

husband and wife; second, it was two weeks before we found out that we were cast.)

9:00 p.m.—Suzy and Squire celebrate!

MON., APRIL 16:

11:00 a.m.—Wardrobe call at Coast. Brought all possible wardrobe for camping. Selections made. Map to location given out. Call time announced.

WED., APRIL 18:

8:00 a.m.—Arrive at location (approx. 1.5-hour drive). Reported to production manager/assistant director.

8:15 a.m.—Reported to makeup.

8:30 a.m.—Got into wardrobe in the motor home.

8:45 a.m.—Reported to the director on the set.

9:30 a.m.—Rough blocking of movements and rehearsing of lines.

10:30 a.m.—Stood in place for final lighting and set adjustments.

11:30 a.m.—Touch up makeup and final rehearsal.

11:45 a.m.—Begin actual shooting of first setup.

1:00 p.m.—Lunch.

1:35 p.m.—Back to makeup. Squire shaves again.

1:45 p.m.—Back to the set. Continue.

5:35 p.m.—Finish shooting last shot. (Called a "wrap" in the business.)

5:45 p.m.—All actors record "wild lines." (Additional recording of audio just in case.)

5:55 p.m.—The A.D. calls a wrap.

6:00 p.m.—After "thank you"s, two tired people head home.

Though you might be tempted to call this a typical workday, the longer you're in the business, the more you realize that there is no day of work that could be called "typical." Workdays are demanding and difficult. The more you are prepared for the difficulties and demands, the better you'll fare.

THE MORNING OF YOUR SHOOT DAY

Here are a few tips to make that morning go a little easier for you.

- Even actors who are seasoned performers have trouble sleeping the night before a shoot day. They're excited about the upcoming day! Don't make it worse for yourself by eating a late dinner of four pizzas the night before. Set yourself up for the best night's sleep possible.

- Make sure you save your voice. Going to a Raiders game and sitting in the "Black Hole" the day before your shoot might not be a good idea.

- Set two alarms for your wake-up. Make sure one is a windup or battery-powered, in case of power failure.

- When you wake up in the morning, you may experience a sudden feeling of panic. It may also happen on the set, and it's a pretty common thing. You might feel like someone is going to discover that you're not qualified to be on the set as an actor. Just tell yourself that you're *excited,* and remind yourself that you competed for this job and got it. Take a deep breath and remind yourself that everyone felt that *you* were the best choice in the entire world for shooting this commercial.

- Leave yourself plenty of time to get to the shoot so you aren't frazzled because of a traffic snarl. There are no excuses for being late.

- Make sure you have everything you need for the day, including the wardrobe you were asked to bring, a hairbrush or a comb, your script, and the directions to the shoot location.

Women should also take makeup (it might be possible to supplement the makeup artist's work), hair curlers if you need them, and hair spray. If your hair needs something special done to it, do it before you leave the house. Men should always take an electric razor along. You may not get a three o'clock shadow, but you might get a nine o'clock shadow. It's very important to look the same at the end of the workday as you did at the beginning.

- Eat a good breakfast before leaving for work. If you don't, you'll be inclined to stuff yourself with unhealthy food from the craft service table when you arrive. There's usually a table on the set with all kinds of tempting food designed specifically to sabotage you and your energy. If you have something to eat, stick to veggies and fresh fruit. Water, sparkling water, and fruit juices are a far cry better than coffee and soft drinks with caffeine. The same holds true for snacks during the day. The wrong foods and drinks can greatly affect your timing and performance. Stay away from all these energy roller-coaster evils.

- You might also want to bring your own supply of water with lemon and honey mixed into it. This can help you out during a long day when your voice starts to give out.

WHAT DO I DO WHEN I ARRIVE ON THE SET?

- If you have a car and parking is limited, ask where you are supposed to park for the day. Parking must be provided for you, so don't park your car on the street with a one-hour coin meter or park it in an illegal area and have it towed. The assistant director will give you this information.

- You'll notice a lot of commotion on the set. There are a lot of people working hard and a lot of people hardly working. It doesn't mean that some are go-getters and some are lazy. Due to the nature of the business, certain groups of people will be

ADVERTISING AGENCY _____ PRODUCER _____

COMMERCIAL TITLE(S) AND
CODE NO.(S) _____ PRODUCT _____

DATES WORKED	WORK TIME FROM/TO	MEALS FROM/TO	TRAVEL TO LOCATION FROM/TO	TRAVEL FROM LOCATION FROM/TO	FITTINGS, MAKEUP, TEST, IF ON DAY PRIOR TO SHOOTING FROM/TO

Multiple Tracking or Sweetening _____ did occur _____ did not occur

Performer's Signature or Initials: _____.

EXHIBIT A-1

STANDARD SCREEN ACTORS GUILD EMPLOYMENT CONTRACT FOR TELEVISION COMMERCIALS

Date _____,20_____

Between _____, Producer, and
_____, Performer.

Check If Applicable
- ☐ Dealer Commercial(s)
  - ☐ Type A   ☐ Type B
- ☐ Seasonal Commercial(s)
- ☐ Test or Test Market Commercial(s)
- ☐ Non-Air Commercial(s)
- ☐ Produced For Cable
- ☐ Work In Smoke Required
- ☐ Spanish Language Translation Services

Producer engages Performer and Performer agrees to perform services
for Producer in television commercials as follows:

Commercial Title(s) and Code No(s) _____

No. of Commercials _____

Such commercial(s) are to be produced by _____
_____ (Advertising Agency)
(Address)

acting as agent for _____
(Advertiser)

_____ (Product(s))

City and State in which services rendered: _____ Place of Engagement: _____

( ) Principal Performer
( ) Stunt Performer
( ) Specialty Act
( ) Dancer
( ) Singer

( ) Solo or duo
( ) Group-3-5
( ) Group-6-8
( ) Group-9 or more
( ) Contractor

( ) Signature - solo or duo
( ) Group-Signature-3-5
( ) Group-Signature-6-8
( ) Group-Signature-9 or more
( ) Pilot

Classification: On Camera _____ Off Camera _____ Part to be Played _____

Compensation: _____ Date & Hr. of Engagement: _____

Check if: Flight Insurance ($11.30) Payable ☐
Wardrobe to be furnished by Producer ☐   by Performer ☐
If furnished by Performer, No. of Costumes @ $16.90_____ @ $28.20_____ Total Wardrobe Fee $ _____
(Non Evening Wear)   (Evening Wear)

☐ Performer does not consent to the use of his/her services made hereunder on the Internet.
☐ Performer does not consent to the use of his/her services in commercials made hereunder as dealer commercials payable at dealer commercial rates.
☐ Performer does not consent to the use of his/her services in commercials made hereunder on a simulcast.

The standard provisions printed on the reverse side hereof are a part of this contract. If this contract provides for compensation at SAG minimum, no addition, changes or alterations may be made in this form other than those which are more favorable to the Performer than herein provided. If this contract provides for compensation above SAG minimum, additions may be agreed to between Producer and Performer which do not conflict with the provisions of the SAG Commercials Contract, provided that such additional provisions are separately set forth under "Special Provisions" hereof and signed by the Performer.

Until Performer shall otherwise direct in writing, Performer authorizes Producer to make all payments to which Performer may be entitled hereunder as follows:
☐ To Performer at _____
(Address)
☐ To Performer c/o _____ at _____
(Address)

All notices to Performer shall be sent to the address designated above for payments and, if Performer desires, to one other address as follows:
To_____
(Name)   (Address)
All notices to Producer shall be addressed as follows:
To Producer at _____
(Address)
This contract is subject to all of the terms and conditions of the applicable Commercials Contract. Employer of Record for income tax and unemployment insurance purposes is _____
(Name)   (Address)
PRODUCER (NAME OF COMPANY) _____
The Performer has the right to consult with his/her representative or Union before signing this contract.

BY_____ PERFORMER _____

Performer hereby certifies that he/she is 21 years of age or over. (if under 21 years of age this contract must be signed below by a parent or guardian.) I, the undersigned, hereby state that I am the _____of the above named Performer and do hereby consent and give my permission to this agreement.
(Mother, Father, Guardian)

_____
(Signature of Parent or Guardian)

SPECIAL PROVISIONS (including adjustments, if any, for Stunt Performers):

Performer acknowledges that he/she has read all the terms and conditions
in the Special Provisions section above and hereby agrees thereto.   _____
(Performer)

IMPORTANT PROVISIONS ON BACK. PLEASE READ CAREFULLY.

2179-123

191

working while others are not. Lighting people may be setting lights while sound people are inactive. Just stay out of the way of those who seem to be working, and watch. Keep those eyes and ears open and you'll learn a lot.

- Everyone you are introduced to is important, whether it's an agency producer or a makeup person. Write down names in your journal and remember them. Hopefully, you will work with them again, and remembering their names is an incredible leg up!

- Report to the A.D. as soon as you arrive. Don't just assume that she knows you're there. Ask where she is, find her, and report in. She will tell you when to report to makeup and wardrobe and will give you a contract to fill out and sign. The previous page has a typical SAG contract.

WHAT DO I DO WHEN THE LOCATION IS OUT OF TOWN?

Yippee! You get a free trip!

- Even though air travel isn't a lot of laughs these days, the flight and the hotel accommodations will be, in most cases, first-class, so you should have a comfortable time.

- Make sure you have your ticket or electronic ticket and passport if you need it; know exactly where you will be staying and how you're supposed to get from the airport to the hotel.

- Always have a contact name and telephone number for both the day and the evening in case of a late plane arrival.

- If it's at all possible, carry your luggage rather than check it in through baggage. You'll not only save yourself time on both ends, but you'll be pretty sure it won't end up being mistakenly shipped to Tehran.

- You'll be given a per-diem amount, usually in cash, for your expenses.

- Save your receipts. The IRS will want proof of your expenditures.

In the old days, flying to location for a job was pretty easy and a lot of fun. You were always in first-class on the airplane, there weren't long lines for check-in, you didn't have to remove your shoes and belt to be screened, and the travel day was pretty much hassle-free. I subscribed to and always carried the North American issue of the OAG flight guide, a monthly schedule of the times of every flight in the country. If I finished a job in New York early, I'd take a quick look at my OAG, see if there was an earlier flight going to Los Angeles out of Newark instead of La Guardia, make a quick phone call, use the same ticket, and get home a couple of hours earlier. I always looked at it as sort of a game in those days.

Unless you're living on another planet and haven't flown anywhere lately, you know that those easy travel days don't exist anymore. Even though you almost always still get to fly first-class, the travel day is tough and the screening lines are long. My advice is that if you have a location job out of town, resist the temptation to make your own travel arrangements and let the ad agency or production company book your flight for you. If you book your own flight and the flight is delayed or canceled, it's your fault and you're in hot water. If the delayed or canceled flight is one that *they* booked, it's not your fault. Still, always double-check the flight arrival and departure times to make sure that a delay will not present a life-and-death situation as far as the shoot is concerned.

And if you have a choice when to fly home, don't opt to be flown out right after the shoot is scheduled to wrap, but choose to fly home the following morning. The job may run late, you'll be looking at your watch, and you'll have put additional stress on yourself.

A thousand years ago I was playing "Hero" in *A Funny Thing Happened on the Way to the Forum* at South Coast Repertory in Costa Mesa, California. I auditioned for (and got) a Right Guard Deodorant commercial that was to shoot in San Francisco the same day as one of the show's evening performances. I double-checked with the production company to see if I could be back in Southern California in time for an eight o'clock p.m. curtain and they assured me there wouldn't be a problem. What I didn't do was tell the theater folks that I had booked a job in San Francisco, thinking the less they knew, the better. So I caught the late, night-before flight out of Orange County to the

City by the Bay, and checked into the hotel room they had set up for me, ready to work the following morning. During the whole workday, I worried that I wouldn't make my flight back to Orange County in time for curtain, kept looking at my watch, and I don't think I did my best work on the commercial. Of course, we finished late, but there was still ample time to make my flight and the show. Unfortunately, as soon as I got to San Francisco airport I discovered (naturally) that the plane had mechanical trouble and was grounded. Panicked, I found out that there were no other flights to Orange County that would arrive in time for me to make curtain, but there *was* a flight on another airline from another terminal headed for LAX leaving in twenty minutes. I ran as fast as I could to the other terminal and got there in time to make a desperate call to the theater (they weren't too pleased) before my flight took off.

One of the theater's front-office folks raced to LAX, picked me up at the curb, and we raced down the freeway at ninety miles per hour, spending much of that time to the right of traffic driving down the shoulder. I changed into my costume in the car (he forgot my sandals), got to the theater at the end of the overture, ran onstage, barefoot, for the first scene ("Hero" sings the first solo), and gave one of the worst adrenaline-pumping performances of my life. (As I recall, I was even wearing my wristwatch.) A total of two bad performances, four hundred miles apart in one day. I learned my lesson, so after that—*no más!*

WHAT CAN I DO TO FIT IN ON THE SET?

This is a tough one. Remember that many of the crew members may have worked with one another before and they might be friends off the set. Just be aware that everyone new to the set will be feeling what you feel. (Remember that first day of school?) Just be nice to everyone and do what you can to get to know people. When someone isn't busy, go over and introduce yourself. Talk to the sound person about what he does, how he got started, and the equipment he has. One thing's for certain, he's a sound professional because he loves sound! Ask his advice on some equipment you're thinking about buying. Talk to the makeup artist and ask about the interesting jobs she's done. Try to learn all you can about what each person does. If you do, you'll be remembered as an actor who is interested and interesting. You'll make some valuable acquaintances and you'll be spending your idle time constructively. Who knows, on the next job you do, some of those same people may be on the crew. Finally, the best way to have people appreciate you and your work as talent is to do what's expected of you and do it well. Know your words, work hard, listen carefully, and be accessible, friendly, and respectful.

WHO IS REALLY IN CHARGE ON THE SET?

Good question. The director, even though he is employed by the ad agency or the production company, is the one in charge of the day. Anyone who wants to give you direction must first go through the director. The purpose of this is to avoid situations where the actor might get conflicting information on how to do something or say a line. If you find that you are getting direction from more than one source, just smile and do what's asked of you by the director. They'll eventually work out their problems. Any questions you have about staging or delivery of lines should be aimed at the director.

For every director in the business, there is a different personality. Some directors like to work with actors; some do not. Keep in mind that the director's personality and style of working were developed long before you walked onto the set. Just smile, do your best work, and don't let someone else's problems affect you. I've worked with a lot of directors over the years. I've seen directors use their power to try to sleep with actresses (and succeed); I've seen directors use foul language with small children; and I've seen directors intimidate and demean actors until they could no longer perform. Some of the kindest people I've ever known also have happened to be directors. Just be prepared. Directors are not required to take a standardized psychological test for compatibility. Some are nice people; some are not.

WILL I GET TIME TO REHEARSE ON THE SET?

Definitely. However, this is not a time to work on your lines. You'll be expected to know them cold. You'll probably be doing each scene many times during rehearsal to work out problems with lighting, timing, camera movement and focus, product placement, and a hundred other things. While everyone else is working on his own area of responsibility, make sure you're working on yours: You'll need to integrate the blocking with your already-memorized words so that there is a logical connection between the two.

Once your business is worked out, the director will want a number of variations. It's not uncommon to do a line or a piece of business a hundred times. If the director asks you to speed up the timing of a line or change a line or the delivery of a line, make sure you try it on your own before you try it out on camera. When you rehearse or are asked to "run through the copy for time," there may be a tendency not to do it full out. Resist that temptation. Do full movements and give full-out readings. If you don't, the timing will change and you will have done the "run-through" for naught. One of the most difficult things for an actor to do is repeat what he did and not vary the reading, business, or timing. It takes careful work during the rehearsal process to iron out and lock in what you're to do. Use the rehearsal time and use it well!

WHAT ABOUT DOING MY OWN STUNTS IN COMMERCIALS?

When an actor is required to do a stunt in a commercial, a full description of the stunt will be disclosed prior to the audition at the time of hiring. The actor is entitled to stunt pay, which should not be less than a scale session fee but may be more if your talent agent is able to negotiate more. But, unless you are qualified, never volunteer to do stunts. Don't think you're being a hero by volunteering. Almost every year, actors (and stuntmen!) are seriously hurt and even killed because they were doing stunts. If it seems unsafe, it is. Just because the camera operator has no qualms about hanging from a rope dangling from a helicopter, it doesn't mean you shouldn't. Sometimes *macho* is just another word for "dumb." If you have any concerns at all, call your talent agent and let her deal with it. It's far better to lose a day's work than to lose an appendage...

I once did a television show where my character (I was a kidnapper!) had to drive fast across some railroad tracks, hit the brakes, skid sideways to a stop, and get out and run. Sounded pretty easy and I drive well, so I told the A.D. that I could probably do the stunt. The A.D. said they had already hired a stuntman to do it, and then he left to set up the shot. What I didn't know was that the stuntman was standing nearby and had heard me talk to the A.D. He approached me after the A.D. had left. In a nice way, he said that my willingness to do the stunt, even though it looked pretty easy, would take away his day's work. I apologized and said I'd learned a lesson. During the shot, the car door malfunctioned as the car was skidding sideways, and the stuntman fell out onto the pavement, getting dragged by the side of the car. He was hurt, but he got up and ran like he was supposed to. They were able to use the shot, but I learned two lessons that day: Stunts can be dangerous, and not doing them myself means that someone else gets to work.

Cris tells of one of his actors who was just starting his career and booked a spot. When he showed up on the set and signed his contract, the riggers put him in a harness and he spent the entire day (with overtime) suspended from a wire. After the day finally ended, the actor went home. When he woke up the next morning, he was black and blue and in enormous pain. He called Cris, who promptly called the casting director. The casting director said that the actor had knowingly signed the contract and there was nothing he could do. Rather than file a claim with SAG and ruffle feathers, Cris decided to just let it go and move on. The actor was sore for a week and, to this day, will not hesitate to call his agent if he has any doubts or questions concerning the shoot.

WHAT ABOUT WORKING WITH CHILDREN?

Working with children is even more difficult than auditioning with them. They're just kids and they usually just act like kids: unpredictable.

Your shoot-day schedule will change because there will be on-the-set schooling and strict time-of-working guidelines that are set up by the governing authorities of each state. Often, if the kids are little, they will cast twins so they can have one child on break while they work with the other. It is always best to leave any directing of the children completely up to the director.

WHAT ABOUT WORKING WITH ANIMALS?

This presents some of the same problems that are on the set when you are working with children. Animals may not have to go to school or have work time restrictions, but, just like kids, they are unpredictable. Don't try to be friendly and bond with the animal. Don't pet the animal unless the on-set animal trainer says you can—and listen very closely to everything the trainer says. Above all, be careful.

I've worked with a kangaroo (stay away from the front feet and the tail), a reindeer (they stink, and their antlers are dangerous), wild turkeys (they spit blood when they're upset), pigeons (they seem to aim before they poop), a cow (one of nature's dumbest animals), a huge crow (who bit me on the ear), a Bengal tiger (who bit one of the actresses on the leg), and the usual array of horses, cats, and dogs. Frankly, I'd rather work with an adult human being.

ARE THERE ANY SECRETS TO SHAVING OFF TENTHS OF SECONDS WHEN READING COPY?

Actually, there is, and an old voice-over veteran taught it to me. If you are doing spokesperson copy and need to shave a tenth of a second off your reading, just give the reading exactly the same delivery and tempo you've been using. When you get to the very last phrase, hurry it up just a touch. No one will notice any difference in your reading, and they'll think you're a technically brilliant actor because you nailed it! If you need to shave two-tenths off, do the same thing with the last two phrases. The trick is to make sure the rest of the copy is always consistent.

ANYTHING I SHOULD DO JUST BEFORE THEY START SHOOTING?

Set yourself up and be prepared for the first piece of business you're going to do or the words you're going to say. Do it just like you did during rehearsal and you'll do fine.

HOW DO I KNOW WHEN THE SHOOTING'S BEGUN AND THE SCENE STARTS?

The assistant director will usually ask for quiet ("Quiet on the set!"), give the cue to the sound person ("Roll sound"), to which the sound person will respond ("Speed"). Then the A.D. will tell camera to begin recording ("Roll camera"), and the camera operator will respond ("Camera's rolling"). At this point, an electronically timed slate or a standard slate with clacker will be put in front of the camera. If it is a standard slate held by an assistant, the clacker will be dropped on the slate to make a sound. The purpose of either slate is to coordinate sound with picture later on for the editor. The director may then ask for quiet again or just say, "Action." At that point, you should wait a split second for your action or words to begin or the scene to start so you don't overlap with the director's command to begin.

A couple of things may happen to unnerve you a bit. When shooting on a soundstage, and the sound person is given the instruction to roll sound, he will also push a button that either blows a horn or rings a loud buzzer. Either one can be disconcerting. You'll notice that things get deathly silent. Another thing you'll notice is that if the camera is tightly focused on your face for a shot, the slate and clacker business will happen right in front of your face. I've found it to be a good idea to start a bit of relevant body movement just before the director says, "Action." It warms you up to begin the scene, gets you moving before you say your first words, and you won't be coming from a dead stop as the scene begins.

WHAT ABOUT OVERTIME?

Yippee! This means you're making more money. Commercial shoots can sometimes last for many, many hours, so it's not a good idea to make plans for the evening. If you've purchased hard-to-get tickets for the latest hit musical after the shoot, you'll end up worrying all day long about making curtain on time.

THAT'S A WRAP!

When the shoot day is over, the director will double-check with the advertising agency folks and the script supervisor to make sure all the shots have been completed to everyone's satisfaction. At that point the A.D. will announce, "That's a wrap for talent!" The day may be over for you as an actor, but the crew will most likely work much later striking the lights and set. Wrap time can be a good time to thank everyone whom you worked with during the day, and if you *do* remember some names when you thank folks, you'll have gained some friends.

It can also be a time to socialize. After wrap is called, on many shoots they will provide some soft drinks, beer, wine, and finger foods, and it's fine to take part. During the postwrap gathering, be as polite, respectful, and nice as you were during the day. But a warning: Never have more than one drink after a wrap. Ever. You don't want to tarnish that professional image you worked so hard to develop and maintain during the day, and word travels fast in this business. If you want to have that second glass of wine, wait until you get home. (On the same note, the postwrap gathering is also not a good time to bare your soul to the craft service gal.)

Congratulations! You've made it through your first workday! You may now, officially, call yourself a professional, working actor! Hopefully, those you worked with were impressed by your preparation, your dedication, your knowledge, your professionalism, your sincerity, and your friendliness. Not only was your goal to do a good job on your first commercial, your goal was to make those whom you worked with want to work with you again.

HOW SOON AFTER I SHOOT THE COMMERCIAL WILL I SEE MYSELF ON TV?

Maybe never. Many commercials run nationally, many run regionally, many run locally, many run in a test market, and many don't run at all. Your agent will know the *intended* use of the spot, but that's about it. Some commercials may be kept in a holding cycle for a long time and then finally see some airtime. Once I did a test commercial for Coast soap (I think I made a bit of a career out of playing the dumb husband). I was paid my session fee and subsequent holding fees every thirteen weeks for what seemed like forever. Following my own advice, I happily put my holding cycle checks in the bank and forgot about the spot. Two *years* later, my agent called. He'd renegotiated and I finally got to see my spot on the air. It ran nationally class A for a very long stretch. Another time, for Breck Shampoo, I was hired to sit on the edge of a water fountain and react to a beautiful girl with great hair who just happened to be walking by. (It wasn't very hard to do.) We filmed that spot on 35 mm film late on a Friday afternoon and the commercial was on the air, nationwide, the following Monday.

WHAT ABOUT SENDING THANK-YOU NOTES?

A great idea! Always be courteous. You can e-mail your note if you'd like, but I think a short, handwritten note is much more effective. (Maybe it's just the commitment of going out to buy a stamp that makes it more memorable.) Write a short note to the casting director who called you in for the job, the director, the client (if a client rep was on the set), the advertising agency folks, and anyone else whom you met and got an address for. There's usually a call sheet on the set that has all the contact information. If you have a photo-postcard or a photo–business card that you can use for your note or include with it, it'd be a good idea. These folks spent the day with you on the set, and they are more apt to recognize your face than remember your name.

IS IT POSSIBLE TO GET A COPY OF THE COMMERCIAL?

Your best contact for this is through the ad agency producer, and writing a thank-you note will help you get a copy. Always mention that you'd love to *pay* for a copy of the spot. Normally, no one likes to release a copy of the spot until it's ready to air, so you might have to wait awhile. Usually, they'll just send you a DVD for no charge. A lot depends on the success of the shoot day, your timing, your contact person, and your thank-you note.

From day one I always tried to get copies of all my commercials. At the beginning, they were sent to you in 16 mm, then in ¾-inch video format, then on Beta, then on VHS videotape, and finally on a DVD. I have literally thousands of them and have had them all converted to DVDs. (Any time you're in the area, stop by and you can watch a "Squire Fridell Film Festival." It's perfect for people who have short, thirty-second attention spans.)

SHOULD I KEEP A FILE ON EACH COMMERCIAL I SHOOT?

You bet. In the same way you recorded all your audition information in your journal, also write down everything about your workday. If you got a contact sheet on the day of the shoot, listing everyone's name, include it. Make notes about the things you learned and write down every person's name you came in contact with and what they did on the shoot. Your goal in this business is to work *again* for some of the same folks you just worked for. You *will* bump into these people again and again. What better way to greet someone than calling them by name and playing "remember when" about the shoot you did together. Amazingly, because I've been around for so long and shot so many commercials, there is not a location I can travel to or a job that I can do where I don't discover either a cast or a crew member on the set whom I've worked with before. Honest.

On the next page is an example of a file that I would use to log my jobs.

ON-CAMERA SPOTS					
DATE	# SPOTS	YTD # SPOTS	TOTAL # SPOTS	PRODUCT	LOCATION/MISCELLANEOUS
4-Jan	2	2	362	Toyota	Nashville for TCAA/Boothby
17-Jan	1	3	363	Alcoa	LA/Gips
28-Jan	1	4	364	Bud Lite	LA/Eggers
9-Feb	6	10	370	Toyota	Boston for TCAA/Boothby
19-Feb	2	12	372	Wicks	LA

CHAPTER 14

THE MONEY

Put money in thy purse.

—*Hamlet*, by William Shakespeare

NOW THAT I'M GOING TO MAKE MY LIVING AS A COMMERCIAL ACTOR, HOW SOON SHOULD I QUIT MY DAY JOB?

Don't do it just yet. A lot of actors will get started, book a couple of commercials, and then make the mistake of giving two weeks' notice. Not a good idea. As long as you can get the time off to go out on auditions during the day, keep your *real* job. Most SAG and AFTRA actors, particularly in the beginnings of their careers, rely on other vocations for their livelihood and supplement that income with acting. Some are secretaries, photographers, computer programmers, clerks, salespeople, teachers, substitute teachers, waiters, bartenders, or parking attendants. And for obvious reasons, many actors find it's easier if they have a day job that starts at the *end* of the normal workday. That's why you'd be hard-pressed to find any actor who hasn't been a waiter or a bartender at one time or another. Me included.

My advice: Keep your real job and try to make the hours flexible enough to squeeze in auditions. That way you'll have enough income to live on, and you won't have that desperate look about you when you go in for an audition. As soon as it becomes a situation where you *must* have that job or you'll be evicted from your apartment, you'll blow the audition. They said it best in *A Chorus Line* with the song "I Really Need This Job"! There's also an old saying: "Nobody hires a hungry actor."

HOW OFTEN WILL I BE GOING OUT ON AUDITIONS SO I CAN GET JOBS AND MAKE MONEY?

Beats me. It depends a lot on what you've done up to this point, how much you can self-promote, how many commercial classes and improv classes you've taken, and how much your talent agent sends you out. It's an enormously competitive business out there and any actor who just sits around waiting for his phone to ring will not be successful. There's no rhyme or reason why things happen when they do (or why things don't happen when they should), so you have to be as proactive as you can. If you hustle, you'll be more successful.

Unless you've sworn to live a life of poverty, everyone likes money, and life is a lot easier and more fun if you have some of it. The purpose of this chapter is to let you know how (and how much) commercial actors are paid. Most important, it's to offer a little advice on how to keep your share of those dollars you've earned.

HOW—AND HOW MUCH—DO I GET PAID?

The current SAG contract is a whopping 236 pages long. A lot of it has to do with the different amounts an actor is to be paid, depending on a lot of criteria, but in a nutshell, this is how to figure it out:

Session Fee
Currently, an on-camera SAG-AFTRA principal actor is to be paid $567.10 for an eight-hour day, which shall also constitute payment for the first commercial made for one designated advertiser. In other words, his salary for the day's work is $567.10 and is called a "session fee." However, each commercial isn't always completed in one day and things can get complicated.

Let's take a look at three scenarios, all of which will pay the actor the same amount for one commercial booking.

SCENARIO ONE

Let's suppose you work as principal talent for three days and appear on camera in one commercial. Your fee will be three days of session fees for a total of $1,701.30 ($567.10 × 3).

SCENARIO TWO

Let's suppose you work as principal talent for three days and appear on camera in three commercials for a designated advertiser. Your session fees will be $1,701.30 ($567.10 × 3).

SCENARIO THREE

Now let's suppose you work as principal talent for one day and appear in three commercials for a designated advertiser. Your fee will be $567.10 for the session fee for the one commercial *plus* an additional $1,134.20 ($567.10 × 2) for a total of $1,701.30 for the extra two commercials.

Each of the above scenarios would pay you $1,701.30 as a principal actor.

THEY ALL AMOUNT TO THE SAME AMOUNT OF MONEY, SO WHAT'S THE DIFFERENCE?

Good question. Which scenario would potentially be best for the actor?
The answer?
The third scenario.

WHY WOULD THAT BE A BETTER OPTION?

In the first scenario, the actor had to work three days to shoot one commercial. Three days' work and only one spot. In the second scenario, the actor had to work three days to shoot three commercials. Three spots are terrific, but it took three days out of his life. In the third scenario, the actor had to work only one day, but he shot three commercials!

WHY IS THAT IMPORTANT?

Two reasons:

- Each commercial is an independent entity worth a holding fee every thirteen weeks. Three commercials equals three holding fees every thirteen weeks!

- If each of those commercials gets on the air, the potential of rerun residuals for three commercials is three times greater! Bingo!

WHAT ARE RESIDUALS AGAIN?

Residuals are what actors thrive on and live for. This is the money that is paid to the actor each and every time his commercial is broadcast on the air. Residual amounts can vary greatly depending on whether a commercial runs prime time, wild spot, local, on cable, on the Internet, or foreign. They all have separate fee structures. The payment amounts are also on a degrading scale until the thirteen-week cycle is over and then payments begin fresh again.

WHAT OTHER THINGS ARE IN THE SAG CONTRACT THAT I NEED TO KNOW ABOUT?

Buyout

It's not uncommon to do a commercial for a buyout, but it's usually not too good for the actor financially. This is an arrangement among the client or agency, the actor, and his talent agent, agreeing on a one-time payment for services rendered with no other fees due, including holding fees and usage. Typically, the buyers expect unlimited usage forever and ever with no further compensation to the actor. Your talent agent is the best judge of whether a buyout is a good option.

Commercials That Are Wild Spots

The session fee for a wild spot commercial is the same, but the commercial is broadcast by noninterconnected, single stations and is aired independent of any program. That means the potential audience is smaller than that of a class-A program commercial, so the pay is considerably less for each airing. Different geographical markets are given different "unit weights" by SAG, and the actor is paid accordingly. A unit weight is calculated according to the number of "television households." Markets with fewer than 700,000 television households are given one unit. Seven hundred thousand to 1,049,999 are given two units, and so on. Philadelphia, for instance, has a unit weight of 8 while San Diego has a unit weight of 2.

Commercials That Are Class A, B, or C

Class A, B, and C spots are all within-program commercials and are rated according to their market share. Class-A commercials are broadcast in over twenty cities; class-B commercials are broadcast in six to twenty cities; and class-C commercials are broadcast in one to five cities. However, New York, Chicago, and Los Angeles count as eleven cities each, so if your commercial is within-program and plays in any two of the above cities, you've got a class-A commercial. These pay the best in residuals.

Commercials That Are Test Spots

A test spot commercial is one that will be aired in a small market and then monitored for its effectiveness. You must be told the commercial will be a test commercial before the audition. Years ago in New York, I did a test commercial for Coca-Cola that the ad agency held on to for years, paying me my holding fee every thirteen weeks. It ended up being renegotiated by Michael Bloom, my New York agent, became a class-A spot, ran nationally for years, and became one of my all-time moneymaker commercials. You never know.

Exclusivity

Your holding fee is paid to maintain your exclusivity to that particular product, and you cannot perform in commercials for any competing products while you're being held. For example, you cannot do two commercials for competing clients in take-out foods, cosmetics, automobiles, or toilet paper. If the ad agency fails to send you your holding fee in the prescribed amount of time, you are automatically released, but I'd make sure to have your talent agent contact the advertiser to be absolutely certain. If a mistake is made on your part, it can be a very sticky and costly situation, so don't assume anything until your agent makes that call to see if you are, in fact, released.

Holding Fee

Every thirteen weeks from your first day of employment, the advertiser must pay you your original session fee in order to keep the commercial viable for airing. If he lets the time period lapse, you are released from that product exclusivity and may appear in a competing product commercial. The holding fee will usually be credited against any use fees or residuals. The exception for this thirteen-week holding fee rule is for seasonal commercials, because they air only during holidays. Advertisers need not pay the thirteen-week holding fees for seasonal spots.

Location

Any exterior setting away from a studio set is referred to as a location. You can be on location close to home within driving distance, but if you go on location away from home, you'll be lodged and flown first-class, depending on the distance. If you travel one thousand or more air miles, first-class transportation shall be provided. Under a thousand miles, you'll usually be flown coach. The client, ad agency, or production company will foot the bill.

Meal Periods

This is your lunch or dinner (or breakfast!) break, and the time is deducted from your day.

Per Diem

Expense money given to you (usually in cash) while on location for each day that you are away from home.

Overscale: Double Scale/Triple Scale

This is two or three times the normal scale residual rate that is some-times successfully negotiated by your talent agent to make you (and him) more money. It usually applies only if the actor's talent agent has been successful in negotiating an overscale contract for the services of a popular actor. After I'd been working for Toyota for a while, for instance, my L.A. agent was successful in negotiating a nice overscale contract. And then, every few years, he would renegotiate.

Overscale: Guarantee

This is usually an increased amount of money for actors who are in demand and work often. An agent may negotiate an overscale guaran-tee of up-front money per thirteen-week cycle, usually with all resid-ual usage deducted from the guarantee. Should the usage exceed the guaranteed amount within any thirteen-week cycle, the in-excess residuals are paid out to the actor.

Sometimes a guarantee will also include a stipulation that the usage be applied at a multiple (two or three times) of scale. My Mc-Donald's long-term contract, for instance, was paid with an overscale guarantee.

Overtime

Over eight hours and up to ten hours, talent will be paid time and a half; over ten hours constitutes double time.

Session Fee

The money you are paid for the initial day's work on a commercial. It is usually a scale amount.

Travel Days

For travel days to and from work you are paid a session fee of $567.10. And, as you know, if you fly one thousand miles or more, you must be supplied with a first-class ticket.

Wardrobe Call

You're paid for your wardrobe call at $70.89 an hour ($567.10 divided by 8 hours). If the advertiser wants you to use your personal wardrobe for the shoot, the use fee is $16.90 per change for nonevening clothing, and $28.20 for each change for evening wear.

Weather Day
If the commercial is to be shot outdoors, you may be given a weather day. It means that if the day is supposed to be sunny and it rains and the shoot day doesn't take place, the day will be postponed until the weather is right for the shoot. When this happens you'll receive a half-day's pay for each of the canceled days.

When You Are Downgraded
This is when someone hires an actor as a principal and then moves her to a lower category. If the commercial is edited so that you cannot be recognized or identified or you are not in the final cut of the commercial, you will be downgraded. You'll still get your daily session fee, but it will eliminate any possible residuals. A bummer.

When You Are Upgraded
The opposite of downgraded, and it's a good thing! If an extra was hired as atmosphere talent and the director used him as a principal, he would then be upgraded and be eligible for residuals. This sometimes happens in commercials where a scene or a moment develops on the set that was not part of the original storyboard, but the agency or director wants to keep it in the scene. Advertisers want to avoid this like the plague. It means they are going to go over budget because they didn't plan on an additional principal nor did they plan on paying additional residuals. I've worked on a bunch of different Toyota spots over the years where an extra was worked into a scene and was upgraded to a principal. It always made me smile.

Working On a Holiday or a Saturday or Sunday
It's called golden time! You're paid a premium of double time if you work on a holiday or a Saturday or Sunday. That's $1,134.20 a day in session fee! Just hope for overtime on top of that!

WHO FIGURES ALL THIS OUT?

Obviously, the amount that you'll end up being paid for a commercial is a big question and there are pages and pages of calculations and formulas. After you've done the commercial, leave the math-checking to your talent agent.

All the monies due you are paid by the advertiser (sometimes through another firm that specializes in talent pay), taxes are taken out, and then the balance is usually forwarded directly to your talent agent, who takes out his 10 percent from the original gross amount. Your agent then sends you a check for your net amount. Agents are entitled to 10 percent of all session fees, holding fees, and residuals. (If it happens to be an AFTRA rather than a SAG job, the agent's 10 percent commission is customarily on top of the total gross amount.)

WHO KEEPS TRACK OF HOW MANY TIMES MY COMMERCIAL IS ON THE AIR?

Believe it or not, the ad agency that hired you.

HOW DO I KNOW I'M NOT BEING CHEATED?

You don't, but most of the mistakes happen only at the local level where somebody's looking for a quick filler on Channel 3 and your spot is thrown on the air. It's pretty rare that abuses happen, and it's of no advantage to the ad agency.

HOW COME?

The advertising agencies have a media package agreement with their clients. They tell them that for a certain amount of money they will put a particular commercial (or campaign of commercials) on the air in a number of markets. They show the client (in great detail) when and where the commercial spots will run and how many times they plan to air the commercials. The talent is then paid according to that report. The client won't cheat you, because they're not in a position to do so. The ad agency doesn't want to cheat you, because if your commercial plays *more* than they've indicated, they'll have to pay the network or the station for that airtime and are not reimbursed by the client. And, unless it's a mistake, a network or local station won't play the spot because nobody's paying to have it aired.

I once did a dozen or so commercials as spokesman for Magic Mountain just north of Los Angeles. They were terrific commercials shot on location at the amusement park, and after a good on-the-air run, I was notified that the campaign was off the air and I was thus released. About a month later, one of my former high school students called me and said he'd seen one of the spots on the air the night before. I quizzed him about the time he'd seen it, and the channel, and then promptly called my agent, who then called the local SAG office. SAG checked into the station's log and discovered that they had "mistakenly aired the spot." I was paid a penalty *plus* an additional thirteen-week holding fee. Yippee! You'll be pleased to note that the following week I rewarded my former student by taking him out to dinner. At McDonald's ...

ONCE I BOOK A COMMERCIAL, HOW MUCH MONEY WILL I MAKE?

Don't quit your day job and buy that new house just yet. Booking a commercial does not guarantee that the commercial will ever see airtime, nor does it guarantee that you will be in the final cut if it does air. A commercial's intended run can also change. You may be told at the time of hiring that it is the intention of the advertiser to air the spot as a national class-A commercial. Again, there's no guarantee. The advertising agency may decide to not run the spot at all, or they may elect to hold the commercial on a thirteen-week cycle. If that's the case, the only money you can count on is your session fee. At the time this book is published, SAG scale for the day is $567.10, based on an eight-hour day with no overtime. You may also have some wardrobe fees if they ask you to use you own clothes, and some rehearsal or audition overtime fees.

HOW MUCH MONEY DOES THE USUAL COMMERCIAL MAKE IN RESIDUALS?

Again, that's hard to say because there's no such thing as a "usual commercial." You can make a session fee and that's all—or the commercial can be a class-A spot and play for years. If that happens, you'll make a bunch of money. My advice is to just do the job and forget it. If it plays, you'll get some surprises in the mail. If it doesn't, you won't be disappointed.

The *least* amount I've ever made on a commercial was the session fee for a day's work (that was a whopping $136 back in the old days). The commercial never aired and after thirteen weeks, I was released. The *most* money for one individual spot that I did was for Coca-Cola. The spot was on the air for over four years and grossed a little over $31,000. That was a good one!

The most profitable individual commercial I've ever shot was for Toyota. It was the first spot for Toyota that I auditioned for, and even though it was originally for one commercial, it was the spot that led to twenty-eight *years* of consecutive work as a spokesperson for Toyota! But since you're asking about averages, I once calculated that the average for me was somewhere around $3,300 per spot. I think that's a little high, but that's what the math said . . .

Cris Dennis tells a story about booking a set of baby twins for a milk commercial. The spot was for a baby and, because of the labor laws, a common practice has always been to hire twins so they can work one at a time while the other rests, allowing a lot more to get done in a day. Even though there was only one child in the commercial, both were paid residuals because they were both used in the spot. The commercial went well, was very funny, and won some awards in the advertising community. The spot ran for a few years and was finally pulled off the air. Then, every few years or so after the spot had stopped airing, Cris would get a call from the agency wanting to rerun the commercial, so he would negotiate a higher rate each time. This happened any number of times, and Cris said that the final negotiation was when the twins were just finishing their fourth year of college. The mother told Cris that both kids had been put through college for that one day's work when they were babies. Now, *that* was a good gig!

Another client of Cris' had two offers of work that came in simulta-neously: One was for a beer commercial that was to shoot for five days in Hawaii and the other was a cat food spot scheduled to shoot for one day in Los Angeles. Both spots were scheduled to run nationally, so the actor chose the Hawaii shoot. I'm probably right in saying that we'd all rather go to Hawaii for a five-day shoot than have a one-day job in L.A. The long and short of it? The beer commercial shot in Hawaii never aired. The cat food spot was edited into multiple spots and became a major campaign involving cats and people dancing together and was on the air for years. Go figure...

HOW CAN I KEEP (AS MUCH AS POSSIBLE OF) THE MONEY THAT I MAKE?

Right off the bat, your agent gets 10 percent off the top if it's a SAG job. (Again, if it's an AFTRA job, customarily he'll make 10 percent of what you made but his commission will be on top of your total gross.) After you take out federal and state taxes, union dues, health and pension deductions, and a little for your IRA, you're looking at about half left over for you.

For some reason, actors are notoriously poor money handlers and because of that, many of them choose to hire business managers. The manager makes a spreadsheet, figures out a budget, pays all the actor's bills, and puts the actor on an allowance. The allowance and the budget are the good parts. The bad part is that business man-agers don't perform this service for free, and they take a big per-centage of the actor's earnings. There are also great risks whenever someone else handles your finances, and the horror stories are not few and far between. An old friend I once did a series with called me a few years back at Christmastime and said he had *good news* and he had *bad news*. The good news was that he'd had the best moneymaking year he'd ever had. The bad news? His business man-ager of the past ten years had "poorly invested" all his money and my buddy was broke.

With a little effort, you can invest well, put *yourself* on a budget, and be proud of the fact that you handle your own money smartly. Remember that it's not how much money you make in a year—it's what you're able to *save* that's important. Here are a few tips that I've found helpful. Some have been said before, but they are worth repeating.

- Don't quit your job when you decide to become an actor. Even if you initially have some luck, it takes time to get to a point where you can depend on acting as your primary source of money. And if you resign from your day job, it is questionable whether you are entitled to unemployment benefits.

- If you *do* make some money, resist the temptation to run out and spend it on all those things you've always wanted. There's a huge difference between *wanting* something and *needing* something.

- Right from the get-go, get yourself a savings plan. If you have another job and the acting income is a plus, live on your other job's wages and put all your acting income in some sort of interest-bearing savings account. Both SAG and AFTRA have credit unions, and a credit union is a great place to start putting your savings. They're owned and operated by the membership and usually pay a higher interest rate than banks, so go talk to them about your savings and let them help you set up a plan.

  As soon as I started to get my feet back on the ground after my "dark year" as an actor, (see The Life of an Actor, page 243) my father gave me a great tip that I took to heart. He told me to take 10 percent of the gross amount of *any* money that I made, whether it was from teaching, bartending, waiting tables, or acting, and put that money into an interest-bearing savings program. Within two years, I'd gotten completely out of debt, had enough money for a hefty down payment on my first house, and started buying some real estate. Because of that 10-percent savings commitment, I was able to make enough investments to guarantee my future and the future of my family. Thanks, Pop!

- As an actor, it is vital that you keep complete and accurate records of all monies spent to further your career. Remember that tax-deductible food item that my wife bought just before her audition for Lipton Lite Lunch? It may have been only a couple of bucks, but it was a write-off! And remember that your appointment book is a legal ledger and can be used in an audit.

• Be aware that your talent agent, in most cases, has your power of attorney—that means you've given him permission to cash your checks. Because I had a problem with my first agent "misappropriating" money from my first commercial job, whenever I do a commercial job, I enter it into a ledger and then list the gross amount of each and every check I get in the mail from my agent.

At the end of the year my figures should match my W-2 forms from each of the advertising agencies I've worked for. If the numbers don't match, there's something wrong. Either the check was lost in the mail (it happens) or somebody's got your earnings (that also happens). I've included an example below of a ledger of gross monies I received one year.

MONEY RECEIVED TO-DATE				
TOYOTA	**STEW STARTER**	**COAST SOAP**	**PILLSBURY**	**SCOTT'S TURF BUILDER**
S - $2,000.00 (1)	S - $ 582.50 (2)	R - $ 637.00 (1)	H - $ 218.00 (2)	S - $1,086.00 (1)
R - $1,793.60 (1)	H - $ 582.50 (5)	R - $ 239.00 (1)		R - $ 68.20 (3)
R - $ 220.00 (2)	H - $ 582.50 (9)	R - $ 478.00 (2)		R - $1,218.00 (4)
R - $ 220.00 (2)	H - $ 582.50 (12)	R - $ 198.00 (2)		H - $1,000.00 (7)
S - $ 582.50 (2)	R - $ 273.00 (12)	R - $ 195.00 (3)		

S = Session Fee; H = Holding Fee; R = Residual; (1)–(12) = Month Received

WHAT THINGS CAN I WRITE OFF?

A lot! But keep good records! There is a terrific, easy-to-use tax planner and organizer to keep track of all your expenses. It even has pockets for your receipts and is the best tax workbook for an actor I've seen. The title is *The Actor's Tax Workbook,* and you can find it either at your local bookstore, if it has a good theater section, or go online to get a copy. It breaks down all your expenses and categorizes them month-by-month. It's a little over twenty bucks *and it's also a write-off!*

You can write off anything you spend while you are looking for, getting, and keeping work as an actor. This would include things like headshots and résumés, demo tapes, trade journals and subscriptions, posting services, voice lessons, dance lessons, dance studio time, classes, and private coaching. Taxi, subway, and bus fares are all deductible if they are for auditions or for work. *You can also write off this book!* With expenses such as cable service, your computer, fax machine, copier, Internet provider, and cell phone, you need to allocate a percentage. For instance, if you're using your cell phone half the time for personal calls and half for business, then you can legitimately write off 50 percent of your phone and your monthly charges. If audited, you might be asked to bring in your bill showing which numbers you called. (It happened to me!) Your automobile expense write-offs would include miles driven to and from auditions, studio classes, voice lessons, and trips to mail your photos. Miles driven between different jobs is a deductible item and miles driven for medical and dental visits are also okay to deduct.

What is most important is that you have receipts and entries in your journal for these items. If you don't, you'll be fine unless you get that *You're being audited by the IRS* note in the mail!

CHAPTER 15

THE LIFE OF AN ACTOR

ACTORS PAY IN ADVANCE

—A sign in the window of a turn-of-the-century pub in London

If you've gotten this far in the book, you should have a pretty good idea of what the life of an actor is all about. That is, unless you've just picked up this book and are perusing it from back to front (I have a habit of doing that). An actor's life isn't an easy life, even if you do have success. In the introduction to this book, I briefly touched on how I got started as an actor and ended up making a pretty darn good living. But I talked only about the good part. Here's the rest of that story—I call it the "dark year."

After teaching high school for three years and acting a lot on the side, I was having some success as an actor, and I did precisely what I'm advising you *not* to do: I quit my day job to devote all my time to my new acting career. Fortunately, I only took a leave of absence (on the stellar advice of my father) and found another teacher who filled my drama teaching assignment.

To make the following year's tragic story very short, I quickly learned that I couldn't make much of a living doing occasional guest-starring parts on television shows. By the time the dark year was over, MasterCard had taken away my credit card, I was evicted from my apartment because I couldn't pay the rent, and I almost lost my car due to lack of payments. It was a dismal time in my life. I decided that being a full-time actor wasn't in the cards for me, so I substitute-taught for the remainder of the year and then, gratefully, took my teaching job back. I taught for six more years, even though I began to work more and more as an actor. After a total of nine years, I finally figured out that I didn't have the time to do both jobs well, so I quit teaching. That was a long time ago, but I still have nightmares remembering that terrible dark year.

HOW DO YOU DEFINE A *SUCCESSFUL* ACTOR?

My definition of a "successful actor" might surprise you. Success as an actor isn't being on the cover of *TV Guide* or having a TV series...or acting in a film and making a lot of money...or doing a commercial that was split into five spots and ran nationally for three years that made you a bunch of money. What makes an actor successful is merely that he or she *is an actor who works as an actor, year after year after year.*

There are some wonderfully gifted Equity actors whom I worked with at South Coast Repertory eons ago who are still there working as actors. They are wonderful actors, supporting themselves and their families, and they act for a living in a wonderful repertory theater group. Would you recognize them outside of Orange County? Probably not. Are they successful? You bet they are!

Each year Suzy and I head north to Ashland for the Oregon Shakespeare Festival, and we marvel at the hundred or so wonderfully gifted actors who are employed almost year-round, doing shows in repertory and providing some of the best theater entertainment in the world. Some of these company members are the most talented actors I've ever seen. Are they recognized outside of Ashland? Probably not. Are they successful? You bet they are! They're working actors! And they work year after year after year!

HOW DO YOU DEAL WITH ALL THE REJECTION?

Rejection is an always-present part of this business and you will always have to live with it. It makes no difference whether you've been in the business for a long time or if you're brand-new. On the one hand, you weren't chosen for the job because you're an untried commodity and you're unproven on the set. On the other hand, you find you're not chosen because you've been *too* successful and the advertiser thinks that you're overexposed. Or maybe you didn't get the job because you have blue eyes, red hair, weigh too much, weigh too little, are too tall or too short, or you look too much like the ad agency producer's ex-wife. For every job that you *do* get there will be many, many more that you did *not* get. Rejection is the nature of this business, and it's much more common than acceptance and employment.

At the height of my commercial career, when I was traveling back and forth between New York and Los Angeles for auditions and jobs, I figured out that my success ratio for commercials was one job for every eight auditions. I didn't know anyone who was working more than I was, but that was *still* seven times more that someone would say "NO!" for every time I heard a "YES!"

When you're into sales, it's a tough job. You're competing with all those other salespeople who also want to sell their brand to the customer. But as a salesperson, it's not too hard to divorce yourself from the product you're trying to sell. You can always rationalize your lack of sales on the fact that someone else's widget is better than your widget. Your ego's not involved with the product. Actors are into sales, too, except that they are selling *themselves. You* are the product and your ego *is* involved. And that makes it very hard to separate your feelings about your product . . . after all, it's *you* they are turning down. When you don't get a job, it's natural to begin to question your acting skills, your talent, your hairline, your figure, or the shape of your nose. After a number of rejections, it can get to the best of us, especially since we actors always seem to be looking for approval and are usually equipped with egos that are pretty fragile. Keep this in mind as you examine acting as a career. No matter how much you want to do it, if you can't face a lot of rejection on a daily basis, then I'd suggest that acting isn't the right choice for you.

Cris Dennis was a working actor and a member of SAG when he was seven years old. He said that he auditioned and booked work until the ripe old age of eleven, when the rejections started affecting him negatively. He and his parents decided to have him walk away and go back to playing Little League baseball. He says he became a much happier, healthier kid. His advice? When it's not fun and you no longer enjoy the process, you should do something else.

There's another pattern that's very disturbing that's come up as I've gotten older—all my friends who started out as young actors at the same time I did and found a degree of success, now find that they're not working very much. They no longer get those audition calls from their talent agents very often. This seems to affect women more than men, but as my friends have grown older, the advertising demographics have changed and the jobs have become increasingly scarce. I have to be honest and say that I know a lot of bitter actors who are contemporaries. A lot of them...

WHAT ABOUT SUCCESS?

Ah, the sweet smell of it.

When you're working, the highs in this business are wonderful. You feel wanted, talented, productive, and useful. Some of the best moments in my life have been associated with acting. There is no greater feeling in the world than making a fantastic living as an actor, doing what you love to do. There is no more exhilarating feeling than having an audience love what you've done. Unfortunately, those highs are scarce and short-lived, and the swing to the lows can be severe.

HOW DO YOU HANDLE THE STRESS?

I think it's good to have a plan of support for yourself so that you can even out those high-to-low periods a bit. These are a few ideas that have worked for me, and suggestions I've offered other actors over the years.

- First and foremost, make sure you have another source of steady income. Even if you happen to land that first commercial with your very first audition (that'd be a record!), make sure you keep that day job until you're *sure* that you can continue to eat, pay your rent, and pay your bills each month. I've already talked about my dark year and how I almost starved to death. (If it weren't for my mom mailing me a weekly care package of food, I would've been in a lot of trouble.)

- If you don't handle stress very well and don't have a way to eliminate stress, this is the wrong business for you. Your goal in life should be to be *happy*—and if trying to be an actor makes you *un*happy, then, for goodness' sake, do something else.

- Live within your income. That means to fully pay off your credit card bills each and every month and *never* just pay the minimum. The interest payments are just this side of a pound of flesh.

- If you can't afford to buy a new car (or anything else other than a house) with cash, don't buy it.

- Stay away from trying to alter your mood or tone down your stress with drink, marijuana, or other drugs. It may work for a bit, but it's a quick road to a questionable future. It can also make for a very short career. (I've got horror stories.)

- Keep busy. Even if you happen to be the favorite nephew of a rich uncle who is paying all your bills, get active and stay as busy and creative as you can. The busier you are, the less time you'll have to feel stress between those auditions. I've said it before and I will say it again: If you *ever* find yourself sitting at home staring at your TV or cell phone, you're both physically and mentally in the wrong place. Join a local theater group, take some acting classes, get some exercise, or just spend time doing things that make you happy, whether it's finding a new hobby or going to a movie. Waiting at home for your career to take off is neither realistic nor healthy.

- More than thirty-five years ago (how the time flies!) I did one of the most intelligent things I've ever done that helped my life and my career: I started Transcendental Meditation (TM), a simple relaxation technique done twice a day for twenty minutes that helps relieve stress and fatigue. It lowered my high blood pressure and gave me a badly needed stress-release valve. Many people in high-stress occupations regularly practice TM. It helped me in auditions and work on the set because I didn't get as stressed out. My wife started doing TM independently before we were married and found that it helped her in her dance career while she was living in New York, touring with the Nikolais Dance Theatre Company. A lot of people, including other actors whom I know well, swear by it and its effectiveness. My wife and I still meditate twice a day. (I just did the math and I figure that I've sat down to do my twenty-minute program over 25,000 times!)

- I talked about affirmations before, but over my office desk are two printed affirmations that I've had up for decades. The first is the last line from the original *Willy Wonka and the Chocolate Factory,* starring Gene Wilder. While in the airplane, he turns to the little boy and says, "Don't ever forget what happened to the man who suddenly got everything he always wanted. He lived happily ever after."

  The second affirmation is a take-off on a line from the film *Field of Dreams.* It reads, "If you want it, it will happen." Do affirmations work? I think so. I also know that it would scare me to stop.

GOT ANY PARTING THOUGHTS?

A couple of them . . .

I don't think that life *just happens.* It seems to be more of a series of connect-the-dot moments where one event in time leads to the next . . . making it possible for one thing to lead to another. Without each of those moments happening *when it did* and *in the sequence it did,* none of us would be where we are at this exact place in time. We might be somewhere, but we wouldn't be right here.

I don't think successful acting careers just happen either. It's fun to arrive at a play early enough to read the bios of the actors in the playbill. All of those actors are all acting in the same show that night, but each of them took a very different path to get there. The only thing they all have in common is that each has had a series of connect-the-dot moments that led her to *this* moment and *this* role in *this* play. In the same regard, when you're sitting in the theater reading that play-bill, there are also a whole series of those connect-the-dots in your life that put you in *that* theater seat to see *that* show on *that* particular night.

Looking back, there were a lot of moments in my life that eventually led me toward the life of an actor. And I never had a clue any of them were important until I'd gotten older and years had gone by. Meeting my longtime agent and friend, Pen Dennis, at precisely the right moment in my young life was a godsend. Being taken under the wing of Leonard Stern, an executive producer at Universal Studios, proved to greatly change the course of my life.

Teachers were enormously important for me. Were it not for the kindness of Mrs. Peck, way back in the fifth grade, the encouragement of Mrs. Moser, my speech teacher in high school, the talent of Harvey Berman, my drama teacher in junior college, the encouragement of Don Duns, the head of the speech department at the University of the Pacific, and the embrace of Omar Paxson at Occidental College . . . my life would be very different. When the first edition of this book appeared on bookshelves, I was able to find the addresses of those teachers and I sent each of them a copy. In it I wrote: "You may not even remember me, but you were a very significant moment in my life. Thank you." And you know what? Without any one of those folks (and plenty of others) in my life, you wouldn't be reading this book.

Well, that's it . . . that's everything I've learned and I can tell you about acting in television commercials. Hopefully, it has been of use to you, you're headed in the right direction, and you're on your way to enjoying success—and happiness!

Let me know if it helps you out. (You don't really have to send me 10 percent!)

Break a leg!

Squire Fridell

LISTING OF SAG AND AFTRA UNION OFFICES

The SAG and AFTRA offices listed in the next few pages are for reference only. Union offices, addresses, and contact information are always in a state of flux, so be sure to reread the Publications and Poopsheets chapter, do your research, and find the most current lists available.

It would be foolish to print all the commercial agents in the United States, and my suggestion is to subscribe to Ross Reports (see Publications and Poopsheets) to get the most up-to-date listings in your area.

Screen Actors Guild Branches

ARIZONA/UTAH BRANCH

3131 E. Camelback Road, Suite 200
Phoenix, AZ 85016
Tel. (602) 383-3780 or (800) 724-0767 ext. 7 / Fax (602) 383-3781
Don Livesay, dlivesay@sag.org

BOSTON BRANCH

20 Park Plaza
Suite 822
Boston, MA 02116
Tel. (617) 262-8001 or (800) 724-0767 ext. 7
Fax (617) 262-3006 or (800) 737-6105

CHICAGO BRANCH

1 East Erie, Suite 650
Chicago, IL 60611
Tel. (312) 573-8081 or (800) 724-0767 ext. 7
Fax (312) 573-0318 or (800) 599-1675
Hotline (312) 867-3710

COLORADO BRANCH
Market Square Center
1400 Sixteenth Street, Suite 400
Denver, CO 80202
Tel. (720) 932-8193 / Fax (720) 932-8194 or (800) 595-4256
Colorado Executive Director: Julie Crane, jcrane@sag.org
Administrative Assistant: Tamara Decker, tdecker@sag.org

DALLAS/FORT WORTH BRANCH
15950 N. Dallas Pkwy, Suite 400
Dallas, TX 75248
Tel. (972) 361-8185 or (800) 724-0767 ext. 7 / Fax (800) 311-3216
Linda Dowell, ldowell@sag.org
Trish Avery, tavery@sag.org
Jessica Oren, joren@sag.org

DETROIT BRANCH
Town Center
2000 Town Center, Suite 1900
Southfield, MI 48075
Tel. (248) 351-2678 or (800) 724-0767 ext. 7 / Fax (248) 351-2679
Marcia Fishman, mfishman@sag.org

FLORIDA BRANCH
7300 N. Kendall Drive, Suite 620
Miami, FL 33156-7840
Tel. (305) 670-7677 / Fax (305) 670-1813
Executive Director: Georgia Branch
Melissa Goodman, mgoodman@aftra.com

GEORGIA BRANCH
455 E. Paces Ferry Road NE, Suite 334
Atlanta, GA 30305
Tel. (404) 239-0131
Assistant Executive Director: Alison Wise, awise@aftra.com

HAWAII BRANCH
949 Kapi'olani Blvd., Suite 105
Honolulu, HI 96814
Tel. (808) 596-0388 / Fax (808) 593-2636
Executive Director: Brenda Ching, bching@sag.org

HOLLYWOOD BRANCH

The Hollywood Branch is the national headquarters in Los Angeles, California. It is the largest division in the Screen Actors Guild, with members residing in greater Los Angeles, Santa Barbara, and Orange and Riverside counties.

5757 Wilshire Blvd., 7th Floor
Los Angeles, CA 90036-3600
Tel. (323) 954-1600 / Fax (323) 549-6603
Executive Director: Ilyanne Morden Kichaven, hollywoodexec@sag.org
For deaf performers only: TTY/TTD (323) 549-6648

HOUSTON BRANCH

(through Dallas Branch)
15950 N. Dallas Pkwy, Suite 400
Dallas, TX 75248
Tel. (972) 361-8185 or (800) 724-0767 ext. 7 / Fax (800) 311-3216
Executive Director: Linda Dowell, ldowell@sag.org
Assistant Executive Director: Trish Avery, tavery@sag.org
Administrative Assistant: Jessica Oren, joren@sag.org

NASHVILLE BRANCH

(through Miami Branch)
7300 North Kendall Drive, Suite 620
Miami, FL 33156-7840
Tel. (305) 670-7677 ext. 226 or (800) SAG-0767, option 5, ext. 226
Fax (305) 670-1813 or (800) 844-5439
Leslie L. Krensky, lkrensky@sag.org

NEVADA BRANCH

(through Los Angeles Branch)
5757 Wilshire Boulevard
Los Angeles, CA 90036-3600
Tel. (323) 549-6440 or (800) 724-0767 ext. 7
Fax (323) 549-6460 or (800) 801-5081
Executive Director: Hrair Messerlian, hmesserlian@sag.org

NEW MEXICO BRANCH

(through Denver Branch)
Market Square Center
1400 Sixteenth Street, Suite 400
Denver, CO 80202
Tel. (720) 932-8193 / Fax (720) 932-8194 or (800) 595-4256
Executive Director: Julie Crane, jcrane@sag.org
Administrative Assistant: Tamara Decker, tdecker@sag.org

NEW YORK BRANCH

(Manhattan)
360 Madison Avenue (corner of Forty-fifth Street and Madison)
12th Floor
New York, NY 10017
Tel. (212) 944-1030 / Fax (212) 944-6774
Membership Services: (212) 944-6243
Executive Director: Jae Je Simmons, (212) 827-1474
nymember@sag/org

PHILADELPHIA BRANCH

(through Michigan Branch)
Town Center
2000 Town Center, Suite 1900
Southfield, MI 48075
Tel. (248) 351-2678 or (800) 724-0767 ext. 7 / Fax (248) 351-2679
Membership Department: (212) 944-6243
Executive Director: Marcia Fishman, mfishman@sag.org

PORTLAND BRANCH

(through Seattle Branch)
800 Fifth Avenue, Suite 4100
Seattle, WA 98104
Tel. (206) 224-5696 or (800) 724-0767 ext. 7
Fax (206) 224-5695 or (800) 978-6741
Executive Director: Dena Beatty, dbeatty@sag.org

SAN DIEGO BRANCH

(through Los Angeles Branch)
5757 Wilshire Boulevard
Los Angeles, CA 90036-3600
Tel. (323) 549-6440 or (800) 724-0767 ext. 7
Fax (323) 549-6460 or (800) 801-5081
Executive Director: Hrair Messerlian, hmesserlian@sag.org

SAN FRANCISCO BRANCH

350 Sansome Street, Suite 900
San Francisco, CA 94104
Tel. (415) 391-7510 / Fax (415) 391-1108
Executive Director: Frank Du Charme

SEATTLE BRANCH

800 Fifth Avenue, Suite 4100
Seattle, WA 98104
Tel. (206) 224-5696 or (800) 724-0767 ext. 7
Fax (206) 224-5695 or (800) 978-6741
Executive Director: Dena Beatty, dbeatty@sag.org

UTAH BRANCH

(through Arizona Branch)
3131 E. Camelback Road, Suite 200
Phoenix, AZ 85016
Tel. (602) 383-3780 or (800) 724-0767 ext. 7 / Fax (602) 383-3781
Executive Director: Don Livesay dlivesay@sag.org

WASHINGTON, D.C.-BALTIMORE BRANCH

4340 East West Highway, Suite 204
Bethesda, MD 20814
Tel. (301) 657-2560 or (800) 724-0767 ext. 7
Fax (301) 656-3615 or (800) 253-9730
Executive Director: Patricia O'Donnell

AFTRA Branches

ATLANTA BRANCH

455 East Paces Ferry Road, NE
Suite 334
Atlanta, GA 30305
Tel. (404) 239-0131 / Fax (404) 239-0137
President: Barry Stoltze
Executive Director: Melissa Goodman
atlanta@aftra.com

BOSTON BRANCH

20 Park Plaza, Suite 822
Boston, MA 02116-4399
Tel. (617) 262-8001 / Fax (617) 262-3006
President: Paul Horn
Executive Director: Dona Sommers
boston@aftra.com

BUFFALO BRANCH

c/o WIVB-TV 2077 Elmwood Avenue
Buffalo, NY 14207
Tel. (716) 879-4989 / Fax (716) 634-0514
Local President: Mylous Hairston, mylous@aol.com

CHICAGO BRANCH

One East Erie, Suite 650
Chicago, IL 60611
Tel. (312) 573-8081 / Fax (312) 573-0318
President: Craig Dellimore
Executive Director: Eileen Willenborg
chicago@aftra.com

CLEVELAND BRANCH

820 West Superior Avenue, Suite 240
Cleveland, OH 44113-1800
Tel. (216) 781-2255 / Fax (216) 781-2257
President: Mike Kraft
Executive Director: Catherine Nowlin
cleveland@aftra.com

DALLAS/FORT WORTH BRANCH

6060 N. Central Expressway, Suite 468
Dallas, TX 75206
Tel. (214) 363-8300 / Fax (214) 363-5386
President: Brent Anderson
Texas Regional Director: T. J. Jones
dallas@aftra.com

DENVER BRANCH

1400 Sixteenth Street, Suite 400
Denver, CO 80202
Tel. (720) 932-8228 / Fax (720) 932-8194
President: Denis Berkfeldt
Executive Director: Julie Crane
denver@aftra.com

DETROIT BRANCH

23800 West Ten Mile Road, Suite 228
Southfield, MI 48034
Tel. (248) 228-3171 / Fax: (248) 223-9223
President: Jayne Bower

Executive Director/National Representative: Lorain Obomanu
Assistant Executive Director: Kim Wilson
detroit@aftra.com

FRESNO BRANCH

(through San Francisco Branch)
350 Sansome Street, Suite 900
San Francisco CA 94104
Tel. (415) 391-7510 or (888) 238-7250 / Fax (415) 391-1108
Local President: Denny Delk
Executive Director: Frank Du Charme
sf@aftra.com

HAWAII BRANCH

(through New York Branch)
260 Madison Ave
New York, NY 10016
Tel. (866) 634-8100
hawaii@aftra.com

HOUSTON BRANCH

6060 N. Central Expressway, Suite 468
Dallas, TX 75206
Tel. (214) 363-8300 / Fax (214) 363-5386
President: Nik Hagler
Texas Regional Director: T. J. Jones
houston@aftra.com

KANSAS BRANCH

P.O. Box 32167
4000 Baltimore, 2nd Floor
Kansas City, MO 64111
Tel. (816) 753-4557 / Fax (816) 753-1234
Local President: Larry Greer
Executive Director: John Miller
Assistant Executive Director: Sylvia Stucky
kansascity@aftra.com

LOS ANGELES BRANCH

5757 Wilshire Blvd., 9th Floor
Los Angeles, CA 90036
Tel. (323) 634-8100 / Fax (323) 634-8246
Local President: Ron Morgan

Executive Director: William F. Thomas
losangeles@aftra.com

MIAMI BRANCH

3050 Biscayne Boulevard, Suite 501
Miami, FL 33137
Tel. (305) 571-9891 / Fax (305) 571-9892
President: Connie Zimet
Executive Director/Southeastern Regional Director: Herta Suarez
miami@aftra.com

NASHVILLE BRANCH

P.O. Box 121087
1108 Seventeenth Avenue South
Nashville, TN 37212
Tel. (615) 327-2944 / Fax (615) 329-2803
President: CeCe DuBois
Executive Director: Randall Himes
nashville@aftra.com

NEW ORLEANS BRANCH

(through Miami Branch)
2750 North Twenty-ninth Avenue, Suite 200N
Hollywood, FL 33020
Tel. (954) 920-2476 or (800) 330-2387 / Fax (954) 920-2560
President: Charles Ferrara
Southeastern Regional Director: Herta Suarez
neworleans@aftra.com

NEW YORK BRANCH

260 Madison Avenue (Between 38th Street & 39th Street),
    7th Floor
New York, NY 10016
Tel. (212) 532-0800 / Fax (212) 545-1238
President: Holter Graham
Executive Director: Stephen Burrow
aftrany@aftra.com

OMAHA BRANCH

3000 Farnam St.
Omaha, NE 68131
Tel. (402) 346-8384
President: Erik Whitmore

PEORIA BRANCH

c/o Station WEEK-TV 2907
Springfield Road
East Peoria, IL 61611
Tel. (309) 698-3737 / Fax (309) 698-2070
Treasurer: Garry Moore, gmoore@week.com

PHILADELPHIA BRANCH

230 South Broad Street, Suite 500
Philadelphia, PA 19102-1229
Tel. (215) 732-0507 / Fax (215) 732-0086
President: Catherine Brown
Executive Director: John Kailin
philadelphia@aftra.com

PHOENIX BRANCH

20325 N. Fifty-first Avenue, Suite 134
Glendale, AZ 85308
Tel. (623) 687-9977 / Fax (623) 362-2218
President: Joe Corcoran
Executive Director: Roxanne Chaisson
phoenix@aftra.com

PITTSBURGH BRANCH

625 Stanwix Street, Suite 2007
Pittsburgh, PA 15222
Tel. (412) 281-6767 / Fax (412) 281-2444
Executive Director: John Haer
pittsburgh@aftra.com

PORTLAND BRANCH

1125 SE Madison, Suite 204
Portland, OR 97214
Tel. (503) 279-9600 / Fax (503) 279-9603
President: Chrisse Roccaro
Administrator: Loraine Heuer
portland@aftra.com

ROCHESTER BRANCH

87 Fairlea Drive
Rochester, NY 14622
President: June Baller, juneballer@hotmail.com

SACRAMENTO/STOCKTON BRANCH

(through San Francisco Branch)
350 Sansome Street, Suite 900
San Francisco, CA 94104
Tel. (415) 391-7510 or (888) 238-7250 / Fax (415) 391-1108
Executive Director: Frank Du Charme
sf@aftra.com

SAN DIEGO BRANCH

(through Los Angeles Branch)
5757 Wilshire Boulevard, 9th Floor
Tel. (866) 634-8100 (San Diego members only) or (323) 634-8118
Fax (323) 634-8246
President: Ed Badrak
Director, Broadcast: Lawrence Mayberry
sd@aftra.com

SAN FRANCISCO BRANCH

350 Sansome Street, Suite 900
San Francisco, CA 94104
Tel. (415) 391-7510 / Fax (415) 391-1108
Local President: Denny Delk
Executive Director: Frank Du Charme
sf@aftra.com

SCHENECTADY BRANCH

c/o WRGB-TV
1400 Balltown Road
Schenectady, NY 12309
Tel. (518) 346-6666 / Fax (518) 346-6249
Shop Coordinators: Jack Aernecke and Peter Brancato

SEATTLE BRANCH

4000 Aurora Avenue, No. 102
Seattle, WA 98103-7853
Tel. (206) 282-2506 / Fax (206) 282-7073
Local President: Steve Krueger
Executive Director: John Sandifer
seattle@aftra.com

ST. LOUIS BRANCH

1310 Papin Street, Suite 103
St. Louis, MO 63103
Tel. (314) 231-8410 or (866) 895-8411 /Fax (314) 231-8412

President: Mary Ann Carson
Executive Director: John Miller
Freelance Specialist: Tracey J. Shanklin
stlouis@aftra.com

TEXAS REGIONAL BRANCH

6060 N. Central Expressway, Suite 468
Dallas, TX 75206
Tel. (214) 363-8300 / Fax (214) 363-5386
Texas Regional Director: T. J. Jones

TRI STATE BRANCH

1056 Delta Avenue, #4
Cincinnati, OH 45208
Tel. (513) 579-8668 / Fax (513) 579-1617
President: Denise Dal Vera
Executive Director: John Haer
National Broadcast Representative: Tim Williams
tristate@aftra.com

TWIN CITIES BRANCH

2610 University Avenue West
Suite 350
St. Paul, MN 55114
Tel. (651) 789-8990 / Fax (651) 789-8993
President: Shawn Hamilton
Executive Director: Colleen Aho
twincities@aftra.com

WASHINGTON, D.C./BALTIMORE BRANCH

7735 Old Georgetown Road, Suite 950
Bethesda, MD 20814
Tel. (301) 657-2560 / Fax (301) 656-3615
President: Joe Krebs
Executive Director: Pat O'Donnell
wash_balt@aftra.com

TELEVISION COMMERCIALS USING SQUIRE FRIDELL AS ON-CAMERA TALENT

With thanks to the following clients and their ad agencies for over 3,250 TV spots!

Beverages

André Champagne
Bud Light Beer
Coca-Cola (*multiple*)
Diet Pepsi
Folgers Coffee (*multiple*)
Folgers Crystals (*multiple*)
Gallo Wine
Iron City Beer
Michelob Beer
Olympia Beer (*my first commercial!*)
Pepsi-Cola
Pepsi Lite
Schaefer Beer
Schlitz Beer
Schmidt's Beer
Stagg Beer (*multiple*)
Wyler's Lemonade

Fast Foods and Restaurants

Burger Chef
Jack in the Box
KFC (*multiple*)
McDonald's (*pre-Ronald*)
McDonald's (*as Ronald McDonald—megamultiple!*)
Red Lobster
Sambo's
Taco Bell

Foods

Ballpark Franks
Canadian Bacon
Crisco
Dole Pineapple
Duncan Hines Cake Mix
Eckrich Hot Dogs
Good Seasons (*megamultiple*)
Heinz Chili
Hellmann's Mayonnaise
Hidden Valley Dressing
Hood Ice Cream
Hunt's Snack Pack
Jell-O
Knudsen Yogurt
Lay's Potato Chips (*multiple*)
M&M's
National Egg Council
Oscar Meyer
Peek Freans
Pillsbury (*multiple*)
(continues on p. 262)

Foods (*continued*)

Rice Krispies
Shake 'n Bake
Squeeze Meeze Snack
Stew Starter
Stouffer's
Sugar Crisp
Sugar Smacks
Sun Giant
Twix

Toothpaste, Toiletries, and Personal

Alka-Seltzer
Aquafresh Toothpaste (*multiple*)
Ban Deodorant
Breck Shampoo
Charmin (*multiple*)
Close-Up Toothpaste (*multiple*)
Coast Soap
Contac
Desenex
Excitement Toothpaste
Extend Mouthwash
Eye World (*multiple*)
Gillette Max Hold
Gillette Track Two
Hai Karate Aftershave
Head and Shoulders Shampoo
Ivory Soap
Johnson & Johnson Diapers
    (*multiple*)
Max Factor
Neet
One A Day Vitamins
Prell Shampoo
Right Guard Deodorant
Safeguard Deodorant
Secret Deodorant
Sinutab
Sure Deodorant (*multiple*)

Household, Yard, and Pet Items

Bounce
Brawny Paper Towels
Charmglow
Cheer Detergent
Clean Sweep
Clorox
Clorox PreSoak
Clorox Window Cleaner
Dawn Dishwashing Liquid
409 Cleaner
Gain Detergent
Glad Bags
HiPro Dog Food
Hudson Napkins
Joy Detergent
Purina Dog Food
Puss 'n Boots
Scotts Turf Builder
Toro Mower

Clothes and Accessories

Converse Tennis Shoes
Haggar Slacks
Happy Legs
Totes Carry Bag
Totes Galoshes
Totes Hats (*multiple*)
Totes Rain Boots (*multiple*)
Totes Scarves
Totes Shoes

Cameras, TVs, and Appliances

Amana Microwave
CB Radios
Kodak (*multiple*)
Polaroid (*multiple*)
RCA TV
Stanley Tools
Texas Instruments (*multiple*)
Zenith

Motorcycles, Autos, and Gas

AMC
Avis
British Petroleum
Buick
Dodge
Honda
International Scout
Kawasaki
Midas Mufflers
National Car Rental
Oldsmobile
Pontiac
Texaco (*multiple*)
Toyota (*megamultiple!*)
Toyota of Canada (*multiple*)
Volkswagen

Airlines

American
Continental
TWA
United

Banks, Utilities, Telephone, and Insurance

Arizona Bank
Birmingham National Bank
Broadview Savings
Dallas National Bank
Denver Bank
El Paso Bank (*multiple*)
General Telephone
Hartford Federal Savings
Kemper Insurance
Lloyds Bank
Mountain Bell Telephone
Mutual of Omaha Insurance
National Bank of Detroit (*multiple*)
North Carolina National Bank
   (*multiple*)
North Carolina Power & Light

SW Bell (*multiple*)
UCB
Union Bank (*multiple*)
US Savings Bonds (*multiple*)
World Savings

Stores, Furniture, and Homes

Abbey Rents
Builders Emporium
Builders Square (*multiple*)
Dallas Homes
Handy Dan (*megamultiple*)
Ralph's Markets
Serta Mattresses
Two Guys (*multiple*)
Wickes Furniture (*multiple*)

Miscellaneous

Alcoa Aluminum
Cinemax (*megamultiple*)
Contel
Cox Toys
De Beers Diamonds
FTD Florist (*multiple*)
Gorilla Toys
H&R Block
Hallmark (*multiple*)
HBO (*megamultiple*)
Jovan
Magic Mountain (*megamultiple*)
Mattel Toys (*multiple*)
Roosevelt Raceway
Tiparillo
Wilt Chamberlain Basketball Game

I'm sure there were others.
Forgive me if I've left out a few . . .

ACKNOWLEDGMENTS

I can no other answer make but thanks, and thanks, and ever thanks.

—William Shakespeare (*and Squire Fridell*)

With great appreciation to Cris Dennis of Film Artists Associates. Without Cris' research and guidance, this updated edition would never have happened.

And to Cris' wife, Martha, who knows more about SAG and AFTRA contracts than the folks at SAG and AFTRA.

To Pen Dennis of Film Artists Associates, my friend and trusty Los Angeles agent for the last (it seems like) one hundred years.

To my literary agent, Faith Hamlin, and her predecessor, the late Diane Cleaver, of Sanford J. Greenburger Associates.

To my editor, Lindsay Orman of Random House.

To Barry Geller and to Maharishi, two coinciding forces that enabled me to write the first edition.

To my wife, Suzy, who has never let me settle for anything less than I should.

To our daughter, Lexy, who now walks some of the same trails as her old man and makes me beam with pride and joy.

To all my students over the years, who always ended up teaching me.

To all the skilled actors I've auditioned and worked with (*and stolen tricks from*) over the years.

Lastly, to everyone who ever hired me (*and even to those who didn't, but thought about it*).